Thinking in LINQ

Harnessing the Power of Functional Programming in .NET Applications

Sudipta Mukherjee

Apress®

Thinking in LINQ: Harnessing the power of functional programing in .NET applications

ISBN-13 (pbk): 978-1-4302-6845-1

ISBN-13 (electronic): 978-1-4302-6844-4

Trademarked names, logos, and images may appear in this book. Rather than use a trademark symbol with every occurrence of a trademarked name, logo, or image, we use the names, logos, and images only in an editorial fashion and to the benefit of the trademark owner, with no intention of infringement of the trademark.

The use in this publication of trade names, trademarks, service marks, and similar terms, even if they are not identified as such, is not to be taken as an expression of opinion as to whether or not they are subject to proprietary rights.

While the advice and information in this book are believed to be true and accurate at the date of publication, neither the authors nor the editors nor the publisher can accept any legal responsibility for any errors or omissions that may be made. The publisher makes no warranty, express or implied, with respect to the material contained herein.

Managing Director: Welmoed Spahr
Lead Editor: James DeWolf
Development Editors: Russell Jones
Technical Reviewer: Fabio Claudio Ferracchiati
Editorial Board: Steve Anglin, Mark Beckner, Gary Cornell, Louise Corrigan, James DeWolf, Jonathan Gennick, Robert Hutchinson, Michelle Lowman, James Markham, Matthew Moodie, Jeff Olson, Jeffrey Pepper, Douglas Pundick, Ben Renow-Clarke, Gwenan Spearing, Matt Wade, Steve Weiss
Coordinating Editor: Kevin Walter
Copy Editor: Sharon Wilkey
Compositor: SPi Global
Indexer: SPi Global
Artist: SPi Global
Cover Designer: Anna Ishchenko

Distributed to the book trade worldwide by Springer Science+Business Media New York, 233 Spring Street, 6th Floor, New York, NY 10013. Phone 1-800-SPRINGER, fax (201) 348-4505, e-mail orders-ny@springer-sbm.com, or visit www.springeronline.com. Apress Media, LLC is a California LLC and the sole member (owner) is Springer Science+Business Media Finance Inc. (SSBM Finance Inc.). SSBM Finance Inc. is a **Delaware** corporation.

For information on translations, please e-mail rights rights@apress.com, or visit www.apress.com.

Apress and friends of ED books may be purchased in bulk for academic, corporate, or promotional use. eBook versions and licenses are also available for most titles. For more information, reference our Special Bulk Sales–eBook Licensing web page at www.apress.com/bulk-sales.

Any source code or other supplementary material referenced by the author in this text is available to readers at www.apress.com. For detailed information about how to locate your book's source code, go to www.apress.com/source-code/.

Sohan, this is for you, my son. You have been my inspiration.

Contents at a Glance

Contents

About the Author

Sudipta Mukherjee is an experienced programmer. Born in Shibpur, a town in the Howrah district of West Bengal in India, he grew up in Bally, another small town in the Howrah district. He has been working with C# and LINQ since they were first released, and is an enthusiastic advocate for LINQ. Sudipta is a prolific author, whose previous books include *Data Structures Using C* (http://goo.gl/pttSh) and *.NET 4.0 Generics: Beginner's Guide* (http://goo.gl/LwVmZ5).

His interests are data structure, algorithms, text processing, machine learning, natural language processing, programming languages, and tools development. When not working at his day job or writing books, Sudipta likes spending time with his family and following his passion of sketching and painting. Sudipta lives in Bangalore and can be contacted via e-mail at sudipto80@yahoo.com or on Twitter @samthecoder.

About the Technical Reviewer

Fabio Claudio Ferracchiati is a senior consultant and a senior analyst/developer using Microsoft technologies. He works at BluArancio SpA (www.bluarancio.com) as a senior analyst/developer and Microsoft Dynamics CRM Specialist. He is a Microsoft Certified Solution Developer for .NET, a Microsoft Certified Application Developer for .NET, a Microsoft Certified Professional, and a prolific author and technical reviewer. Over the past ten years, he's written articles for Italian and international magazines and coauthored more than ten books on a variety of computer topics.

Acknowledgments

A book like this can't be published without continuous support from the publisher, editors, and the technical reviewer. I am very thankful to James T. DeWolf and Kevin Walter of Apress for being patient and supportive. I had incredible support from my development editor, Russell Jones. I also want to thank Fabio Claudio Ferracchiati for his invaluable help in reviewing and running each and every program that I wrote. Thanks a lot, gentlemen.

Anybody who has ever written a technical book will probably tell you that it is not easy to follow this path until the end. It requires a lot of patience and support. Thanks to God, I have a lot a patience. And I had tremendous support, especially from my wife, Moue, and everybody in my family. Thank you, sweetheart! Last but not least, I want to thank God once again for giving me my little angel, Sohan. It is such a joy to be with him. I have learned a lot from him; his perseverance especially has helped me overcome some of my own stumbling blocks in life.

Introduction

This book won't teach you the basics of LINQ. It will teach you how to use it appropriately. Having a jackhammer is great only if you know how to use it properly; otherwise, you are not much better off than someone with a hammer. LINQ is powerful. Powerful beyond measure. I hope you will see some of that power by following the examples in the book.

Here is a brief walk-through of the chapters:

- Chapter 1: Thinking Functionally

    Our generation of programmers has been raised with object-oriented programming ideas. This initial chapter is dedicated to showing how functional programming is different from object-oriented programming. This chapter sets the context for the rest of the book.

- Chapter 2: Series Generation

    This chapter has recipes for generating several series using LINQ. For example, it shows how to generate recursive patterns and mathematical series.

- Chapter 3: Text Processing

    Text processing is a blanket term used to cover a range of tasks, from generation of text to spell-checking. This chapter shows how to use LINQ to perform several text-processing tasks that are seemingly commonplace.

- Chapter 4: Refactoring with LINQ

    Legacy code bases grow, and grow fast—faster than you might think they would. Maintaining such huge code blocks can become a nightmare. When is the last time you had trouble understanding what some complex loop code does? This chapter shows how to refactor your legacy loops to LINQ.

- Chapter 5: Refactoring with MoreLINQ

    MoreLINQ is an open source LINQ API that has several methods for slicing and dicing data. Some of these operators are easily composable using other LINQ operators. But some are also truly helpful in minimizing the total number of code lines. This chapter shows how you can benefit from using MoreLINQ.

- Chapter 6: Creating Domain-Specific Languages Using LINQ

    Domain-specific languages (DSLs) are gaining in popularity because they convey the intent of the programmer very nicely. This chapter shows how to create several DSLs.

- Chapter 7: Static Code Analysis

    LINQ treats everything as data. Code is also data. This chapter shows how, by using LINQ-to-Reflection, you can do a lot of meta programming in .NET.

- Chapter 8: Exploratory Data Analysis

  This chapter shows how you can use LINQ to solve several data analysis tasks. I hope you find this chapter enjoyable, because the examples are really interesting.

- Chapter 9: Interaction with the File System

  I have always wished that Windows Explorer included better features for querying the file system. However, by using LINQ, you can build your own custom queries quickly. This chapter shows you some examples that can be useful in the real world.

- Appendix A: Lean LINQ Tips

  LINQ is an API that provides several operators to express your intent. Although that is super powerful, it comes with a price. If you don't know how these operators work internally, you might end up using a combination that results in slower code. This appendix provides some hard-earned knowledge about how to glue LINQ operators together for optimum performance.

- Appendix B: Taming Streaming Data with Rx.NET

  Being reactive is important when dealing with streaming data. Microsoft's über-cool framework, Rx.NET, is a fantastic API for dealing with streaming data and async operations. This appendix shows how to use Rx.NET to tackle streaming data.

CHAPTER 1

Thinking Functionally

As you begin this book, I urge you to forget everything you know about programming and bear with me while I walk you through a high-level view of what *I* think programming is. To me, to program is to *transform*. I'll give you a few simple examples to explain my viewpoint.

First, suppose you have some data in a database and you want to show some values in a website after performing some calculations on that data. What are you actually doing here? You are transforming the data.

That first example is obvious, but there are many other less obvious examples. Spell-checking, for example, is a transformation of a list of dictionary words to a set of plausible spelling-correction suggestions. Generating a series of numbers that follow a pattern (such as the Fibonacci series) is also a transforming operation, in which you transform the initial two values to a series.

1-1. Understanding Functional Programming

Transforming data often requires intermediate transformations. You can model each such intermediate transformation by a function. The art of gluing together several such functions to achieve a bigger transformation is called *functional programming*. Note that functional programming is nothing new. It's just high-school math in disguise.

For example, suppose you have the following functions:

```
f(x) = x + 1
g(x) = x + 2
z(x,y) = x == y
```

Using these functions, you can create several *composite functions* in which the arguments are functions themselves. For example, f.g (read as *f of g*) is shown as follows:

```
f(g(x)) = f(x+2) = x + 2 + 1 = x + 3
```

Similarly g.f (read as *g of f*) is as follows:

```
g(f(x)) = g(x+1) = x + 1 + 2 = x + 3
```

I will leave it up to you to determine that z(f.g) is equal to z(g.f) for all values of x.

Now, imagine that your goal is to add 6 to x using these two functions. Try to find the function call sequence that will do this for you.

To think of it another way, functional programming is programming using functions but without worrying about the internal state of the variables. Functional programming allows programmers to concentrate more on *what* gets done than how exactly *how* it gets done.

With that in mind, imagine that you want a cup of coffee. You go to the local coffee shop, but when you ask for coffee at the sales counter, you don't worry in painful detail about how the coffee has to be made. A great video by Dr. Don Syme, the man behind Microsoft's functional programming language, F# explains this concept better than I ever could. I strongly recommend that you watch it (www.youtube.com/watch?v=ALr212cTpf4).

1-2. Using Func<> in C# to Represent Functions

You might be wondering how to port such functions to C#. Fortunately, it's quite straightforward. C# includes a class called Func. Using this class, you can create functional methods much as you create variables of any primitive type, such as integers. Here's how you could write the functions described in the previous section:

```
Func<int,int> f = x => x + 1; // describing f(x) = x + 1
Func<int,int> g = x => x + 2; // describing g(x) = x + 2
```

Here's how to define f.g (read *f of g*) by using Func<>:

```
Func<Func<int,int>,Func<int,int>,int,int> fog = (f1,g1,x) => f1.Invoke(g1.Invoke(x));
```

In the preceding definition, fog is a function that takes two functions as arguments and calls them to obtain the final output. The initial argument to the first function is provided in x. Note how the function itself is passed as an argument to the composite function.

The Func<> class has several constructors that can be used to represent functions. In each constructor, the last argument represents the return type. So, for example, a declaration such as Func<int,int> represents a function that takes an integer and returns an integer. Similarly, the function z (z(x,y) = x == y) declared previously can be represented as Func<int,int,bool> because it takes two integers and returns a Boolean value.

1-3. Using Various Types of Functions

Several kinds of functions can be classified broadly into four major categories, as shown in Figure 1-1: generator functions, statistical functions, projection functions, and filters.

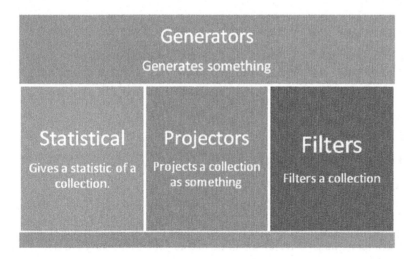

Figure 1-1. *Classification of several types of functions*

Generator Functions

A *generator function* creates values out of nothing. Think of this as a method that takes no arguments but returns an `IEnumerable<T>`.

Enumerable.Range() and Enumerable.Repeat() are example of generator functions.

A generator function can be represented by the following equation, where T represents any type:

```
() => T[]
```

Statistical Functions

Statistical functions return some kind of statistic about a collection. For example, you might want to know how many elements are present in a collection, or whether a given element is available in a collection. These types of operations are statistical in nature because they return either a number or a Boolean value.

Any(), Count(), Single(), and SingleOrDefault() are examples of statistical functions. A statistical function can be represented by either of the following equations:

```
T[] => Number
T[] => Boolean
```

Projector Functions

Functions that take a collection of type T and return a collection of type U (where U could be the same type as T) are called *projector functions*.

For example, suppose you have a list of names, and the first and last names are separated by whitespace. You want to project only the last names. Because the full names are represented as strings, and the last name is a substring of the full name, it's also a string. Thus the result type of the projection is the same as that of the source collection (string). So in this case, U is the same as T.

Here's a situation where U and T don't match: Say you have a list of integers, and each integer represents a number of days. You want to create a DateTime array from these numbers by adding the day values to DateTime.Today. In this case, the initial type is System.Int32, but the projection type is DateTime. In this case, U and T don't match up.

Select(), SelectMany(), and Cast<T>() are other examples of projector functions. A projector function can be represented by the following equation, where U can be the same as T:

```
T[] => U[]
```

Filters

Filters are just what you would think they are. These functions filter out elements of a given collection that don't match a given expression.

Where(), First(), and Last() are examples of filter functions. A filter function can be represented by either of the following equations:

T[] => T[]: The function output is a list of values that match a given condition.

T[] => T: The function output is a single value that matches a given condition/predicate.

1-4. Understanding the Benefits of Functional Programming

I'll walk you through the top five benefits of using a functional programming approach. However don't bother trying to memorize these. After you get comfortable with functional programming, these will seem obvious. The five top benefits are as follows:

- Composability
- Lazy evaluation
- Immutability
- Parallelizable
- Declarative

Composability

Composability lets you create solutions for complex problems easily. In fact, it's the only good way to combat complexity. Composability is based on the *divide and rule* principle. Imagine you are planning a party and you want everything to be done properly. You have a bunch of friends who are willing to help. If you could give each friend a single responsibility, you could rest assured that everything would be done properly.

The same is true in programming. If each method or loop has a single responsibility, each will be easier to refactor as new methods, resulting in cleaner and thus more maintainable code. Functional programming thrives because of the composability it offers.

Lazy Evaluation

Lazy evaluation is a concept that provides the results of queries only when you need them. Imagine that you have a long list of objects, and you want to filter that list based on a certain condition, showing only the first ten such matching entries in your user interface. In imperative programming, each operation would be evaluated. Therefore, if the filter operation takes a long time, your user would have to wait for it to complete. However, functional programming languages, including implementations such as F# or LINQ, allow you to take advantage of *deferred execution* and *lazy evaluation*, in which the program performs operations such as this filter only when needed, thus saving time. You'll see more about lazy evaluation in Chapter 6.

Immutability

Immutability lets you write code that is free of side effects. Although functional programming doesn't guarantee that you will have code free of side effects, the best practices of functional programming preach this as a goal—with good reason. Side effects such as shared variables not only may lead to ambiguous situations, but also can also be a serious hindrance in writing parallel programs. Imagine you are in a queue to buy movie tickets. You (and everyone else) have to wait until it's your turn to buy a ticket, which prevents you from going directly into the theater. Shared states or shared variables are like that. When you have a lot of threads or tasks waiting for a single variable (or collection), you are limiting the speed with which code can execute. A better strategy is more like buying tickets online. You start your task or thread with its own token/variable/state. That way, it never has to wait for access to shared variables.

Parallelizable

Functional programs are easier to *parallelize* than their imperative counterparts because most functional programs are side-effect free (immutable) by design. In LINQ, you can easily parallelize your code by using the AsParallel() and AsOrdered() operators. You'll see a full example in Chapter 4.

Declarative

Declarative programming helps you write very expressive code, so that code readability improves. Declarative programming often also lets you get more done with less code. For example, it's often possible to wrap an entire algorithm into a single line of C# by using LINQ operators. You'll see examples of this later in this book, in Chapters 6 and 8.

1-5. Getting LINQPad

You can enter and execute all the examples in this book with a useful tool called LINQPad. LINQPad is a free C#/VB.NET/F# snippet compiler. If you're serious about .NET programming, you should become familiar with LINQPad—it does more than just let you test LINQ statements.

You can download LINQPad from `www.linqpad.net/GetFile.aspx?LINQPad4Setup.exe`.

■ **Note**　I highly recommend you download and install LINQPad now, before you continue.

Some of the examples in this book run in LINQPad with the LINQPad language option set to C# Expressions. The rest of the examples run in LINQPad with the LINQPad language option set to C# Statement(s). I've made an effort to add reminders throughout the book where appropriate, but if you can't get an example to run, check the LINQPad Language drop-down option.

CHAPTER 2

Series Generation

LINQ helps you generate series by using intuitive and readable code. In this chapter, you will see how to use several LINQ standard query operators (LSQO) to generate common mathematical and recursive series. All these queries are designed to run on LINQPad (www.linqpad.net) as C# statements.

Series generation has applications in many areas. Although the problems in this chapter may seem disconnected, they demonstrate how to use LINQ to solve diverse sets of problems. I have categorized the problems into six main areas: math and statistics, recursive series and patterns, collections, number theory, game design, and working with miscellaneous series.

The following problems are related to simple everyday mathematics and statistics.

2-1. Math and Statistics: Finding the Dot Product of Two Vectors

The *dot product of two vectors* is defined as the member-wise multiplication of their coefficients.

Problem

The problem is to write a function that finds the dot product of two vectors.

Solution

Use the Zip() standard query operator, passing it a function delegate that multiplies two values at the same location in the arrays.

Listing 2-1 generates the dot product of these two vectors. Figure 2-1 shows the result.

Listing 2-1. Finding a dot product

```
int[] v1 = {1,2,3}; //First vector
int[] v2 = {3,2,1}; //Second vector

//dot product of vector
v1.Zip(v2, (a,b) => a * b).Dump("Dot Product");
```

Figure 2-1. *The dot product of two vectors {1, 2, 3} and {3, 2, 1}*

How It Works

Zip() is a LINQ standard query operator that operates on two members at the same location (or index). The delegate passed to Zip() denotes the function used to generate a zipped single value from the members at the same index in two series. For a vector dot product, the function is a simple multiplication denoted by (a,b) => a * b.

2-2. Math and Statistics: Generating Pythagorean Triples

A *Pythagorean triple* is a tuple of three integers that can form the sides of a right-triangle.

Problem

Use LINQ to generate a Pythagorean triple.

Solution

The most common Pythagorean triple is {3, 4, 5}. The obvious scheme for generating more of these triples is to multiply an existing triple by some number. For example, multiplying {3, 4, 5} by 2 yields {6, 8, 10}—another Pythagorean triple. However, Babylonians came up with a more general formula for generating Pythagorean triples: The base and height assume the values of c * c –1 and 2 * c, respectively, where c represents a number greater than or equal to 2. The hypotenuse, the longest side of a right triangle, is always one greater than the square of that number (c).

Listing 2-2 generates Pythagorean triplets by using the old and simple Babylonian formula.

Listing 2-2. Generating Pythagorean triples with the Babylonian formula

```
Enumerable.Range(2,10)
    .Select (c => new {Length = 2*c,
                       Height = c * c - 1,
                       Hypotenuse = c * c + 1})
    .Dump("Pythagorean Triples");
```

This generates the output shown in Figure 2-2.

Pythagorean Triplets

Length	Height	Hypotenuse
4	3	5
6	8	10
8	15	17
10	24	26
12	35	37
14	48	50
16	63	65
18	80	82
20	99	101
22	120	122
130	495	515

IEnumerable<> (10 items)

Figure 2-2. *Pythagorean triplets generated by the Babylonian method*

How It Works

This example uses an anonymous type. Note that the code doesn't define a type with properties or fields named Length, Height, or Hypotenuse. However, LINQ doesn't complain. LINQPad clearly shows that the type of the projected collection is anonymous. Check out the tool tip shown in Figure 2-3.

```
Enumerable.Range(2,10)
.Select (c => new {Length = 2*c, Height = c * c - 1, Hypotenuse = c * c + 1})
.ToList(
.Dump();  (extension) List<{anonymous}> Enumerable.ToList (this IEnumerable<{anonymous}> source)  F1 for help
```

Figure 2-3. *A tool tip that shows the projection of the anonymous type*

This feature is useful because it saves you from having to create placeholder classes or using tuples. (The example could have used a Tuple<int,int,int> in place of the anonymous method, but using the anonymous type improves readability.) If, however, you project the result to a List<T> and then try to dereference it by using an index, you will see the properties Length, Height, and Hypotenuse as shown in Figure 2-4—just as if you had defined a strongly typed collection of some type with those public properties.

```
var q = Enumerable.Range(2,10)
                  .Select (c => new {Length = 2*c, Height = c * c - 1, Hypotenuse = c * c + 1})
                  .ToList();

q[0].
        Dump
        Equals
        GetHashCode
        GetType
        Height
        Hypotenuse
        Length
        ToString
```

Figure 2-4. *The properties of the anonymous type show up in IntelliSense*

2-3. Math and Statistics: Finding a Weighted Sum

Finding vector dot products has real-world applications, the most common of which is finding a weighted sum.

Problem

Suppose every subject in an exam has a different weight. In such a setting, each student's score is the weighted sum of the weight for each subject and the score obtained by the student in that subject. The problem here is to use LINQ to find the weighted sum.

Solution

Mathematically, the weighted sum is the sum of the coefficients of the vector dot product, which you can obtain easily with LINQ, by using Zip() and Sum(). Listing 2-3 shows the solution.

Listing 2-3. Finding a weighted sum

```
int[] values = {1,2,3};
int[] weights = {3,2,1};

//dot product of vector
values.Zip(weights, (value,weight) =>
          value * weight) //same as a dot product
    .Sum() //sum of the multiplications of values and weights
    .Dump("Weighted Sum");
```

Figure 2-5 shows the results.

```
Weighted Sum
10
```

Figure 2-5. *The weighted sum of two vectors*

How It Works

The call to Zip() creates a dot product, while the call to Sum() adds the results of multiplying the values and weights.

2-4. Math and Statistics: Finding the Percentile for Each Element in an Array of Numbers

Percentile is a measure most often used to analyze the result of a competitive examination. It gives the percentage of people who scored below a given score obtained by a student.

Problem

Imagine you have a list of scores and want to find the percentile for each score. In other words, you want to calculate the percentage of people who scored below that score.

Solution

Listing 2-4 shows the solution.

Listing 2-4. Score percentile solution

```
int[] nums = {20,15,31,34,35,40,50,90,99,100};
nums
    .ToLookup(k=>k, k=> nums.Where (n => n<k))
    .Select(k => new KeyValuePair<int,double>
       (k.Key,100*((double)k.First().Count()/(double)nums.Length)))
    .Dump("Percentile");
```

The code creates a lookup table in which each score becomes a key, and the values for that key are all the scores less than the key. For example, the first key is 20, which has a single value: 15 (because 15 is the only score less than 20). The second key is 15, which has no values (because that's the lowest score).

Next, the code creates a list of KeyValuePair objects, each of which contains the key from the lookup table, and a calculated percentile, obtained by multiplying the number of values that appear under each key in the lookup table by 100 and then dividing that by the number of scores (10 in this case).

This code generates the output shown in Figure 2-6.

Percentile

▲ IEnumerable<KeyValuePair<Int32,Double>> (10 items) ▶

Key	Value ≡
20	10
15	0
31	20
34	30
35	40
40	50
50	60
90	70
99	80
100	90
	450

Figure 2-6. *Score and percentile obtained by students*

Finding the *rank* of each mark is also simple, as you obtain rank from percentile. The student with the highest percentile gets the first rank, and the student with the lowest percentile gets the last rank, as shown in Listing 2-5.

Listing 2-5. Obtaining score ranking from percentile

```
int[] marks = {20,15,31,34,35,50,40,90,99,100};
marks
    .ToLookup(k=>k, k=> marks.Where (n => n>=k))
    .Select (k => new {
        Marks = k.Key,
        Rank = 10*((double)k.First().Count()/(double)marks.Length)
    })
    .Dump("Ranks");
```

Figure 2-7 shows the ranks of the students derived from the percentile.

Ranks

▲ IEnumerable<> (10 items) ▶	
Marks ≡	**Rank** ≡
20	9
15	10
31	8
34	7
35	6
50	4
40	5
90	3
99	2
100	1
514	55

Figure 2-7. *Student rank derived from percentile*

How It Works

This example uses a lookup table to find out the percentile. The keys in the lookup table hold the number, and the values are all those numbers that are smaller than that number. Later the code finds the percent of these values against the total number of items. That yields the percentile for the particular number represented by the key.

2-5. Math and Statistics: Finding the Dominator in an Array

A *dominator* is an element in an array that repeats in more than 50 percent of the array positions.

Problem

Assume you have the following array: {3, 4, 3, 2, 3, -1, 3, 3}. There are eight elements, and 3 appears in five of those. So in this case the dominator is 3. The problem is to use LINQ to find the dominator in an array.

Solution

The first algorithm that comes to mind to find a dominator has to loop through the array twice and thus has quadratic time complexity, but you can improve the efficiency by using a lookup. Listing 2-6 shows the solution.

Listing 2-6. Finding the array dominator

```
int[] array = { 3, 4, 3, 2, 3, -1, 3, 3};
array.ToLookup (a => a).First (a => a.Count() >
     array.Length/2).Key.Dump("Dominator");
```

This generates the result shown in Figure 2-8.

```
Dominator
3
```

Figure 2-8. *The dominator of an array*

How It Works

`array.ToLookup (a => a)` creates a lookup table in which the keys are the values. Because there are duplicates, there will be many values. However, you are interested in only the first value. So an item that has occurred more than `array.Length / 2` times is the dominator. And you will find that dominator as the key of this element in the lookup table.

2-6. Math and Statistics: Finding the Minimum Number of Currency Bills Required for a Given Amount

Machines that process financial transactions involving cash, such as ATM machines or self-service grocery checkout stations, must be able to make change efficiently, providing users with the minimum number of bills required to add up to a specific amount.

Problem

Given all the currencies available in a country and an amount, write a program that determines the minimum number of currency bills required to match that amount.

Solution

Listing 2-7 shows the solution.

Listing 2-7. Finding minimum number of currency bills

```
//These are available currencies
int[] curvals = {500,100,50,20,10,5,2,1,1000};

int amount = 2548;

Dictionary<int,int> map = new Dictionary<int,int>();

curvals.OrderByDescending (c => c)
        .ToList()
        .ForEach(c => {map.Add(c,amount/c); amount = amount % c;});

map.Where (m => m.Value!=0)
    .Dump();
```

13

When you run this query in LINQPad, you will see the output shown in Figure 2-9. The Key column shows the face value of various bills, while the Value column shows the number of those bills required to add up to the target value.

IEnumerable<KeyValuePair<Int32,Int32>> (6 items) ▶	
Key	Value ≡
1000	2
500	1
20	2
5	1
2	1
1	1
	8

Figure 2-9. *Output of the minimum currency bill count query*

How It Works

The algorithm to find the minimum number of currency bills required is recursive. It is a continuous division of the value by the largest currency value that results in an integer greater than or equal to 1, repeated against the remainder until the value of the amount diminishes to zero.

amount/c (amount divided by c) calculates the number of currency bills required with value c. The remaining amount is the remainder, as calculated by amount % c.

The data is stored as a currency and currency count pair in the C# dictionary map. Each dictionary key is a currency bill face value, and the value is the number of such currency bills required to total the given amount, using the minimum number of currency bills. Thus, any nonzero value in the map is what you should look for. The LINQ query map.Where (m => m.Value!=0) does just that. And that's about it!

LINQPad has a cool feature that sums up the values in the Value column. In this case, that summation is 8. That means it will require a minimum of eight currency bills to make 2,548.

The first call to OrderByDescending() makes sure that you start with the highest available currency value.

2-7. Math and Statistics: Finding Moving Averages

Finding a moving average is a problem that often arises in time series analysis, where it's used to smooth out local fluctuations. A *moving average* is just what it says—an average that "moves." In other words, it is the average of all elements that fall within a moving window of a predefined size. For example, suppose you have the numbers 1, 2, 3, 4, and the window size is 2. In that case, there are three moving averages: the average of 1 and 2, the average of 2 and 3, and the average of 3 and 4.

Problem

Create a program that finds the moving average of given window size.

Solution

Listing 2-8 shows the solution.

Listing 2-8. Finding a moving average

```
List<double> numbers = new List<double>(){1,2,3,4};
List<double> movingAvgs = new List<double>();

//moving window is of length 4.
int windowSize = 2;

Enumerable.Range(0,numbers.Count - windowSize + 1)
          .ToList()
          .ForEach(k => movingAvgs.Add(numbers.Skip(k).Take(windowSize).Average()));
//Listing moving averages
movingAvgs.Dump();
```

This generates the output shown in Figure 2-10.

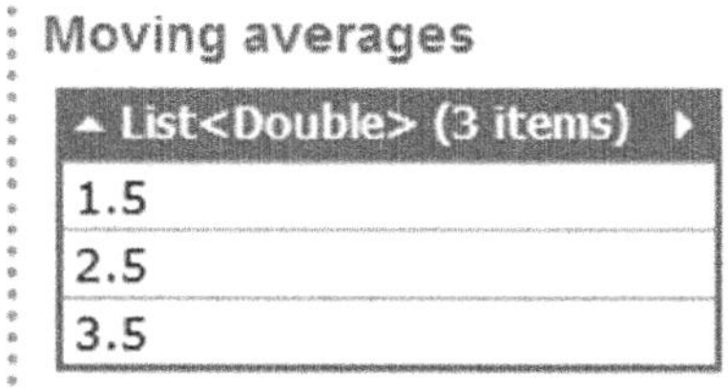

Moving averages

▲ List<Double> (3 items) ▶
1.5
2.5
3.5

Figure 2-10. *The moving average of 1, 2, 3, 4 with window size 2*

How It Works

The first step toward calculating the moving average is to find the moving sum. And to find the moving sum, you need to find the elements currently available under the window.

Figure 2-11 shows the movement of the sliding window as the gray rectangle in each row. The moving window slides across the array for a given window size of 2.

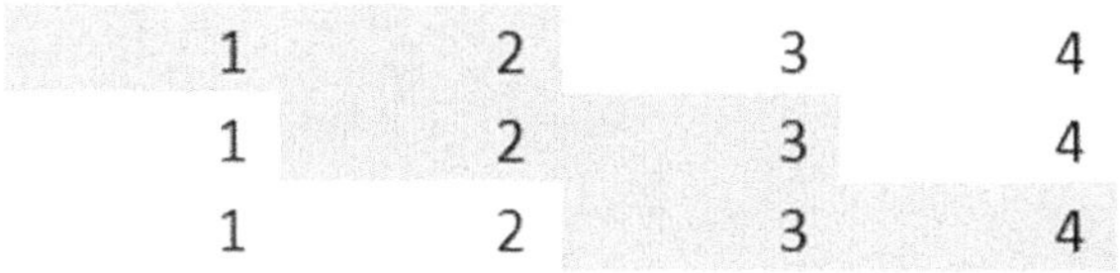

1	2	3	4
1	2	3	4
1	2	3	4

Figure 2-11. *A sliding window over example input data for calculating the moving average*

At first the sliding window has two elements: 1 and 2. Then it slides toward the right by one position. The movement of the sliding window can be described as follows: At first, no element is skipped and the 2 element is taken. Then the 1 element is skipped and the 2 element is taken, and so forth. Thus in general you can find the elements currently present in the sliding window by using the following LINQ query numbers.Skip(k).Take(windowSize), where k ranges from 0 to numbers.Count - windowSize + 1.

The LSQO Average() finds the average of the sequence. Thus all the moving averages are stored in listmovingAvgs.

2-8. Math and Statistics: Finding a Cumulative Sum

To find the growth of a variable, you have to measure it at regular intervals.

Problem

Let's say you have a list of numbers that represent the value of some business entity, which varies year to year. You want to measure the growth percentage for that entity from year to year. Remember that the numbers in the list represent entity values for a particular year, not a cumulative amount up until that year. However, to measure growth, you need a value that represents the previous total. This value is called a *cumulative sum*. The problem is to write a function to find the cumulative sum of a given sequence by using LINQ standard query operators.

Solution

Listing 2-9 shows the solution.

Listing 2-9. Cumulative sum solution

```
List<KeyValuePair<int,int>> cumSums =
    new List<KeyValuePair<int,int>>();
var range = Enumerable.Range(1,10);
range.ToList().ForEach( k => cumSums.Add(
    new KeyValuePair<int,int>(k,range.Take(k).Sum())));
cumSums.Dump("Numbers and \"Cumulative Sum\" at each level");
```

This generates the output shown in Figure 2-12.

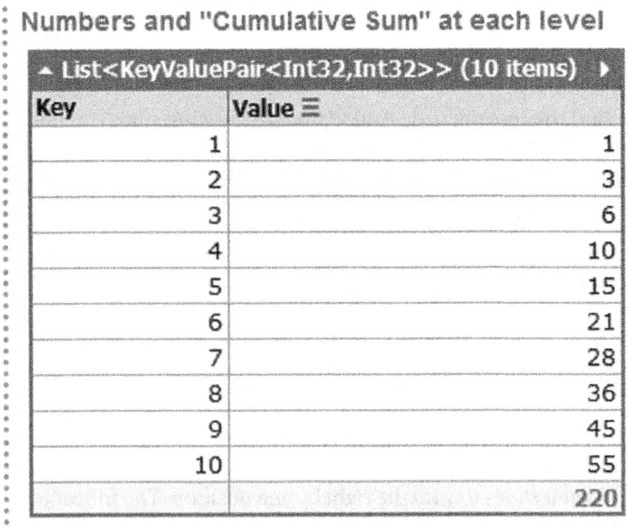

Numbers and "Cumulative Sum" at each level

▲ List<KeyValuePair<Int32,Int32>> (10 items) ▶

Key	Value ≡
1	1
2	3
3	6
4	10
5	15
6	21
7	28
8	36
9	45
10	55
	220

Figure 2-12. *A sequence and the cumulative sum of the sequence at each stage*

How It Works

The code is fairly self-explanatory. If you were to describe the cumulative sum (sometimes referred to as a *cumsum*) algorithm to your grandma, you might say, "Grandma, take the first element, then the sum of the the first two elements, then the sum of the first three elements, and so on until you run out of elements." Now look at the code. Doesn't it look just like that? To show a number and then the cumulative sum up to that number, I am using a List<KeyValuePair<int,int>>.

A pattern that can be expressed using a recurrence relation is known as a *recursive pattern*. For example, fractals are recursive patterns. Their entire fractal structure resembles the smallest building block. In the following problems, you will explore how to use LINQ to generate such patterns.

2-9. Recursive Series and Patterns: Generating Recursive Structures by Using L-System Grammar

Aristid Lindenmayer was a Hungarian biologist who developed a system of formal languages that are today called *Lindenmayer systems*, or L-systems (see http://en.wikipedia.org/wiki/L-system). Lindenmayer used these languages to model the behavior of plant cells. Today, L-systems are also used to model whole plants.

Problem

Lindenmayer described the growth of algae as follows: At first the algae is represented by an *A*. Later this *A* is replaced by *AB*, and *B* is replaced by *A*. So the algae grows like this. The letter *n* denotes the iteration:

```
n = 0 : A
n = 1 : AB
n = 2 : ABA
n = 3 : ABAAB
n = 4 : ABAABABA
n = 5 : ABAABABAABAAB
n = 6 : ABAABABAABAABABAABABA
n = 7 : ABAABABAABAABABAABABAABAABABAABAAB
```

The problem here is to simulate the growth of algae by using a functional programming approach.

Solution

Listing 2-10 simulates the growth of algae as described by an L-system.

Listing 2-10. Algal growth using L-system grammar

```
string algae = "A";

Func<string,string> transformA = x => x.Replace("A","AB");
Func<string,string> markBs    = x => x.Replace("B","[B]");
Func<string,string> transformB = x => x.Replace("[B]","A");

int length = 7;
Enumerable.Range(1,length).ToList()
    .ForEach ( k => algae = transformB(transformA(markBs(algae))));

algae.Dump("Algae at 7th Iteration");
```

This generates the algae at its seventh iteration, as shown in Figure 2-13.

```
Algae at 7th Iteration
ABAABABAABAABABAABABAABAABABAABAABAAB
```

Figure 2-13. *Algae at its seventh iteration*

How It Works

The trick is to identify which Bs to modify for the current iteration. Because A gets transformed to AB and B gets transformed to A, you need to do the transformation for A first, followed by the transformation of B. The code `transformB(transformA(markBs(algae)))` does that in the described order.

2-10. Recursive Series and Patterns Step-by-Step Growth of Algae

The previous example shows only the final stage of the algae. However, by modifying the example slightly, you can show the growth of the algae at each stage.

Problem

Modify the program in Listing 2-10 so that it shows the growth of the algae at each stage.

Solution

The bold code in Listing 2-11 shows the changes made to the previous example.

Listing 2-11. Algal growth shown by stages

```
string algae = "A";

Func<string,string> transformA = x => x.Replace("A","AB");
Func<string,string> markBs    = x => x.Replace("B","[B]");
Func<string,string> transformB = x => x.Replace("[B]","A");

int length = 7;
Enumerable.Range(1,length)
.Select (k => new KeyValuePair<int,string>(
    k,algae = transformB(transformA(markBs(algae)))))
.Dump("Showing the growth of the algae as described by L-System");
```

This shows the growth of the algae at each stage, as shown in Figure 2-14.

Showing the growth of the algae as described by L-System

Key	Value
1	AB
2	ABA
3	ABAAB
4	ABAABABA
5	ABAABABAABAAB
6	ABAABABAABAABABAABABA
7	ABAABABAABAABABAABABAABAABABAABAAB

▲ IEnumerable<KeyValuePair<Int32,String>> (7 items) ▶

Figure 2-14. *The growth of the algae at each iteration*

How It Works

Unlike the previous version, this version stores the state of the algae at each stage, projected as a key/value pair, where the key represents the number of the iteration, and the value represents the stage of the algae at that iteration. Interestingly, the length of the algae string always forms a Fibonacci series. At the second iteration (the number 1 in the preceding output), the value of the algae is AB, so the length of the algae is 2. At the third iteration, the algae is ABA, and the length is 3. At the fourth iteration, the algae is ABAAB, and the length is 5 (the next Fibonacci number after 3), and so on.

You can project the length of the algae by using Listing 2-12; changes from the preceding example are shown in bold.

Listing 2-12. Projecting the length of algal strings

```
int length = 5;
Enumerable.Range(1,length)
    .Select (k => new Tuple<int,string,int>(k,algae =
        transformB(transformA(markBs(algae))),algae.Length))
    .Dump("The length of the alage forms the Fibonacci Series");
```

This generates the output shown in Figure 2-15.

The length of the alage forms the Fibonacci Series

Item1 ≡	Item2	Item3 ≡
1	AB	2
2	ABA	3
3	ABAAB	5
4	ABAABABA	8
5	ABAABABAABAAB	13
15		31

▲ IEnumerable<Tuple<Int32,String,Int32>> (5 items) ▶

Figure 2-15. *The length of the algae at each iteration forms the Fibonacci series*

This table has three columns: Item1, Item2, and Item3. The first column, Item1, shows the serial number depicting the stage of the algae growth. Item2 shows the algae, and Item3 shows the length of the algae at that stage. At each stage, the length of the algae is a Fibonacci number.

2-11. Recursive Series and Patterns: Generating Logo Commands to Draw a Koch Curve

Logo is a computer language created for teaching programming. One of its features is *turtle graphics*, in which the programmer directs a virtual onscreen turtle to draw shapes by using simple commands such as turn left, turn right, start drawing, stop drawing, and so on.

Problem

You can generate several fractals, including the Sierpinksi Triangle, Koch curve, and Hilbert curve by using the L-system and a series of generated turtle graphics commands. These commands consist of constants and axioms. For example, here are the details to generate a Koch curve:

- *Variables*: F

- *Constants*: +, –

- *Start*: F

- *Rules*: (F → F+F–F–F+F) //This means at each iteration, "F" has to be replaced by "F+F-F-F+F"

Here, F means *draw forward*, plus (+) means *turn left 90°*, and minus (–) means *turn right 90°* (for a more complete explanation, see http://en.wikipedia.org/wiki/Turtle_graphics). The problem here is to generate a Koch curve and related patterns by using LINQ.

Solution

Listing 2-13 shows the code that generates the Logo commands to create a Koch curve.

Listing 2-13. Generate Logo commands to create a Koch curve

```
string koch = "F";
Func<string,string> transform = x => x.Replace("F","F+F-F-F+F");

int length = 3;

//Initialize the location and direction of the turtle
string command = @"home
setxy 10 340
right 90
";
```

```
//Finish it in the next line so a new line appears in the command
command += Enumerable.Range(1,length)
    .Select (k => koch = transform(koch))
    .Last()
    .Replace("F","forward 15")
    .Replace("+",Environment.NewLine + "Left 90" +
        Environment.NewLine)
    .Replace("-",Environment.NewLine + "Right 90" +
        Environment.NewLine);

command.Dump();
```

How It Works

This generates the output partially shown in Figure 2-16.

```
home
setxy 10 340
right 90
forward 15
Left 90
forward 15
Right 90
forward 15
Right 90
forward 15
Left 90
forward 15
Left 90
forward 15
```

Figure 2-16. *The first few generated Logo commands to draw a Koch curve*

■ **Note**   To see how a Koch curve is drawn in Logo, go to `http://logo.twentygototen.org/` and paste the generated command in the text box on the right-hand side. Then click Run Normally or Run Slowly to see how the curve is drawn. I have uploaded a demo. You can check it out at `www.youtube.com/watch?v=hdSMPp607tI&feature=youtu.be`.

2-12. Recursive Series and Patterns: Generating Logo Commands to Draw a Sierpinski Triangle

By following a pattern similar to that discussed in the previous section, you can generate Logo commands to draw Sierpinski triangles.

Problem

The rules to draw a Sierpinski triangle are as follows:

- *Variables*: A, B
- *Constants*: +, −
- *Start*: A
- *Rules*: (A → B − A − B), (B → A + B + A)
- *Angle*: 60°

Here, *A* and *B* both mean *draw forward*, a plus sign (+) means *turn left by some angle*, and a minus sign (−) means *turn right by some angle*. The problem here is to use LINQ to follow the rules and draw a Sierpinski triangle.

Solution

Listing 2-14 shows the code to generate the Logo commands that draw the Sierpinski triangle.

Listing 2-14. Generate Logo commands to draw a Serpinski triangle

```
string serpinskiTriangle = "A";

Func<string,string> transformA = x => x.Replace("A","B-A-B");
Func<string,string> markBs    = x => x.Replace("B","[B]");
Func<string,string> transformB = x => x.Replace("[B]","A+B+A");

int length = 6;

Enumerable.Range(1,length)
.ToList()
.ForEach (k => serpinskiTriangle =
    transformB(transformA(markBs(serpinskyTriangle))));

serpinskiTriangle
    .Replace("A", "forward 5" + Environment.NewLine)
    .Replace("B", "forward 5" + Environment.NewLine)
    .Replace("+", "left 60" + Environment.NewLine)
    .Replace("-", "right 60" + Environment.NewLine)
    .Dump("LOGO Commands for drawing Serpinsky Triangle");
```

How It Works

You can follow the same structure to generate several other fascinating space-filling graphs such as the dragon curve or the Hilbert curve. To see these fractals generated at each iteration, visit www.kevs3d.co.uk/dev/lsystems/.

2-13. Recursive Series and Patterns: Generating Fibonacci Numbers Nonrecursively (Much Faster)

Generating a Fibonacci series is one of the classic recursive algorithms. You may already be familiar with the Fibonacci series; however, for the sake of completeness, here's a brief explanation. The Fibonacci series is a recursive series in which each item is the sum of the previous two items in the series.

Problem

Here are the first few terms in the Fibonacci series: 1, 1, 2, 3, 5, 8, 13, 21. Generating those is simple enough. However, recursively calculating Fibonacci numbers takes quite some time and sometimes can cause overflow. By using a collection and saving the last two numbers to add, you can make it much faster. The problem here is to write some LINQ code that uses the faster method.

Solution

Listing 2-15 shows the solution. For each item in the initial range, the query checks to see if it's less than or equal to 1. If so, it adds a 1 to the `fibonacciNumbers` list. Otherwise, it adds the sum of the last two numbers in the `fibonacciNumbers` list.

Listing 2-15. Generating Fibonacci numbers with LINQ

```
List<ulong> fibonacciNumbers = new List<ulong>();
Enumerable.Range(0,200)
        .ToList()
        .ForEach(k =>
                fibonacciNumbers.Add(k <= 1 ? 1:
                fibonacciNumbers[k-2] + fibonacciNumbers[k-1]));

fibonacciNumbers.Take(10).Dump("Fibonacci Numbers");
```

This displays the first ten Fibonacci numbers, as shown in Figure 2-17.

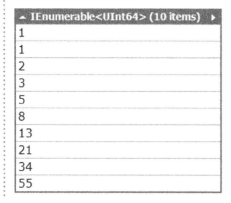

Figure 2-17. *The first ten Fibonacci numbers*

How It Works

The problem with recursion is that it's stateless. In plain English, that means recursive algorithms are forgetful—they don't remember what they calculated in previous iterations.

To solve this, you need a collection to hold the previously calculated values. After you have that collection, the next entry to be added is the sum of the two preceding elements denoted by `fibonacciNumbers[k-2]` and `fibonacciNumbers[k-1]`.

The technique represented in the preceding example is a scheme to make this recursive program run faster. There are several such problems, and because the pattern of these problems is the same, you can create a common generic structure to generate the results.

2-14. Recursive Series and Patterns: Generating Permutations

Generating permutations of a sequence is important in several applications. The following code generates all permutations of a given string. However, the algorithm can be extended to use with any data type.

Problem

Generate permutations of a given sequence.

■ **Tip**   For this code to work, you have to change the LINQPad language combo box to C# Program.

Solution

Listing 2-16 shows the solution.

Listing 2-16.

```
private HashSet<string> GeneratePartialPermutation(string word)
{
    return new HashSet<string>(Enumerable.Range(0,word.Length)
    .Select(i => word.Remove(i,1).Insert(0,word[i].ToString())));
}
void Main()
{
        HashSet<string> perms = GeneratePartialPermutation("abc");

        Enumerable.Range(0,2)
        .ToList()
        .ForEach
        (
           c=>
           {
                    Enumerable.Range(0,perms.Count ())
                    .ToList()
                    .ForEach
```

```
            (
              i => GeneratePartialPermutation(
                    perms.ElementAt(i))
            .ToList().ForEach(p=>perms.Add(p))
            );

            Enumerable.Range(0,perms.Count ())
            .ToList()
            .ForEach
            (
                i => GeneratePartialPermutation(new string
                    (perms.ElementAt(i).ToCharArray()
                    .Reverse().ToArray())
            )
            .ToList().ForEach(p=>perms.Add(p)));

    });
    perms.OrderBy (p => p).Dump("Permutations of 'abc'");
}
```

This generates the output shown in Figure 2-18.

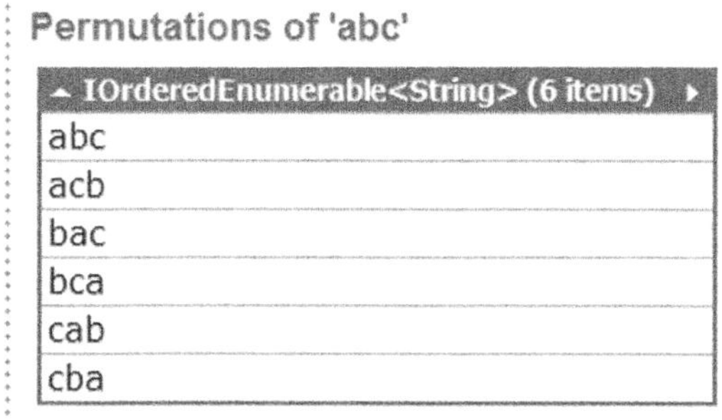

Permutations of 'abc'

▲ IOrderedEnumerable<String> (6 items) ▶
abc
acb
bac
bca
cab
cba

Figure 2-18. *Permutations of the string abc*

How It Works

The first step in generating permutations is to generate rotated versions of the given sequence. To do this, you bring each character to the front, leaving the order of the other characters unchanged. That's what the method GeneratePartialPermutation() does. So if the word is *abcd*, GeneratePartialPermutation() will return a set containing the items {"abcd", "bacd", "cabd", "dabc"}.

The next step is to generate the partial permutation for each of these and then the reverse of each. By running this process twice, you can ensure that you have traversed all possible permutations of the given string.

Finally, the code sorts the generated set of permutations alphabetically by using OrderBy().

2-15. Recursive Series and Patterns: Generating a Power Set of a Given Set

A *power set* is a set that contains all possible sets that can be created from the elements of the given set.

Problem

For the set {'a', 'b', 'c'}, the power set will be {"a", "ab", "bc", "ca", "abc"}. The problem is to write some LINQ code to generate the power set from any given set.

Solution

Listing 2-17 generates a power set from all the characters of a given string.

Listing 2-17. Create a power set from a given string

```
void Main()
{
        string word = "abc";
        HashSet<string> perms = GeneratePartialPermutation(word);
        Enumerable.Range(0,word.Length).ToList().ForEach(x=>
        Enumerable.Range(0,word.Length)
        .ToList()
        .ForEach( z=>
        {
                perms.Add(perms.ElementAt(x).Substring(0,z));
                perms.Add(perms.ElementAt(x).Substring(z+1));
        }));
     perms.Select (p => new string(p.ToCharArray()
          .OrderBy (x => x)
          .ToArray()))
          .Distinct()
          .OrderBy (p =>p.Length )
          .Dump("Power-set of 'abc'");
}
```

This code generates the power set of the string abc, as shown in Figure 2-19.

Power-set of 'abc'

▲ IOrderedEnumerable<String> (8 items) ▶
a
c
b
bc
ab
ac
abc

Figure 2-19. *The power set of the set formed from the characters of the string abc*

How It Works

This solution starts by creating the partial permutation list of the given word. Note that to get the elements of the power set, it is sufficient to split each partial permutation at each index and take the first and last token. For example, the word *abc* will generate these three element pairs: {"a", "bc"}, {"ab", "c"}, {"abc"}. By doing this for all the partial permutations, you are guaranteed to have generated all elements of the power set. However, this technique produces duplicate elements. Therefore, the final step sorts the characters of these tokens alphabetically and removes duplicates by using a Distinct() call. This leaves us with all the elements of the power set of the characters of the given word: *abc*, in this case.

We have all written code to manipulate in-memory collections by using a traditional loop-and-branch style. However, with LINQ, these types of manipulations become easy. In the following sections, some of these are solved using LINQ operators that appear often as subproblems in our code.

2-16. Collections: Picking Every *n*th Element

Picking every *n*th element from a given collection is a common problem that often appears as a subproblem of other problems such as shuffling or load distribution. The idea is to pick every *n*th element without dividing the index to figure out whether to include an entry.

Problem

Write an idiomatic LINQ query to find every *n*th element from a given sequence.

Solution

The code in Listing 2-18 shows the solution.

Listing 2-18. Picking every *n*th element from a given collection

```
int n = 20; //Pick every 20th element.
List<int> numbers = Enumerable.Range(1,100).ToList();
List<int> nthElements = new List<int>();
Enumerable.Range(0,numbers.Count()/n)
        .ToList()
        .ForEach(k => nthElements.Add(numbers.Skip(k*n).First()));
nthElements.Dump();
```

The output of the program is shown in Figure 2-20.

▲ List<Int32> (5 items) ▶
1
21
41
61
81

Figure 2-20. *The result of picking every 20th element*

How It Works

This example uses `Skip()` and `First()` in unison. This is idiomatic LINQ usage that you'll find in many applications. If you want to pick every *n*th element, there will be exactly `(numbers.Count()/n) + 1` elements after the pick, starting at the first index. In this case, the value for k ranges from 0 to 4. Thus the code snippet `numbers.Skip (k*n).First()` picks the first element after skipping k*n items from the left for all values of k starting at 0 and ending at 4. So when k is 1, the query skips the first 20 (because k*n is 20) elements, and then picks the next element (the 21st element in this case). This process continues until the end of the series.

2-17. Collections: Finding the Larger or Smaller of Several Sequences at Each Index

Finding the minimum or the maximum value at each location from several collections of the same length is useful for many applications.

Problem

Imagine that the numbers in some collections denote the bidding values for several different items. You want to find the maximum and minimum bid values for all the items. The problem is to write a generic LINQ query to find such values easily.

Solution

Listing 2-19 shows the solution.

Listing 2-19. Picking minimum or maximum values from multiple collections

```
List<int> bidValues1 = new List<int>(){1,2,3,4,5};
List<int> bidValues2 = new List<int>(){2,1,4,5,6};

bidValues1.Zip(bidValues2, (firstBid,secondBid) =>
    Math.Max(firstBid,secondBid))
    .Dump("Maximum bids");

bidValues1.Zip(bidValues2, (firstBid,secondBid) =>
    Math.Min(firstBid,secondBid))
    .Dump("Minimum bids");
```

This generates the output in Figure 2-21, which shows the minimum and maximum bid values at each stage.

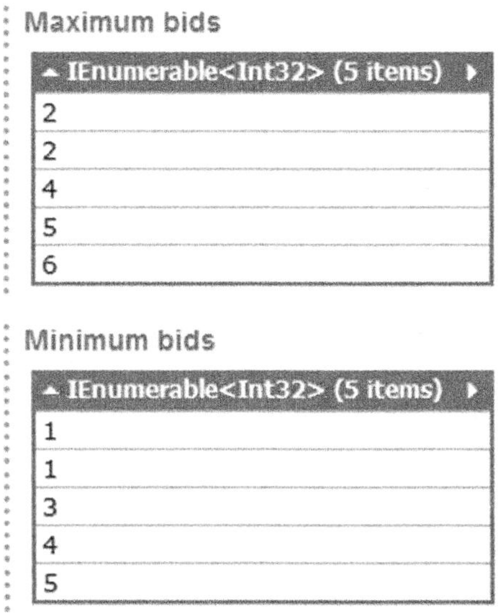

Maximum bids

▲ IEnumerable<Int32> (5 items) ▶
2
2
4
5
6

Minimum bids

▲ IEnumerable<Int32> (5 items) ▶
1
1
3
4
5

Figure 2-21. *Member-wise maximum and minimum values*

This example uses only two collections; however, in a real setting, you might need to extract minimum and/or maximum values at one or more specified locations from many collections.

While the code shown so far works, LINQ provides a cleaner way to solve the problem (see Listing 2-20).

Listing 2-20. A better LINQ solution for picking minimum and maximum values from multiple collections

```
List<List<int>> allValues = new List<List<int>>();
List<int> bidValues1 = new List<int>(){1,2,3,4,5};
List<int> bidValues2 = new List<int>(){2,1,4,5,6};
List<int> bidValues3 = new List<int>(){4,0,6,8,1};
List<int> bidValues4 = new List<int>(){9,2,4,1,6};

//Add all collections in this list of collections.
allValues.Add(bidValues1);
allValues.Add(bidValues2);
allValues.Add(bidValues3);
allValues.Add(bidValues4);

//Showing the maximum values compared at each location for 4 collections
allValues
.Aggregate((z1,z2) => z1.Zip(z2,(x,y) => Math.Max(x,y)).ToList())
.Dump("Maximum values : Generalized Approach");

//Showing the minimum values compared at each location for 4 collections
allValues
.Aggregate((z1,z2) => z1.Zip(z2,(x,y) => Math.Min(x,y)).ToList())
.Dump("Minimum values : Generalized Approach");
```

The preceding code generates the output in Figure 2-22, which shows minimum and maximum bid amounts at each stage.

Maximum values : Generalized Approach

▲ List<Int32> (5 items) ▶
9
2
6
8
6

Maximum values : Generalized Approach

▲ List<Int32> (5 items) ▶
1
0
3
1
1

Figure 2-22. *Maximum and minimum values from several collections at each location*

How It Works

This is a little tricky. The solution aggregates a list of lists over their zipped values. It may take some time to wrap your head around this.

Consider the following code:

```
Aggregate((z1,z2) => z1.Zip(z2,(x,y) => Math.Min(x,y)).ToList())
```

Here, z1 and z2 are of type List<int>. The inner call to Zip() uses the minimum value at each location to find out what the result should be at that location. Thus, at each level of aggregation (which processes two lists at a time), you always have a collection that has the minimum values at each location for all the collections aggregated thus far, as shown in Figure 2-23.

List1	List2	At first pass	Result	List3	At second pass	Result	List4	At third pass
1	2	1	1	4	1	1	9	1
2	1	1	1	0	0	0	2	0
3	4	3	3	6	3	3	4	3
4	5	4	4	8	4	4	1	1
5	6	5	5	1	1	1	6	6

Figure 2-23. *How the minimum values get picked at each stage*

These tables illustrate how the code finds the minimum number at each location and at each stage. The resulting collection, containing the minimum value at each location for the initial two lists, serves as the first argument in the next step. Changed values at each step are in the third column of the table.

Number theory has some fascinating examples of series generation in action. Most of us were taught programming using these examples. If you have been programming for a while, you likely are familiar with the number sequences described here. That choice is deliberate. I wanted to show how LINQ can help us approach the problem differently.

2-18. Number Theory: Generating Armstrong Numbers and Similar Number Sequences

In recreational mathematics, an *Armstrong number* is a topic of interest. An Armstrong number is a number that is the same as the sum of its digits raised to the power of three. For example, consider the number 153, as shown in Figure 2-24.

$$153 = 1^3 + 5^3 + 3^3$$

Figure 2-24. *An Armstrong number*

Note that the number is obtained by summing up all its digits raised to the power of three.

A *Dudeney number* is a positive integer that is a perfect cube, such that the sum of its decimal digits is equal to the cube root of the number. Consider the number 512. The sum of the digits in 512 is 8. And the cube of 8 is 512. Stated another way, the cube root of 512 is 8, which is the sum of the digits of 512.

A *sum-product number* is an integer that in a given base is equal to the sum of its digits times the product of its digits. Or, to put it algebraically, given an integer n that is l digit long in base b (with dx representing the xth digit), if the following condition shown in Figure 2-25

$$n = (\sum_{i=1}^{l} d_i)(\prod_{j=1}^{l} d_j)$$

Figure 2-25. *Equation of a sum-product number*

A *factorion* is a natural number that equals the sum of the factorials of its decimal digits. For example, 145 is a factorion because 1! + 4! + 5! = 1 + 24 + 120 = 145.

Problem

Given a range, can you find all the Armstrong numbers, Dudeney numbers, sum-product numbers, or factorions in that range?

Solution

Because all these number definitions deal with the digits of integer numbers, you can first create a method to extract the individual digits of a number from a given integer. Listing 2-21 shows the code for an extension method that extracts digits from a given integer number.

Listing 2-21. Finding Armstrong numbers, Dudeney numbers, sum-product numbers, and factorions in a range

```
public static class NumberEx
{
     public static IEnumerable<int> Digits(this int n)
     {
         List<char> chars = new List<char>() {'0','1','2','3','4','5','6','7','8','9'};
         List<int> digits = new List<int>();
           foreach (char c in n.ToString())
                 digits.Add(chars.IndexOf(c));
           return digits.AsEnumerable();
     }
}

void Main()
{

    Enumerable.Range(0,1000)
    .Where(k => k.Digits().Select (x => x * x * x).Sum() == k)
       .Dump("Armstrong Numbers");

    Enumerable.Range(0,1000)
    .Where(k => {
        var digits = k.Digits();
        if(digits.Sum() * digits.Aggregate ((x,y) =>x*y) == k)
            return true;
        else
            return false;
    }).Dump("Sum Product Numbers");
    Enumerable.Range(0,1000)
        .Where (e => Math.Pow(e.Digits().Sum(),3) == e)
        .Dump("Dudeney Numbers");

    Enumerable.Range(1,1000)
        .Where (e => e.Digits()
        .Where (d => d > 0)
        .Select(x =>Enumerable.Range(1,x)
        .Aggregate((a,b) => a*b)) //Calculating factorial of each digit
        .Sum() //Calculating summation of factorials
        == e) //when summation matches number it's a factorion
        .Dump("Factorions");
}
```

This generates the output shown in Figure 2-26.

Armstrong Numbers

▲ IEnumerable<Int32> (6 items) ▶
0
1
153
370
371
407

Sum Product Numbers

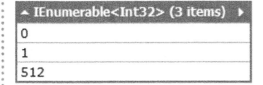

▲ IEnumerable<Int32> (4 items) ▶
0
1
135
144

Dudeney Numbers

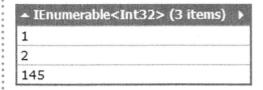

▲ IEnumerable<Int32> (3 items) ▶
0
1
512

Factorions

▲ IEnumerable<Int32> (3 items) ▶
1
2
145

Figure 2-26. *Armstrong numbers and other similar numbers*

How It Works

At the heart of these examples is the Digits() extension method that returns a List<int> containing the individual digits. For example, 153.Digits() returns a List<int> containing the values {1, 5, and 3}.

Let's start with Armstrong numbers. The following code projects each digit of the number k as its cube, and then sums the projected values:

```
k.Digits().Select (x => x * x * x).Sum()
```

For example, if k is 153, then k.Digits().Select (x => x * x * x) returns {1 , 125, 27}, The Sum() operator totals these projected values. Because the sum of 1, 125, and 27 is 153, 153 is a valid Armstrong number. To find the sum-product numbers, you need to find the sum and the product of digits. digits.Sum() returns the sum of the digits, and digits.Aggregate ((x,y) =>x*y) finds the product of the digits. If the product of these two figures matches the number itself, you can declare that the number is a sum-product number.

The code for finding Dudeney numbers couldn't be more straightforward. It is one of those perfect examples that shows how LINQ can make code look more intuitive and yet be more readable at the same time.

The code for finding factorions is a little trickier; however, the algorithm is simple. First, find all the digits of the number. Then discard all zeros because a factorial of zero doesn't make sense. Then, for all such nonzero digits, go to that digit starting from 1. Multiply all the digits you encounter along the way. This will give you the factorial of each digit. If you want to avoid this step, you can precalculate and save the factorials of digits 1 to 9 in a dictionary. At the end, you sum these factorials. If the sum matches the number, that number is a factorion.

2-19. Number Theory: Generating Pascal's Triangle Nonrecursively

In mathematics, Pascal's triangle is a triangular array of the binomial coefficients. It is named after the French mathematician Blaise Pascal. The first few rows of the Pascal triangle are shown in Figure 2-27.

```
          1
        1   1
      1   2   1
    1   3   3   1
  1   4   6   4   1
1   5  10  10   5   1
```

Figure 2-27. *The first few rows of Pascal's triangle*

The structure is recursive. Apart from the first and the last column, every value is the sum of the elements just above it. For example, the 4 in the next-to-last row in Figure 2-27 is the result of adding 1 and 3 immediately above it. Classically, these number triangles are created by calling a function recursively, passing the row and column position. But as the number of rows increases, this method becomes very slow and may even throw an out-of-memory exception because the stack overflows. However, you can avoid the recursion by using extra storage.

Problem

The problem here is to avoid recursion by using external storage. In functional programming, this technique is known as *memoization*.

Listing 2-22 shows some code that generates the Pascal's triangle without recursion. It's much faster than the recursive version.

Solution

Listing 2-22 shows the solution.

Listing 2-22. Generating a Pascal's triangle without recursion

```
List<Tuple<int,int,int>> pascalValues = new List<Tuple<int,int,int>>();
pascalValues.Add(new Tuple<int,int,int>(1,1,1));
pascalValues.Add(new Tuple<int,int,int>(2,1,1));
pascalValues.Add(new Tuple<int,int,int>(2,2,1));

for(int i=1;i<10;i++)
{
    int currentRow = pascalValues.Last().Item1  + 1;
    int currentCol = pascalValues.Last().Item2 + 1;
    for(int j = 1;j<=currentCol;j++)
    {
        if(j==1 || j== currentCol)
            pascalValues.Add(new Tuple<int,int,int>(currentRow,j,1));
        else
            pascalValues.Add(new Tuple<int,int,int>(currentRow,j,
            pascalValues.First (v => v.Item1 == currentRow - 1 &&
                v.Item2 == j - 1).Item3 +
            pascalValues.First (v => v.Item1 == currentRow - 1 &&
                v.Item2 == j).Item3 ));
    }
}
//Show the table
pascalValues
.ToLookup(t=>t.Item1,t=>t.Item3.ToString())
.Select (t => t.Aggregate ((x,y)  => x + " " + y ))
.Aggregate ((u,v)  => u + Environment.NewLine + v)
.Dump("Pascal's Triangle");
```

This generates the output shown in Figure 2-28.

```
Pascal's Triangle
1
1 1
1 2 1
1 3 3 1
1 4 6 4 1
1 5 10 10 5 1
1 6 15 20 15 6 1
1 7 21 35 35 21 7 1
1 8 28 56 70 56 28 8 1
1 9 36 84 126 126 84 36 9 1
1 10 45 120 210 252 210 120 45 10 1
```

Figure 2-28. *The first ten rows of Pascal's triangle*

How It Works

You can represent number triangles as a series of tuples, where each tuple stores the row, column, and the value at the row, col position. For example, you can use a List<Tuple<int,int,int>> in C# where the first item in the tuple represents the row, the second item represents the column, and the third/last item represents the value at that (row, col) position in the triangle.

These three lines store the first three items of the triangle:

```
pascalValues.Add(new Tuple<int,int,int>(1,1,1));
pascalValues.Add(new Tuple<int,int,int>(2,1,1));
pascalValues.Add(new Tuple<int,int,int>(2,2,1));
```

For the first and the last column, the value is always 1. The following code takes care of filling that correctly:

```
if(j==1 || j== currentCol)
    pascalValues.Add(new Tuple<int,int,int>(currentRow,j,1));
```

Every other element is the sum of the element directly above it (same column, previous row) and the element diagonally above it (previous column, previous row). The following code obtains this value:

```
pascalValues.Add(new Tuple<int,int,int>(currentRow,j,
pascalValues.First (v => v.Item1 == currentRow - 1 && v.Item2 == j - 1).Item3  +
pascalValues.First (v => v.Item1 == currentRow - 1 && v.Item2 == j).Item3 ));
```

You can apply similar logic to generate all other number triangles.

2-20. Game Design: Finding All Winning Paths in an Arbitrary Tic-Tac-Toe Board

Most tic-tac-toe boards are 3×3 grids. Tic-tac-toe game implementations usually hard-code the winning paths in the code. However, if you want to create a game that uses an arbitrary-size tic-tac-toe board, you have to find out the winning paths at runtime—whenever the user changes the board size. Because tic-tac-toe boards are square, you can represent a 3×3 board by the integer 3.

Problem

Generate all winning paths of an arbitrarily sized tic-tac-toe board, starting the cell numbering at 1. For a 3×3 board, the cells range from 1 to 9. For a 4×4 board, cells range from 1 to 16.

Solution

Listing 2-23 shows the solution.

Listing 2-23. Generate winning paths for a tic-tac-toe board

```
int boardSize = 3;
var range = Enumerable.Range(1,boardSize*boardSize);

List<List<int>> winningPaths = new List<List<int>>();
//Horizontal Paths
Enumerable.Range(0,boardSize)
    .ToList()
    .ForEach(k => winningPaths.Add(range.Skip(k*boardSize)
        .Take(boardSize).ToList()));

//Vertical Paths
Enumerable.Range(0,boardSize)
    .ToList()
    .ForEach(k => winningPaths.Add(winningPaths.Take(boardSize)
        .Select(p => p[k]).ToList()));

//Diagonal Paths
//Main diagonal
winningPaths.Add(range.Where((r,i) =>
    i % (boardSize + 1) == 0).ToList());

//reverse diagonal
winningPaths.Add(range.Where ((r,i) =>
    i % (boardSize - 1) == 0).Skip(1).Take(boardSize).ToList());
//printing all the paths; one path on each line.
winningPaths.Select(x => x.Select (z => z.ToString()).Aggregate
    ((a,b)=> a.ToString () + " " + b.ToString() ))
    .Dump("All winning paths for a Tic-Tac-Toe board of size 3");
```

This generates the output shown in Figure 2-29.

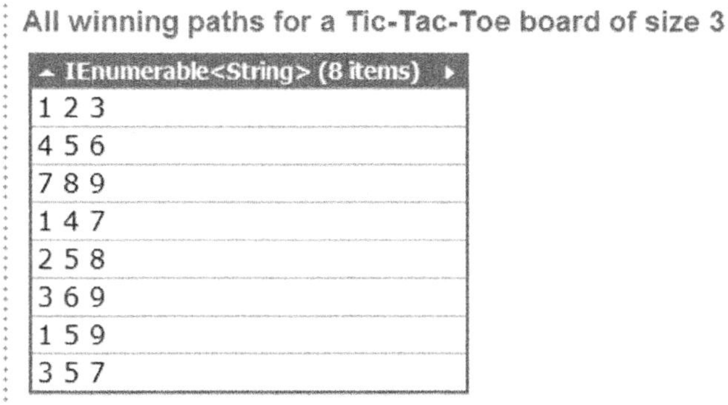

All winning paths for a Tic-Tac-Toe board of size 3

▲ IEnumerable<String> (8 items) ▶
1 2 3
4 5 6
7 8 9
1 4 7
2 5 8
3 6 9
1 5 9
3 5 7

Figure 2-29. *All winning paths of a 3×3 tic-tac-toe board*

How It Works

Tic-tac-toe boards have four types of winning paths, as shown in Figure 2-30. Follow this hint to find how the code works.

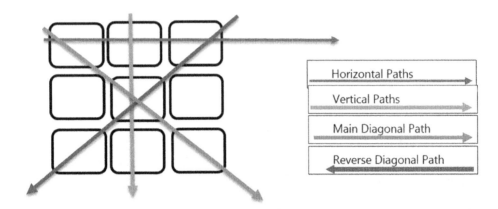

Figure 2-30. *The direction of all winning paths in a tic-tac-toe board*

Finding horizontal paths is simple. At each stage, you need to take as many elements as the board size. So if the board size is 3×3, you have to take three elements at each stage. Skip() followed by Take() achieves that. This is a common technique. Whenever you want to skip a few elements at each stage and then take one or more, this LINQ idiom comes in handy.

For vertical paths, note that each element in each vertical path is selected from its respective index of the corresponding horizontal paths. Or in other words, vertical paths are a transposition of the matrix created from the horizontal paths.

Finding elements of the main diagonal path is also simple. Elements at the main diagonal appear at a gap of (boardSize + 1). In other words, elements of the main diagonal form an arithmetic progression (AP) with a difference of (boardSize + 1).

The code var range = Enumerable.Range(1,boardSize*boardSize); generates a range of all cell values. Subsequently, the code range.Where ((r,i) => i % (boardSize - 1) == 0) filters the range, skipping the first element, and then picking boardSize elements, leaving you with the elements of the reverse diagonal.

2-21. Series in Game Design: Solving Go Figure

Go Figure is a puzzle to figure out a mathematical expression involving four unique digits (0 to 9), that evaluate to a given answer. For example, if the set of digits is {1, 2, 4, and 9} and the answer is 10, then (9 + 4) – (2 + 1) is a valid expression. The puzzle challenges players to use mathematical symbols (+, -, and *) and brackets to create an expression. Evaluating the expression results in the given answer.

Problem

Write a program that generates answers for a Go Figure puzzle.

Solution

The program in Listing 2-24 solves the puzzle.

Listing 2-24. Generating answers for a Go-Figure puzzle

```
//Assume the answer we want to reach is "10"
int answer = 10 ;

//And we want to create 10 using 1, 2, 4 and 9
List<int> set = new List<int>() {1,2,4,9};

List<KeyValuePair<int,string>> query =
set.SelectMany ((s,i) => set.Where (se => se!=s)
    .Select (se => new KeyValuePair<int,string>
    (se+s,se.ToString()+"+"+s.ToString()))).ToList();

query.AddRange(
set.SelectMany ((s,i) => set.Where (se => se!=s)
    .Select (se => new KeyValuePair<int,string>
    (se*s,se.ToString()+"*"+s.ToString()))));

query.AddRange(
set.SelectMany ((s,i) => set.Where (se => se!=s)
    .Select (se => new KeyValuePair<int,string>
    (se-s,se.ToString()+"-"+s.ToString()))));

List<string> expressions = new List<string>();
for(int i=0;i<query.Count();i++)
{
    for(int j=0;j<query.Count ();j++)
    {
        if(i!=j)
        {
            if(!Regex.Matches(query[i].Value,"[0-9]")
                .Cast<Match>()
                .Select (m =>Convert.ToInt16(m.Value))
                .OrderBy (m => m)
                .Any(z => Regex.Matches(query[j].Value,"[0-9]")
                .Cast<Match>()
                .Select (m =>Convert.ToInt16(m.Value))
                .OrderBy (m => m)
                .Contains(z)))
            {
                if(query[i].Key  + query[j].Key == answer)
                {
                    expressions.Add("(" + query[i].Value + ") +
                        (" + query[j].Value +")");
                    break;
                }
```

```
                    if(query[i].Key - query[j].Key == answer)
                    {
                        expressions.Add("(" + query[i].Value + ") -
                            (" + query[j].Value +")");
                        break;
                    }
                    if(query[i].Key * query[j].Key == answer)
                    {
                        expressions.Add("(" + query[i].Value + ")
                            * (" + query[j].Value +")");
                        break;
                    }
                }
            }
        }
}

expressions.Dump("Expressions");
```

This generates the output shown in Figure 2-31.

Expressions

▲ List<String> (9 items) ▶
(9+4) - (2+1)
(4+9) - (2+1)
(2*1) * (9-4)
(1*2) * (9-4)
(4-1) + (9-2)
(9-1) + (4-2)
(4-2) + (9-1)
(9-2) + (4-1)
(9-4) * (2*1)

Figure 2-31. *All expressions that result in the answer*

How It Works

At the core of this solution is the logic that calculates all the possible values that can be reached by adding, subtracting, or multiplying the given values in the set.

For example, the following code generates a list of key/value pairs, where the keys represent the summation and the values represent the expressions that resulted in the summation. For the given set {1, 4, 2, and 9}, one such entry in this list is represented by the following key and value combination: key = 5, value = 9 – 4.

```
List<KeyValuePair<int,string>> query =
set.SelectMany ((s,i) => set.Where (se => se!=s )
.Select (se => new KeyValuePair<int,string>(se+s,se.ToString()+"+"+s.ToString()))).ToList();
```

Similarly, other expressions and their resultant values are calculated and are added to the query. So when * is used between 9 and 4, you get 36 as the value and 9 * 4 as the expression. However, there isn't any check to identify that 9 * 4 and 4 * 9 are same. Can you bring that in? That would be a good exercise.

After constructing the list of results and expressions, you need to iterate over the list to find the final expression that results in the given answer. However, you must avoid expressions that share the same digit. For example, if you choose 9 – 4 as the first part of the expression, you can't subsequently use any expression containing either of those digits. The following code checks that.:

```
if(!Regex.Matches(query[i].Value,"[0-9]")
                        .Cast<Match>()
                        .Select (m =>Convert.ToInt16(m.Value))
                        .OrderBy (m => m)
                        .Any(z => Regex.Matches(query[j].Value,"[0-9]")
                            .Cast<Match>()
                            .Select (m =>Convert.ToInt16(m.Value))
                            .OrderBy (m => m)
                            .Contains(z)))
```

2-22. Miscellaneous Series: Finding Matching Pairs from Two Unsorted Collections

Assume you have two or more unsorted collections and you want to find a pair of entries from these collections that match.

Problem

Here's a more concrete example. Imagine two arrays containing English words. You want to find words in one array that rhyme with one or more words in the other array. Further, for the purposes of this example, assume that if the last three letters of two words are identical, they probably rhyme. For example, rubble and bubble rhyme, and so do brush and rush. Obviously, this rule doesn't work for all words. Remember that the solution shouldn't involve sorting, because that can be computationally expensive—precisely what you should avoid.

Solution

Listing 2-25 shows the solution.

Listing 2-25. Finding matching pairs in two unsorted collections

```
//finding matching pairs
string[] words1 = {"orange", "herbal", "rubble", "indicative", "mandatory",
                    "brush", "golden", "diplomatic", "pace"};

string[] words2 = {"verbal", "rush", "pragmatic", "story", "race",
                    "bubble", "olden"};

//Checking whether the last three characters match.
//is a rudimentary way to tell if two words rhyme.
Func<string,string,bool> mightRhyme = (a,b) =>
 a[a.Length-1]==b[b.Length - 1]
 && a[a.Length-2]==b[b.Length - 2]
 && a[a.Length-3]==b[b.Length - 3];
```

```
words1
.Select(w => new KeyValuePair<string,string>(w, words2.FirstOrDefault(wo => mightRhyme(w,wo))))
.Where(w => !String.IsNullOrEmpty(w.Value))
.Dump("Matching Pairs");
```

This query when run on LINQPad generates the output shown in Figure 2-32.

Matching Pairs

▲ IEnumerable<KeyValuePair<String,String>> (7 items) ►	
Key	Value
herbal	verbal
rubble	bubble
mandatory	story
brush	rush
golden	olden
diplomatic	pragmatic
pace	race

Figure 2-32. *The result of matching pair extraction from unsorted collections*

How It Works

At first glance, this problem seems to have a straightforward nested loop-based quadratic time solution. You just have to loop through the collections and find the matching pairs one at a time. The preceding code is just a LINQ implementation of this method.

words2.FirstOrDefault(wo => mightRhyme(w,wo)) will return the matching pair for w in words2 or it will return null when there no matching pair exists. In this case, the binary predicate is the method mightRhyme, which takes two strings and returns true if their three trailing characters match.

```
Select(w => new KeyValuePair<string,string>(w, words2.FirstOrDefault(wo => mightRhyme(w,wo))))
```

This code generates an IEnumerable<KeyValuePair<string,string>>, where the keys hold each word in the array words1 and the values hold rhyming pairs found in the array words2, if any, or null if no matches exist.

The following code filters out pairs for which no rhyming was found:

```
Where (w => !String.IsNullOrEmpty(w.Value)) That leaves us with rhyming pairs.
```

2-23. Miscellaneous Series: Using a Lookup-Based Approach

The solution you have explored in this section works. However, it takes quadratic time because it has to loop through the other collection to find rhyming words. So this method is neither scalable nor efficient.

Fortunately, a linear-time solution exists. Because you are finding matching words by matching their last three letters, you can treat the three trailing characters from each word as a hash of each word. So *bal* is the hash of *verbal*. The word *herbal* also has the same *ble* hash.

Problem

Find pairs of possible rhymes in two lists using a lookup-based approach.

Solution

If you create a lookup table based on the hash (that is, just the last three characters of each word), then wherever the hashes match (a collision, in other words), you have a likely candidate for a rhyming pair. The following query generates the hash-based lookup table and finds potential rhyming words using the same two word lists used in the previous solution:

```
string[] words1 = {"orange", "herbal", "rubble", "indicative", "mandatory",
                   "brush", "golden", "diplomatic", "pace"};

string[] words2 = {"verbal", "rush", "pragmatic", "story", "race",
                   "bubble", "olden"};
words1
 .Concat(words2)
 .ToLookup(w => w.Substring(w.Length-3))
 .Where(w => w.Count() >= 2)
 .Select(w => w.Aggregate((m,n)=>m+", "+n))
 .Dump("Showing rhyming pairs comma separated");
```

This generates the output shown in Figure 2-33.

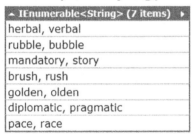

Comma-separated rhyming pairs

▲ IEnumerable<String> (7 items) ▶
herbal, verbal
rubble, bubble
mandatory, story
brush, rush
golden, olden
diplomatic, pragmatic
pace, race

Figure 2-33. *Rhyming pair of words selected from two unsorted collections of words*

How It Works

`words1.Concat(words2)` returns the list of all the words.

`ToLookup (w => w.Substring(w.Length-3)))` creates a lookup table, where the hash is the last three characters of each word. The lookup table looks like Figure 2-34.

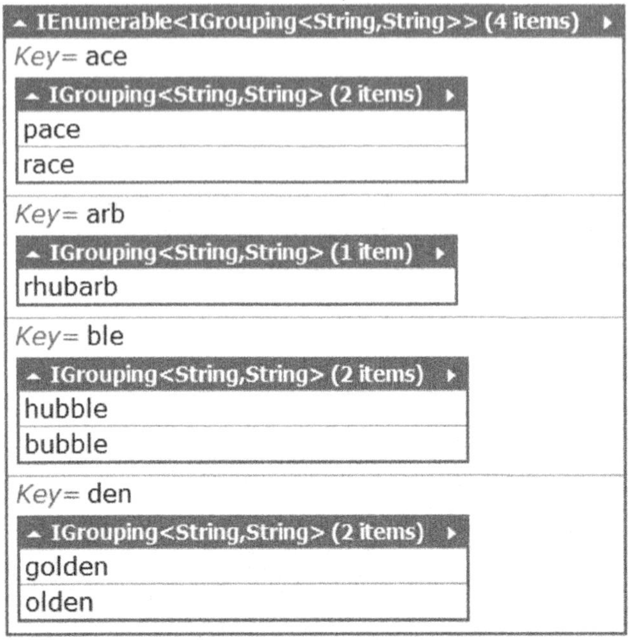

Figure 2-34. *A lookup table with a hash-key consisting of the last three characters of each word*

Now take a close look at the table. The pairs that rhyme have two items. For example, *brush* and *rush* share the same hash—*ush*. So it will be sufficient to find those entries from the lookup table that contain two or more entries. That filtering operation is performed by the code Where (w => w.Count() >= 2). In the final stage, these filtered entries are projected as comma-separated values by Select(w => w.Aggregate((m,n)=>m+", "+n)).

2-24. Miscellaneous Series: Solving the FizzBuzz Challenge in a LINQ One-Liner

The FizzBuzz problem has been used as a litmus test of programming capability among aspiring programming job candidates, which—by itself—makes it worth a bit of study.

Problem

Write a program that prints the numbers from 1 to 100. But for multiples of 3, print *Fizz* instead of the number, and for the multiples of 5, print *Buzz*. For numbers that are multiples of both 3 and 5, print *FizzBuzz*.

Solution

Listing 2-26 shows the solution.

Listing 2-26. Solving the FizzBuzz Challenge with LINQ

```
List<string> fizzBuzzes = new List<string>();
Enumerable.Range(1,100).ToList().ForEach(k =>
    fizzBuzzes.Add(k % 15 == 0 ? "FizzBuzz" : k % 5 == 0 ? "Buzz"
                                           : k % 3 == 0 ? "Fizz"
                                           : k.ToString()));
fizzBuzzes.Take(20).Dump(); //show the first 20 elements
```

This generates the output shown in Figure 2-35.

Figure 2-35. *The first 20 elements of the FizzBuzz series*

How It Works

Solving the FizzBuzz problem requires nothing but a straightforward `if-else` structure described by the following pseudo code:

```
If the number is divisible by 15
    Replace with FizzBuzz
Else if the number is divisible by 5
    Replace with Buzz
Else if the number is divisible by 3
    Replace with Fizz
Else // for everything else
    Don t do anything. Just show that number.
```

Using the ternary operator (? :), you can write this logic in a single line of code. The following line does just that:

```
k % 15 == 0 ? "FizzBuzz" : k % 5 == 0 ? "Buzz" : k % 3 == 0 ? "Fizz" : k.ToString()
```

However, because 15 is a multiple of both 3 and 5, you can optimize for that and eliminate the division by 15. The next example demonstrates that.

2-25. Miscellaneous Series: Solving the FizzBuzz Challenge by Using Set Theory

The previous solution used division by 15. However, because 15 is a multiple of 3 and 5, you can avoid computationally expensive divisions by 15 by relying on the fact that sets divisible by 15 are also divisible by 3 and 5. This boils down to the following solution using set theory properties. The code might look a bit clumsy, but it will offer better performance for longer sequences because it avoids the unnecessary division by 15.

Problem

Rewrite the FizzBuzz Challenge code to eliminate the division by 15.

Solution

Listing 2-27 shows the solution.

Listing 2-27. Solving the FizzBuzz Challenge using set theory

```
var range = Enumerable.Range(1,40);
var mod3 = range.Where(e => e % 3 == 0);
var mod5 = range.Where(e => e% 5 == 0);
var mod15 = mod3.Intersect(mod5);

//Find numbers that are divisible by 3 but not by 5 or 15
mod3 = mod3.Except(mod15);

//Find numbers that are divisible by 5 but not by 3 or 15
mod5 = mod5.Except(mod15);
```

```
//Find integers that are not divisible by either 3 or 5
var neither = range.Except(mod3.Concat(mod5).Concat(mod15));

//Project each of these numbers as per the rule of the challenge.
neither.Select (n => new KeyValuePair<int,string>(n, n.ToString()))
    .Concat(mod3.Select (m => new KeyValuePair<int,string>(m, "fizz")))
    .Concat(mod5.Select (m => new KeyValuePair<int,string>(m, "buzz")))
    .Concat(mod15.Select (m => new KeyValuePair<int,string>(m, "fizzbuzz")))

    //Sort the projected values as per the integer keys
    .OrderBy (n => n.Key)

    //But show the values only.
    .Select (n => n.Value)

    .Take(20) //showing first 20 elements
    //Dump the result
    .Dump ("Fizz Buzz Challenge");
```

How It Works

Although this solution looks overwhelmingly large compared to the previous version, it is simple. If you denote all numbers divisible by 3 as a set, and all numbers divisible by 5 as another set, then the intersection of these two sets will be the set of numbers divisible by 15.

```
//Creates a set of multiples of the number 3
var mod3 = range.Where (e => e % 3 == 0);
var mod5 = range.Where(e => e% 5 == 0); //does so for the number 5.
```

Except() returns elements present in one set but not in the other. Because the numbers divisible by 15 will be present in both sets, you can remove those items. The following lines of code do that:

```
//Find numbers that are divisible by 3 but not by 5 or 15
mod3 = mod3.Except(mod15);
//Find numbers that are divisible by 5 but not by 3 or 15
mod5 = mod5.Except(mod15);
```

So at this point, mod3 contains only elements divisible by 3, while mod5 contains elements only divisible by 5, and mod15 contains elements divisible by 15. The rest of the numbers in the range are not divisible by any of these numbers (3, 5, or 15). These numbers are found and stored in the variable neither.

The following line of code projects the integers and their corresponding values as per FizzBuzz rule:

```
IEnumerable<KeyVlauePair<int,string>>
neither.Select (n => new KeyValuePair<int,string>(n, n.ToString()))
    .Concat(mod3.Select (m => new KeyValuePair<int,string>(m, "fizz")))
    .Concat(mod5.Select (m => new KeyValuePair<int,string>(m, "buzz")))
    .Concat(mod15.Select (m => new KeyValuePair<int,string>(m, "fizzbuzz")))
```

OrderBy (n => n.Key) sorts this projected range of keys in ascending order. Finally, the values for the FizzBuzz series are projected by Select (n => n.Value).

Summary

Congratulations on finishing a long chapter! The problems here were selected to represent real-world applications while keeping variety and simplicity in mind. The key takeaway from this chapter is that you can apply LINQ to solve problems in several domains. The code in this chapter illustrates several idiomatic usages of LINQ. By now you should have a solid grasp of how to apply such LINQ idioms to generate several sequences. The advantage is that using LINQ operators makes your query look clean and concise. In the next chapter, you will see how to apply LINQ to solve several types of text-processing tasks.

CHAPTER 3

■ ■ ■

Text Processing

Text processing is a blanket term used to describe any kind of string processing. Checking whether a pair of words are anagrams of each other is one example of text processing. Generating suggestions for an autocomplete or assisted input process is another. Some types of text processing, such as spell-check and correction features, have become so commonplace that software users now expect them to be present in virtually every program they use.

LINQ changes the way developers deal with text because it lets you write intuitive code to solve complex text-processing tasks. In this chapter, you will have a chance to solve some fun—yet useful—text-processing challenges. The examples in this chapter vary widely in terms of difficulty. They are intended to serve as basic examples of how LINQ can help solve numerous text-processing problems.

The problems in this chapter fall into three broad but related categories:

- *Human-computer interactions* that deal with various input strategies and spell-check

- *Text generation and manipulation*, such as the anagram problem mentioned earlier

- *Information extraction*, such as pulling content from a document

3-1. Simulating a T9 Word Suggestion

Typing on mobile phones wasn't easy in the early days, so several schemes were invented to make it simpler. Autocompletion of words using a T9 dictionary was one such early solution. Figure 3-1 shows a typical basic mobile phone keypad.

Figure 3-1. *The keypad of a mobile phone, with the letters on each key*

A typical mobile phone has the entire alphabet on its keys. This type of keypad enables users to enter predictive text using a T9 dictionary.

Problem

Given a set of T9 key presses, select all possible matching words from a dictionary.

Solution

The code in Listing 3-1 implements an algorithm to pull all the words from T9 that match the keystrokes entered from the keypad. Words that share the same key combination are known as *textonyms*. For example, the key combination 4663 matches the words *good, home, gone,* and *hood.* Those words are textonyms of each other. So when a user types 4663 on a T9-enabled keypad of a mobile phone, the phone offers all the textonyms as suggestions to pick from. Sometimes these suggestions can be quite amusing. For example, *select* and *reject* are textonyms, because they both use the key combination 735328.

Listing 3-1. Find words that match T9 keypresses

```
string keyPad =    @"2 = ABC2
                    3 = DEF3
                    4 = GHI4
                    5 = JKL5
                    6 = MNO6
                    7 = PQRS7
                    8 = TUV8
                    9 = WXYZ9";

Dictionary<char,char> keyMap = new Dictionary<char,char>();

//4663 can lead to "good","home" etc
string key = "4663";

//"735328";//select/reject
//"select" and "reject" can be typed using the key combination "735328"

List<KeyValuePair<string,string>> keyAndLetters =
    keyPad.ToLower()
    .Split(new char[]{'\r','\n'},StringSplitOptions.RemoveEmptyEntries)
    .Select
    (
        p =>
        new KeyValuePair<string,string>(p.Split('=')[0].Trim(),p.Split('=')[1].Trim()))
                .ToList();

foreach (var keyL in keyAndLetters)
{
    foreach (char c in keyL.Value.ToCharArray())
        keyMap.Add(c,Convert.ToChar(keyL.Key));
}
```

```
StreamReader sr = new StreamReader ("C:\\T9.txt");
string total = sr.ReadToEnd();
sr.Close();

var query = total
            .Split(new char[]{'\r','\n',' '},StringSplitOptions.RemoveEmptyEntries)
            .Where (t => t.Length==key.Length)
                .Select (t => t.Trim());

query
    .ToList()
    .Select(w=> new KeyValuePair<string,string>(w,
        new string(w.ToCharArray().Select (x => keyMap[x]).ToArray())))
    .Where (w => w.Value==key)
    .Select (w => w.Key)
    .Dump("Word suggestions");
```

I have used this code in a Windows application that simulates T9 typing. You can see it in action on YouTube (www.youtube.com/watch?v=Su4-_v2qGvQ&feature=youtu.be). Of course, the program is also in the downloadable code that accompanies this book.

When you run the program, you will see a list of suggested words that correspond to the key combination 4663. On a T9-enabled mobile keypad, entering 4663 matches several words, including *gone, good, goof,* and *home,* as you can see in Figure 3-2.

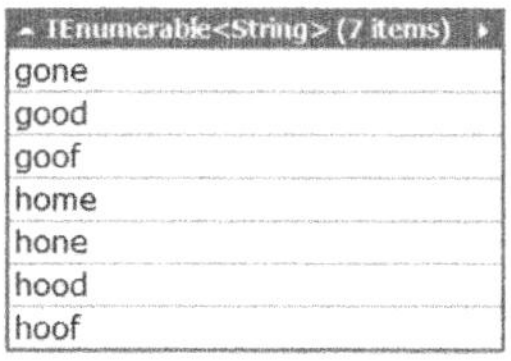

Figure 3-2. Suggestions for the keystrokes 4663 on a T9-enabled keyboard

How It Works

The task is to locate all the possible words from a given dictionary that match a given a key combination. If you approach this problem from another direction, you can think of it as replacing all the characters in a given word with the key on which that letter is available. For example, because *a, b,* and *c* are all available on the 2 key, you can replace all occurrences of these three letters with 2. Doing so re-creates the numeric combination used to enter the word.

For example, suppose you enter the word *home.* To determine the set of numeric keys required to enter *home,* replace each letter with its corresponding numeric digit from the keypad. Referring to the keypad shown in Figure 3-1, you can see that *h* is on key 4, *o* and *m* are both on key 6, and *e* is on key 3. Thus the numeric key for the word *home* is 4663.

Figure 3-3 represents the entire keypad. Each line shows the numeric key and the corresponding letters that can be entered by pressing that key. The Key column represents a key on the mobile phone's keypad. The Value column represents all the characters a user can enter with that key. So the first line shows, for example, that by pressing the 2 key, users can enter an *a, b, c,* or of course the number 2.

Keys and Letters

▲ List<KeyValuePair<String,String>> (8 items) ▶	
Key	**Value**
2	abc2
3	def3
4	ghi4
5	jkl5
6	mno6
7	pqrs7
8	tuv8
9	wxyz9

Figure 3-3. *The keys and the corresponding letters that can be typed by using them*

If you reverse this so that each character is a key, and each mobile phone key number is a value, you end up with a one-to-one mapping, in which each character is matched with its corresponding digit, as shown (partially) in Figure 3-4.

▲ IEnumerable<KeyValuePair<Char,Char>> (8 items) ▶	
Key	**Value**
a	2
b	2
c	2
2	2
d	3
e	3
f	3
3	3

Figure 3-4. *A one-to-one mapping of each character and its corresponding key on the mobile phone keypad*

The following code creates a list of KeyValuePairs, where the keys are words from the dictionary and the values are the corresponding numeric keys:

```
query.ToList()
    .Select(w=> new KeyValuePair<string,string>(w,
        new string(w.ToCharArray().Select (x => keyMap[x]).ToArray())))
```

At the next stage, this list of key/value pairs is filtered by the following Where clause:

```
Where (w => w.Value==key)
```

This returns the list of those key/value pairs whose value is 4663. So keys of these filtered values are textonyms of each other. Projecting the keys of the filtered values by using the final Select() call Select (w => w.Key) leaves us with the textonyms.

3-2. Simulating a Gesture Keyboard

Touch-enabled mobile devices introduced a new era of human-computer interaction. This posed several challenges for interaction designers. Because mobile devices come in all shapes and sizes (also known as *form factors*), it proved truly difficult to design a touch keyboard that worked well on all devices (an approach known as *form factor–agnostic design*). Simply porting traditional keyboard layout and interaction logic from desktops and laptops proved to be a poor solution for touch keypads on mobile devices.

Using an onscreen keyboard on small mobile devices had long been a pain point for users. The problem is largely one of size and accuracy. Users too often tap a different character than the one they intend, which can be annoying. To solve this frustration, interaction designers came up with the idea of gesture typing. This technology lets the user input (note that I didn't write *type*) a word by sliding their fingers over the letters on the keypad, essentially drawing a line from one letter to the next. The Swype app, for example, uses this technology.

Gesture keyboards use multiple algorithms, including machine learning, to predict words that users might have intended. However, at the core of these algorithms is a simple string-processing algorithm called *finding the longest common subsequence*. A subsequence of a string is another string, where the letters of the latter occur in the first at monotonically increasing indices. In a *monotonically increasing sequence*, each element is followed by another greater than itself. For example, the sequence {1,2,4,6} is a monotonically increasing sequence because 1 is less than 2, 2 is less than 4, and 4 is less than 6. However, the sequence {1,2,0,5} isn't monotonically increasing because 0 is less than 2.

Here are couple of amusing examples. The word *wine* is a subsequence of the phrase *world is not enough*. As another example, *rental* is a subsequence of *ornamental*. In the first example, the letters of the word *wine* (*w*, *i*, *n*, and *e*) occur at the indices {0,6,9,13}. These indices are monotonically increasing. Thus *wine* is a subsequence of the phrase *world is not enough*. I will leave it up to you to prove that the word *rental* is also a monotonically increasing subsequence of the word *ornamental*.

Suppose a user wants to type *rental* but the path she traces with her finger touches the letters *rewsantdal*. Several English words are subsequences of this character sequence—to list a few: *rat*, *want*, *rant*, *sand*, and *rental*. As you can see, *rental* is the longest common subsequence between the word *rental* and the character sequence *rewsantdal*. Thus, when the longest common subsequence of the word and the traced-character sequence is the word itself, that's probably a correct entry. When it isn't, however, the longest of such matches should be first in the list of suggested words, because that's most likely what the user intended to input. Now let's see how this can prove helpful in predicting words.

Problem

Given a gesture-typed string generated by a user, generate a list of suggested words by using LINQ to select the best matches from a dictionary.

Solution

Find the longest common monotonically increasing subsequences that are words in the dictionary, and list them for the user.

The code in this solution uses simulated gesture typing. Assume the user wants to type *understands* but touches the following characters along the way: *ujnbvcderesdftrewazxcvbnhgfds*. You will see that *understands* is the longest common subsequence of this character sequence that is also an English word.

This example in Listing 3-2 uses the `LongestCommonSubsequence()` method from the .NET open source string-processing API StringDefs (see `www.codeplex.com/stringdefs`). I started that project to get better string-processing capabilities in .NET.

Listing 3-2. Find closest-match words from a dictionary

```
void Main()
{
        // Define other methods and classes here
        StreamReader sr = new StreamReader ("C:\\T9.txt");
        string total = sr.ReadToEnd();
        sr.Close();

        List<string> suggestions   = new List<string>();
        var query = total.Split(new char[]{'\r','\n',' '},StringSplitOptions.RemoveEmptyEntries)
                .Select (t => t.Trim());

        //should show understand. See the bold characters.
        string path = "ujnbvcderesdftrewazxcvbnhgfds";

        query.Where(word => LongestCommonSubsequence(path,word).Equals(word))
            .OrderByDescending (word => word.Length)
            .ThenByDescending (word => word )
            .Take(4)//Show first 4 suggestions.
            .Dump("Suggestions");
}
```

The simulation generates the suggestions shown in Figure 3-5. These are all the words suggested/predicted by the gesture keyboard algorithm that the user might have intended to type.

Suggestions

▲ IEnumerable<String> (4 items) ▶
understand
unversed
undersea
underfed

Figure 3-5. All the suggestions derived from the gesture keyboard input

How It Works

Those words for which the longest common subsequence of it and the character sequence is the word itself are possible candidates for word suggestions/predictions. However, the longer the word, the higher the probability of it being the intended word. Thus the matching words are sorted by length, in descending order. Finally, the items are sorted in reverse alphabetical order. This is required because you want to preserve the prefix. Because the user started with a *u*, it is reasonable to assume that the intended word starts with a *u*.

3-3. Cloning Peter Norvig's Spelling-Correction Algorithm

Peter Norvig wrote a great spelling-correction program in about 20 lines of Python code. You can find the code and algorithm discussed at great length at http://norvig.com/spell-correct.html. At the heart of the Python code lies a concept called *list comprehension* (see http://en.wikipedia.org/wiki/List_comprehension).

LINQ is perfect for moving list comprehension from theory to practice in C#.

Problem

Use LINQ to clone Peter Norvig's Python code in C#.

Solution

The code in Listing 3-3 shows the solution.

Listing 3-3. Implementing spelling correction

```
Dictionary<string,int> NWords = new Dictionary<string,int>();
public IEnumerable<string> Edits1(string word)
{
    char[] alphabet = {'a','b','c','d','e','f','g','h','j','k','l','m','n','o',
                        'p','q','r','s','t','u','v','w','x','y','z'};
    var splits = Enumerable.Range(1,word.Length)
            .Select(i =>
                new {First = word.Substring(0,i),
                    Second = word.Substring(i+1)});

    var deletes = splits.Where (split  => !string.IsNullOrEmpty(split.Second))
                        .Select (split => split.First + split.Second.Substring(1));

    var transposes = splits
                        .Where  (split => split.Second.Length>1)
                        .Select (split => split.First + split.Second[1] + split.Second[0]
                                + split.Second.Substring(2));

    var replaces = splits
                        .Where (split => !string.IsNullOrEmpty(split.Second))
                        .SelectMany(split => alphabet
                        .Select (c => split.First + c + split.Second.Substring(1)));

    var inserts = splits
                        .Where (split     => !string.IsNullOrEmpty(split.Second))
                        .SelectMany(split => alphabet
                                    .Select (c => split.First + c + split.Second));
    return deletes
                .Union(transposes)
                .Union(replaces)
                .Union(inserts);
}

public Dictionary<string,int> Train(IEnumerable<string> features)
{
    Dictionary<string,int> model = new Dictionary<string,int>();
    Features
            .ToList()
            .ForEach(f => {if (model.ContainsKey(f)) model[f] += 1; else model.Add(f,1);});
    return model;
}
```

```
public IEnumerable<string> KnownEdits2(string word)
{
      List<string> knownEdits2 = new List<string>();
      return Edits1(word)
            .SelectMany(e1 => Edits1(e1)
            .Where (x => NWords.ContainsKey(x)));
}
public IEnumerable<string> Known(IEnumerable<string> words)
{
      return words.Intersect(NWords.Select (v => v.Key));
}
public IEnumerable<string> Correct(string word)
{
      List<string> candidates = new List<string>();
      candidates.AddRange(Known(new List<string>(){word}));
      candidates.AddRange(Known(Edits1(word)));
      candidates.AddRange(Known(Edits1(word)));
      candidates.AddRange(KnownEdits2(word));
      candidates.Add(word);
      return candidates
            .Where (c => NWords.ContainsKey(c)).OrderByDescending (c => NWords[c]);
}
void Main()
{
      StreamReader sr = new StreamReader ("big.txt");
      string total = sr.ReadToEnd();
      sr.Close();
      NWords = Train(Regex.Matches(total,"[a-z]+")
            .Cast<Match>()
            .Select (m => m.Value.ToLower()));
      string word = "mysgtry"; //should return "mystery"
      Correct(word)
            .Distinct()
            .OrderByDescending (x => x.Length)
            .Dump("Did you mean");
}
```

This produces the output shown in Figure 3-6.

Figure 3-6. *Results of the spelling-correction algorithm*

How It Works

At the heart of the Python implementation is the edits1() method, as shown in this Python code snippet:

```
def edits1(word):
    splits     = [(word[:i], word[i:]) for i in range(len(word) + 1)]
    deletes    = [a + b[1:] for a, b in splits if b]
    transposes = [a + b[1] + b[0] + b[2:] for a, b in splits if len(b)>1]
    replaces   = [a + c + b[1:] for a, b in splits for c in alphabet if b]
    inserts    = [a + c + b     for a, b in splits for c in alphabet]
    return set(deletes + transposes + replaces + inserts)
```

The list splits contains list of key/value pairs, in which the keys are substrings of the words through the specified index i and the values are substrings of the words from the index i + 1.

Here is the clone of splits:

```
var splits = Enumerable.Range(1,word.Length).Select(i => new {First = word.Substring(0,i),
                                                      Second = word.Substring(i+1)});
```

In contrast, the deletes collection contains the keys of splits and the substring of the value from the second index onward should the value field exist. Note that every other variable in the edits1() method is declared in terms of splits(). LINQ achieves list comprehension by using filtering—a call to Where() followed by the required projection, followed by calls to Select() or SelectMany().

I have used the same variable names and method names as those used in the original Python code. You can see how the original Python code and my clone compares at http://consulttoday.com/PeterNorvigsSpellingCorrection.html.

3-4. Reversing a Sentence Word by Word

Reversing the words in a sentence may seem simple. However, the classical solution, which uses loops, requires using intermediate storage and looping constructs.

Problem

Write LINQ code to reverse the words in a given sentence.

Solution

Listing 3-4 shows the solution.

Listing 3-4. Reversing a sentence

```
//Reversing a sentence word-by-word
string line = "nothing know I";

line.Split(' ').Aggregate ((a,b) => b + " " + a).Dump();
```

This program prints the following:

```
"I know nothing"
```

How It Works

`Line.Split(' ')` returns a list of the words in the sentence *nothing know I*. The `Aggregate()` function then takes one pair at a time and writes them in reverse order. At the end, the string is completely reversed. You might also find `Reverse()` used to reverse a word collection and then `Aggregate()` used to stitch those reversed words together to get the reversed sentence. However, you see that's not needed, because you can do the same with `Aggregate()` just by swapping the arguments in the body of the lambda function.

3-5. Creating a Word Triangle

A *word triangle* is one of those puzzles that nearly everyone encountered during their formative years. This simple problem sets the context for more-sophisticated problems later.

Problem

Write a program using LINQ to generate a word triangle from a given word.

Solution

The LINQ statement in Listing 3-5 prints a word triangle for the word *umbrella*.

Listing 3-5. Create a word triangle

```
//Word Triangle
string word = "umbrella";
Enumerable
        .Range(1, word.Length)
        .Select (k => new string(word.ToCharArray().Take(k).ToArray()))
        .Concat
        (
            Enumerable.Range(1, word.Length)
                    .Select(k => new string(word.ToCharArray()
                                    .Take(word.Length - k)
                                    .ToArray())))
        )
        .Aggregate ((m,n) => m + Environment.NewLine + n)
        .Dump("Word Triangle");
```

This generates the output shown in Figure 3-7. A triangle is formed with the letters of the given word. The program starts with the first letter. Then it takes the first two, then the first three, and so on, until it prints the whole word. Then the program repeats, but taking letters from the end, instead, until only one letter remains.

```
Word Triangle
u
um
umb
umbr
umbre
umbrel
umbrell
umbrella
umbrell
umbrel
umbre
umbr
umb
um
u
```

Figure 3-7. *Output for the word triangle*

How It Works

The line `Enumerable.Range(1, word.Length)` creates a range from 1 to the length of the given word. The resultant values are projected to obtain a sequence of characters that increases in length by one each time, starting from the left side of the given word. Here's the projection code:

```
Select (k => new string(word.ToCharArray().Take(k).ToArray()))
```

As the value of k changes from 1 to `word.Length`, this leaves you with a substring of the given word, of length k starting from the zero index position, at each stage. So when k is 1, you get *u*. When k is 2, you get *um*, and so on. When k finally hits the `word.Length` value, you get the entire word, *umbrella*. So that portion of the code provides the upper part of the triangle.

For the bottom part of the word triangle, you just need to reverse this process. You take every character from the left, except the last one in the first call, except the last two in the next call, and so on. You concatenate these two sequences by using `Concat()`.

Finally, you can use the `Aggregate()` operator to place the incremental and decremented substrings of the given words so that each one appears right after the previous one in a new line.

3-6. Finding Anagrams

Anagrams are fascinating. *Anagrams*, which are words created by transposing the letters of another word, are also useful to point out and correct obvious spelling mistakes. For example, if you type *hte* in Microsoft Word, it will be autocorrected to *the*, because *hte* is not a word in the dictionary, and *the* is an anagram that is frequently used in English.

Problem

Write a query using LINQ that takes two phrases and returns `true` if they are anagrams of each other; otherwise, it returns `false`.

Solution

The query in Listing 3-6 checks whether two phrases are anagrams of each other. It considers only the alphabetic characters—not any punctuation. The easiest way to tell whether two words are anagrams of each other is to sort the characters and then compare the resultant sequences for equality. For example, the words *oriental* and *relation* are anagrams. When sorted alphabetically, the characters in both words are *aeilnort*.

Listing 3-6. Determining whether two phrases are anagrams of each other

```
string phrase1 = "the eyes";
string phrase2 = "they see";

phrase1.ToCharArray().Where (p => Char.IsLetterOrDigit(p))
      .OrderBy (p => p)
      .SequenceEqual(phrase2.ToCharArray().Where (p => Char.IsLetterOrDigit(p))
      .OrderBy (p => p))
      .Dump();
```

This query outputs true, because the phrases are anagrams of each other.

How It Works

IsLetterOrDigit()filters anything except a letter or a digit.

The code phrase1.ToCharArray().Where (p => Char.IsLetterOrDigit(p)) returns a list of characters only. Because in this case all the characters match the condition, you end up with IEnumerable<char> {'t','h','e','e','y','e','s'}. The OrderBy() clause sorts this character sequence, generating eeehsty. The same call for phrase2 generates the same character sequence. Using the SequenceEqual() operator proves these two sequences are equal.

SequenceEqual() cares about the order of the elements in the source collections. That's why you have to sort the sequences first, using the OrderBy() clauses.

3-7. Checking for Anagrams Without Sorting Characters

The solution in the previous section, which sorts the characters and then checks for anagrams, works fine. However, it's resource-intensive when the input phrases grow big. In this section, you'll try another approach.

Problem

Write a method to determine whether two strings are anagrams of each other, without sorting the characters of the phrases.

Solution

In such situations, you can compare the character histograms of both phrases instead. A *character histogram* is a character frequency table that stores the number of times each character occurs in the phrase. For example, in the phrase *the eyes*, the character frequency for the letter *e* is 3, because *e* occurs three times. Listing 3-7 creates character histograms and then compares them to determine whether the phrases are anagrams of each other instead of sorting. For big strings, this method yields faster results.

Listing 3-7. Checking for anagrams without sorting

```
string phrase1 = "the eyes";
string phrase2 = "they see";

var characterHistogram1 = phrase1
                          .ToCharArray()
                          .Where (p => Char.IsLetterOrDigit(p))
                          .ToLookup (p => p)
                          .ToDictionary (p => p.Key, p=>p.Count ());
var characterHistogram2 = phrase2
                          .ToCharArray()
                          .Where (p => Char.IsLetterOrDigit(p))
                          .ToLookup (p => p)
                          .ToDictionary (p => p.Key, p=>p.Count ());

bool isAnagram = characterHistogram1.All(d =>
                    characterHistogram2[d.Key] == characterHistogram1 [d.Key]);
```

How It Works

As you can see, the filtering part is same as the solution in the previous section. The code ignores anything except a letter or digit. Later, this is projected as a lookup table by calling the ToLookup() operator. Figure 3-8 shows the lookup table for the first phrase, *the eyes*.

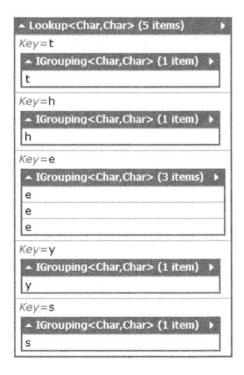

Figure 3-8. *Lookup table for the phrase the eyes*

At the next stage, this lookup table is converted to a dictionary by using the ToDictionary() operator. p.Count() returns the number of elements in each group. Thus the process generates the character histogram shown in Figure 3-9.

Character Histogram of 'the eyes'

▲ Dictionary<Char,Int32> (5 items) ▶	
Key	Value ≡
t	1
h	1
e	3
y	1
s	1
	7

Figure 3-9. *The character histogram for the phrase the eyes*

In Figure 3-9, the Key column represents the characters of the phrase, while the Value column represents the frequency of that character in the given phrase.

After obtaining a character histogram for each phrase, you can test their equality to see whether the phrases are anagrammatic pairs.

The operator All() returns true when all the values in the calling collection match the given predicate. If the two phrases are anagrams, their values will match for every key. The predicate characterHistogram2[d.Key] == dic1[d.Key] validates that.

3-8. Creating a Rudimentary Programming Language Identifier and Automatic Syntax Highlighter

Syntax highlighting is important because it improves the readability of code. Using LINQ and SyntaxHighlighter, you can create an automatic syntax highlighter that can parse code in any language and highlight the code. SyntaxHighlighter is an open source JavaScript API for providing lightweight syntax highlighting support. Most blogging engines already support it.

Problem

From raw text input, identify the programming language and then apply a proper syntax highlighter brush for that language.

Solution

Listing 3-8 reads raw code in any language from the file SampleCode.txt and generates a syntax-highlighted version. LINQ is used to identify the language based on keywords.

Listing 3-8. Adding syntax highlighting to code

```csharp
Dictionary<string, List<string>> langKeywords = new Dictionary<string, List<string>>();

string directory = @"C:\syntaxhighlighter_3.0.83";
string[] files = Directory.GetFiles(directory,"*.js");

foreach (string file in files)
{
        try
        {
                string key = new FileInfo(file).Name.Replace("shBrush", string.Empty)
                                                .Replace(".js", string.Empty);
                langKeywords.Add(key, new List<string>());
                langKeywords[key] = Regex.Matches(File.ReadAllText(file)
                                        .Split(';')
                                        .FirstOrDefault(m => m.Contains("var keywords"))
                                                                .Split('=')[1], "[a-z]+")
                                        .Cast<Match>()
                                                .Select(m => m.Value).ToList();
        }
        catch
        {
                continue;
        }
}

string sampleCode = File.ReadAllText("C:\\SampleCode.txt");

Dictionary<string,int> confiMap = new Dictionary<string,int>();
foreach (var lang in langKeywords.Keys)
{
        foreach(var kw in langKeywords[lang])
        {
                if(sampleCode.Contains(kw))
                {
                        if(!confiMap.ContainsKey(lang))
                                confiMap.Add(lang,1);
                        else
                                confiMap[lang]++;
                }
        }
}
Dictionary<string,string> brushAliases = new Dictionary<string,string>();
brushAliases.Add("CSharp","csharp");
brushAliases.Add("Python","python");
brushAliases.Add("Ruby","ruby");
brushAliases.Add("Perl","perl");
brushAliases.Add("CPP","cpp");
```

```
StreamReader sr = new StreamReader ("C:\\rudiSynTemplate.html");
string total = sr.ReadToEnd();
sr.Close();
total = total.Replace("{brushAlias}",brushAliases[confiMap.OrderByDescending (m => m.Value )

.First ().Key]);
total = total.Replace("<code>",sampleCode);

StreamWriter sw = new StreamWriter (@"C:\syntaxhighlighter_3.0.83\synh.html");
sw.WriteLine(total);
sw.Close();

System.Diagnostics.Process.Start(@"C:\syntaxhighlighter_3.0.83\synh.html");
```

How It Works

I tested this code with the edits1() method from Peter Norvig's spell-checker. The automatic syntax highligher correctly identified that the code is written in Python and applied SyntaxHighlighter's Python brush. Figure 3-10 shows the result as rendered on the browser.

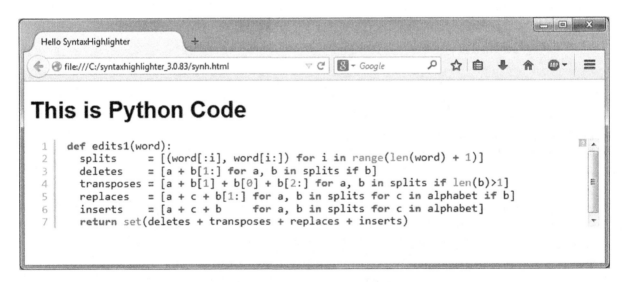

Figure 3-10. Result of applying automatic syntax highlighting on Python code

To execute this, you need to download SyntaxHighlighter. SyntaxHighlighter has a highlighter brush for several programming languages, and each brush has a keyword section that stores all the keywords in the language. For example, here is the list of Ruby keywords from the Ruby brush:

```
var keywords = 'alias and BEGIN begin break case class def define_method defined ' +
    'do each else elsif END end ensure false for if in module new next nil not or raise ' +
    'redo rescue retry return self super then throw true undef unless until when while yield';
```

The program keeps track of all the keywords for all the languages in the one-to-many dictionary langKeywords. Figure 3-11 shows a collapsed view of the dictionary for a few languages.

▲ Dictionary<String,List<String>> (7 items) ▶	
Key	**Value**
Cpp	▾ List<String> (69 items) ▶
CSharp	▾ List<String> (78 items) ▶
Java	▾ List<String> (53 items) ▶
Perl	▾ List<String> (37 items) ▶
Php	▾ List<String> (58 items) ▶
Python	▾ List<String> (29 items) ▶
Ruby	▾ List<String> (42 items) ▶

Figure 3-11. *Dictionary holding language names and their keywords*

Next, the program finds these keywords that have to be highlighted in the sample code. Based on the number of keywords found in the sample code, the program guesses the programing language. The frequency of matches are maintained in a dictionary called confiMap. For the preceding Python example, Figure 3-12 shows the content of confiMap.

Confidence Score

▲ IOrderedEnumerable<KeyValuePair<String,Int32>> (7 items) ▶	
Key	**Value ≡**
Python	7
Ruby	6
Cpp	5
CSharp	5
Php	4
Java	3
Perl	3
	33

Figure 3-12. *Confidence score for the code to apply syntax highlighting*

You see that seven Python keywords were found in the sample code, which is the highest number. Thus the program guesses that the sample code is written in Python.

3-9. Creating a Word-Ladder Solver

Word ladder, or doublets, (http://en.wikipedia.org/wiki/Word_ladder) is a game in which players change one letter at a time while trying to find a path between a given pair of start and end words of the same length. One interesting example is the path from *myth* to *fact*, as shown here:

myth ➤ math ➤ mate ➤ fate ➤ face ➤ fact

   Notice that at each step, only one letter is changed to get to the next word.

Problem

Write a program to solve a word-ladder game. Given two words, print the path between these two words if one exists.

Solution

Listing 3-9 provides a program that prints the word-ladder path between two given words if it exists; otherwise, it prints *no path*. To run this, you have to change the language combo value to C# Program in LINQPad.

Listing 3-9. A LINQ-based word-ladder solver

```
/// <summary>
/// Calculates the Hamming Distance between two strings
/// </summary>
// <param name="first">The first string</param>
/// <param name="second">The second string</param>
/// <returns></returns>
public static int HammingDistance(string first, string second)
{
        return first.ToCharArray().Where((f,i) => second[i]!=f).Count();
}
void Main()
{
        <string> transitions = new List<string>();

        List<string> allWords = new List<string>();
        StreamReader t9Reader = new StreamReader(@"C:\T9.txt");
        string total = t9Reader.ReadToEnd();
        t9Reader.Close();
        //Start and End words
        string start = "myth";
        string end = "fact";

        string startCopy = start;

        transitions.Add(start);

        allWords.AddRange(total.Split(new char[] { ' ', '\r', '\n' },
                                  StringSplitOptions.RemoveEmptyEntries));
```

```
    allWords = allWords    .Where(word => word.Length == start.Length)
                .ToList();

    allWords.Add(end);

    Dictionary<string, List<string>> wordEditDistanceMap =

   allWords.ToLookup (w => w)
          .ToDictionary
        (
            //key selector
            w => w.Key,
            //value selector
            w => allWords.Where(a =>
                        HammingDistance(a,w.Key)==1).ToList()
        );

//At this point we have the dictionary separated by edit distance 1
bool noPath = false;

 List<string> currentList = new List<string>();
 do
 {

    string[] currents = wordEditDistanceMap[start]
      .Where(word => HammingDistance(word, end) ==
          wordEditDistanceMap[start].Min(c => HammingDistance(end, c))).ToArray();
        do
        {
                foreach (string c in currents)
                {
                        if (!currentList.Contains(c))
                        {
                                currentList.Add(c);
                                break;
                        }
                        if ((currents.Length == 1 && currentList.Contains(c)))
                        {
                                Console.WriteLine("There is no such path !");
                                noPath = true;
                                break;
                        }
                }

                if (noPath)
                        break;
        } while (currentList.Count == 0);
        if (noPath)
                break;
        transitions.Add(currentList[currentList.Count - 1]);
```

```
                if(transitions.Count >=2 && transitions[transitions.Count -2]==transitions.Last ( ))
                {
                        Console.WriteLine("There is no such path");
                        noPath=true;
                        break;
                }

                start = currentList[currentList.Count - 1];
        } while (!start.Equals(end) || noPath==true );
        (!noPath)
                transitions.Dump("Transition");// from \"" + startCopy + "\" to \"" + end +"\"");
}
```

How It Works

In this solution, you find the next word through a neighborhood forest of words that are one edit distance away at each step. The *edit distance* of two equal-length strings is defined as the number of characters that differ (this is also called the *hamming distance*). For example, the edit distance between *myth* and *math* is 1. Although the entire solution doesn't use LINQ; however, key elements are expressed using LINQ, illustrating a couple of idiomatic LINQ usages that you will find useful elsewhere too.

The first LINQ usage is the edit distance calculation. This uses the indexed version of the Where() operator. Consider the following code:

```
first.ToCharArray().Where((f,i) => second[i]!=f).Count();
```

This checks the number of occasions that the *i*th element of the second string doesn't match its corresponding character from the first string. The indexed version of Where() is handy for removing a nested looping situation like this one. Or, in other words, in the absence of an indexed version, you would have to code it like this:

```
int count = 0;
foreach(var f in first)
        for(int i = 0; i<second.Length;i++)
                if(f != second[i])
                        count++;
```

The second idiom is ToLookup() followed by ToDictionary():

In this example, this idiom is used to create a dictionary in which the keys are all the words in the T9 dictionary and the values are all other words that are one edit distance away from the T9 words. Figure 3-13 shows an entry of this dictionary.

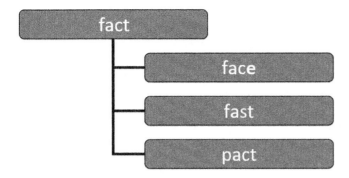

Figure 3-13. *Words that are one edit distance away are stored in the dictionary*

Notice that the words *face*, *fast*, and *pact* are all one edit distance away from the word *fact*. So these words end up in the value list of the word *fact*.

The next challenge in solving this puzzle is to locate the best candidate, the one that is closest to the target word. So if we start with *myth* and are going toward fact, the next word we should pick is *math* and not *moth*, because *moth* is further from *fact* than *math*. The hamming distance between *moth* and *fact* is 4. The hamming distance between *math* and *fact* is 3. Thus, in this case, *math* is a better choice than *moth* in our journey from *myth* to *fact*. To determine this next candidate, the following code is used:

```
string[] currents = wordEditDistanceMap[start]
        .Where(word => HammingDistance(word, end) ==
            wordEditDistanceMap[start].Min(c => HammingDistance(end, c))).ToArray();
```

This code returns all words that are one edit distance away from the current starting word, and for which the edit distance is the minimum from the target word.

At each step, these identified next-best-candidate words get added to the transition path by the following code:

```
transitions.Add(currentList[currentList.Count - 1]);
```

The remaining code is used to avoid infinite looping. So whenever we come back to any word we've already visited and that is not our target word, then there can't be any path.

3-10. Formatting on the Fly

To format free-form text, you have likely been writing specific functions. For example, assume you have a list of social security numbers from all users, but those numbers are not formatted well. Another example might be a list of unformatted phone numbers. Although these examples are similar, you would typically have to write separate functions to apply the right formatting to them. By using LINQ, you can generate these random formatting functions on the fly. Using LINQ in this manner is much like teaching a human how to format a given type of string and then asking that person to format a bunch of those strings. If you have used the new Flash Fill feature of Microsoft Excel, this solution will look similar. However Flash Fill is a much more complex feature that uses machine learning.

Problem

Create a function that returns a transformer given an example transformation. Later, this generated transformer function can be applied to other values.

Solution

Listing 3-10 shows how to create a function that can transform given text to another format.

Listing 3-10. On-the-fly formatting

```
public Func<string,string> FormatLikeThis(string transformation)
{
        string[] tokens = transformation.Split(new string[]{"=>"},StringSplitOptions.
        RemoveEmptyEntries);
        string start = tokens[0];
        string end = tokens[1];
        Dictionary<int,char> insertCharMap = new Dictionary<int,char>();
        Enumerable.Range(0,end.Length).Where(k => !start.Contains(end[k]))
                                .ToList()
                                        .ForEach(k => insertCharMap.Add(k,end[k]));

        Func<string,string> transformer = x =>
        {
                insertCharMap.ToList().ForEach(z => x = x.Insert(z.Key,z.Value.ToString()));
                return x;
        };
        return transformer;
}

void Main()
{
        string[] someVals = {"234567890","345678901","456789012"};
        List<string> modifiedVals = new List<string>();
        var transformer = FormatLikeThis("123456789=>123-456-789");
        someVals.ToList().ForEach(k => modifiedVals.Add(transformer.Invoke(k)));
        someVals.Dump("Before");
        modifiedVals.Dump("After");
}
```

This generates the output shown in Figure 3-14.

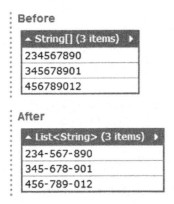

Before

▲ String[] (3 items) ▶
234567890
345678901
456789012

After

▲ List<String> (3 items) ▶
234-567-890
345-678-901
456-789-012

Figure 3-14. *Values before and after formatting*

How It Works

This code works by inserting characters that aren't present in the current string. At the first stage, the given transformation is broken into two pieces. The first part is the starting text, and the last part is the transformed text. The transformed text may have characters that aren't part of the starting string. Consider the following code:

```
Enumerable.Range(0,end.Length).Where(k => !start.Contains(end[k]))
                            .ToList()
                                    .ForEach(k => insertCharMap.Add(k,end[k]));
```

This code stores the locations and new characters that have been introduced. For the example, the transformations 123456789=>123-456-789 and the content of insertCharMap are shown in Figure 3-15.

▲ Dictionary<Int32,Char> (2 items) ▶	
Key	**Value**
3	-
7	-

Figure 3-15. *Characters to insert and indices*

After this character-insert mapping is created, this is used to generate a function by implementing the definition of this function dynamically.

Consider the following code:

```
insertCharMap.ToList().ForEach(z => x = x.Insert(z.Key,z.Value.ToString()));
```

This code inserts characters in the starting text to make it the target text. Another way to think about this is that the strategy to transform one text to another remains the same; only the implementations change during runtime. I encourage you to experiment with other formatting problems.

3-11. Solving Eric Lippert's Comma-Quibbling Problem

Eric Lippert posed a question on his blog that received more attention than he originally expected. The question asks readers to insert a comma between all words in a given collection, but to insert the word *and* (instead of a comma) before the last word, and then wrap the output in curly braces.

Here are four scenarios from Eric's blog:

1. If the sequence is empty, the resulting string is {}.

2. If the sequence is a single item ABC, the resulting string is {ABC}.

3. If the sequence is the two-item sequence ABC, DEF, the resulting string is {ABC and DEF}.

4. If the sequence has more than two items—for example, ABC, DEF, G, H—the resulting string is {ABC, DEF, G and H}. (Note that the G is not followed by a comma.)

Problem

Write a method to return comma-delimited text by using the preceding rules.

Solution

The program in Listing 3-11 solves this comma-quibbling problem.

Listing 3-11. One comma-quibbling problem solution

```
string[] input = {"ABC", "DEF", "G", "H"};
string result =
"{" //starting/opening brace
+ input.Take(input.Length - 1).Aggregate((f,s) => f + ", " + s)
+ " and "
+  input.Last()
+ "}";//closing brace
result.Dump("Eric's Comma Quibbling");
```

This query generates the output shown in Figure 3-16.

```
Eric's Comma Quibbling
{ABC, DEF, G and H}
```

Figure 3-16. *Sample output from Eric Lippert's comma-quibbling challenge*

How It Works

The challenge is to place a comma between every pair except the last word/entry in the input sequence. input.Length gives the length of the input sequence. In this case, that's 4. So input.Take(input.Length - 1) returns an IEnumerable<string> that contains the first three elements: ABC, DEF, and G in this case.

The call to Aggregate in Aggregate((f,s) => f + ", " + s) takes a pair of elements, starting from the leftmost, one at a time, and joins these with a comma followed by a space. This returns the string ABC, DEF, G. To make the text read well, you need to insert an *and* before the last word in the series. The code does just that: it adds the *and* and then calls Last() to get the last element of the input sequence (H, in this case), and appends that to the end of the result string.

Finally, the code places curly braces at the start and end of the result.

This solution will work only when the list contains two or more values. To completely solve the problem, you would also need to handle an empty sequence or one containing only a single value as described in the previous scenarios.

3-12. Generating Random Serials

Random serial generation is a common problem. Two examples are random password generation and serial key generation to be used as license keys.

Problem

Write a program to generate random serials.

Solution

Listing 3-12 shows a way to generate random serials of length 8. The serials will consist of letters (lowercase and uppercase) and numbers.

Listing 3-12. Generating random serials

```
//Serial generation
for(int i=0;i<5;i++)
{
    Enumerable
        .Range(65,26)
        .Select (e => ((char)e).ToString())
    .Concat(Enumerable.Range(97,26).Select (e => ((char)e).ToString()))
    .Concat(Enumerable.Range(0,10).Select (e => e.ToString()))
    .OrderBy (e => Guid.NewGuid())
    .Take(8)
    .ToList().ForEach (e => Console.Write(e));
     //Give a line break between two random serials
     Console.WriteLine();
}
```

This generates five random serials, as shown in Figure 3-17. Each random serial consists of uppercase and lowercase characters and numbers, and has a length of 8.

```
PGCpFodz
cC5XatzS
6vKRwonA
WpUlgZRj
3TxaevKd
```

Figure 3-17. *Five generated random serials*

How It Works

At the heart of this algorithm is the ability to randomly and easily sort a collection by using OrderBy(). In the following code, OrderBy (e => Guid.NewGuid()) sorts the collection in random order, because for each element, a new GUID is generated. The ASCII code for *a* is 97, and the code for *A* is 65. Take a look at the following two lines:

```
Enumerable.Range(65,26)
  .Select (e => ((char)e).ToString())
```

This code generates the sequence ABCDEFGHIJKLMNOPQRSTUVWZYZabcdefghijklmnopqrstuvwxyz. Next, we have the following line:

```
.Concat(Enumerable.Range(97,26).Select(e => ((char)e).ToString()))
```

This line appends the digits 0 to 9, so the sequence becomes ABCDEFGHIJKLMNOPQRSTUVWZYZabcdefghijklmnopqrstuvwxyz0123456789. Then the final call to OrderBy() randomly sorts the characters in this sequence, creating a different sequence every time. Finally, it picks the first eight characters—and there you have it: a random serial.

3-13. Generating All Substrings of a Given String

Generating all substrings of a given string is a problem you are likely to encounter in many different situations. For example, in some plagiarism-detection algorithms, substrings from several sources are extracted and then the number of tokens are checked for a match. The total percentage of tokens that are same in both sources give an impression of how much those two sources match. This is sometime referred as a *similarity measure* or a *proximity score*.

Problem

Write a program to generate all the substrings of a given string.

Solution

The program in Listing 3-13 prints all the substrings of the given string.

Listing 3-13. Generating all substrings of a given string

```
public static List<string> NGrams(string sentence, int q)
{
        int total = sentence.Length - q;
        List<string> tokens = new List<string>();
        for (int i = 0; i <= total; i++)
            tokens.Add(sentence.Substring(i, q));
        return tokens;
}
void Main()
{
    string name  = "LINQ";
    Enumerable.Range(0,name.Length+1)
            .SelectMany(z => NGrams(name,z))
            .Distinct()
            .Where (b => b.Length!=0)
            .Dump("All substrings of 'LINQ'");
}
```

This generates the output shown in Figure 3-18: all substrings of the string LINQ.

All substrings of 'LINQ'

▲ IOrderedEnumerable<String> (10 items) ▶
LINQ
LIN
INQ
LI
IN
NQ
L
I
N
Q

Figure 3-18. *All substrings of the string LINQ*

How It Works

At the heart of this implementation is the NGrams() method. This method returns all the tokens of size q. So if q is 2, and you call NGrams() with the string LINQ, it will generate three substrings: LI, IN, and NQ. Some computing texts refer to this process as a *sliding window*.

So if you call the NGrams() method with all possible sizes (in this case, that's 1, 2, 3, and 4) because the string LINQ has a length of 4), you will end up with all the possible substrings of LINQ.

Enumerable.Range(0,name.Length+1) calculates the length range for which you want to generate N-Grams. Because NGrams() returns a collection of items, you get a one-to-many relationship from one integer length to a set of substrings. This relationship is aptly represented by the projection using SelectMany():

```
SelectMany(z => NGrams(name,z))
```

Because there might be duplicates, it is good to clean the results with a call to Distinct().

3-14. Creating a Scrabble Cheater

Scrabble is a game to showcase word power. The more words you can make from a set of given letters, the more you score.

Problem

Write a program that can generate all other possible words that can be formed by using all the letters or a subset of those letters of the given word.

Solution

The following program generates a list of all words that can be made from a subset of the letters of the given word. For example, if the given word is *what*, players can form the words *hat, thaw, a*, and *at* }.

Listing 3-14 finds all words that can be formed using the letters of the given word or a subset of those letters. It uses a T9 dictionary to locate words.

Listing 3-14. Find all words that can be formed from a given set of letters

```
Func<string,Dictionary<char,int>> ToHist =
                              word => word.ToCharArray()
                                          .ToLookup (w => w)
                                          .ToDictionary(w => w.Key, w => w.Count());
//Scrabble Cheat
string GivenWord = "what";

StreamReader sr = new StreamReader("C:\\T9.txt");
string total = sr.ReadToEnd();
sr.Close();
List<string> allWords = Regex.Matches(total,"[a-z]+")
                             .Cast<Match>()
                             .Select (m => m.Value)
                             .Distinct()
                             .ToList();

Dictionary<string,Dictionary<char,int>> forest =
               new Dictionary<string,Dictionary<char,int>>();

allWords.ForEach(w => forest.Add(w, ToHist(w)));

Dictionary<char,int> hist = ToHist(GivenWord);

List<string> scrabbleCheats = new List<string>();

foreach (string w in forest.Keys)
{
   if(
       //keys should match
       forest[w].Select (x => x.Key).All(x => hist.Select (h => h.Key).Contains(x))
       &&
       //values should be less than or equal to that of hist
       forest[w].All (x => hist[x.Key]-forest[w][x.Key] >= 0)
     )
     scrabbleCheats.Add(w);
}

scrabbleCheats.OrderBy (c => c.Length).Dump("Scrabble Cheats");
```

This generates the words shown in Figure 3-19: all the words that can be generated from the word *what*.

Scrabble Cheats

▲ IOrderedEnumerable<String> (7 items) ►
a
at
hat
haw
taw
thaw
what

Figure 3-19. *All the words that can be formed using the letters of the word what*

How It Works

To locate words that can be formed from all the characters of a given word or a subset of those characters, you locate the words for which the character histogram is equal to or is a subset of the character histogram of the given word.

OK, that might sound heavy. Here's an example. Let's say we want to find all words that can be formed with the letters of the word *what*. The first step is to construct a character histogram of *what*. This histogram is shown in Table 3-1.

Table 3-1. *The character histogram of the word what*

Character	Frequency
W	1
H	1
A	1
T	1

Note that the histogram for the word *hat* is a subset of this histogram. In other words, to create *hat*, we need one *h*, one *a*, and one *t*. We have one of each in *what*. So the word *hat* can be formed using the letters of the word *what*.

In the code, the C# dictionary forest holds all the character histograms for all words in the T9 dictionary. The forest keys represent the words in the dictionary, and the values store their character histograms.

The delegate ToHist generates the histogram of a given word. ToHist() uses ToLookup() to generate a lookup table of characters. This call is followed by a ToDictionary() call, where each key is a character of the word, and each value is a character's frequency (the number of times that character occurs in a given string).

Figure 3-20 shows the intermediate lookup table, created by ToLookup(), for the word *cool*. Here all the unique characters are keys, and the values represent the occurrences.

Lookup of 'cool'

```
▲ Lookup<Char,Char> (3 items)        ▶
Key= c
    ▲ IGrouping<Char,Char> (1 item)  ▶
    c
Key= o
    ▲ IGrouping<Char,Char> (2 items) ▶
    o
    o
Key= l
    ▲ IGrouping<Char,Char> (1 item)  ▶
    l
```

Figure 3-20. *The lookup table created for the word cool*

So this lookup table is converted to a dictionary, displayed as a table in Figure 3-21. The table has two columns: Key and Value. The Key column lists the distinct characters of the word *cool*. The Value column stores the frequency of the characters in the word.

Character Histogram of 'cool'

▲ Dictionary<Char,Int32> (3 items) ▶	
Key	**Value ≡**
c	1
o	2
l	1
	4

Figure 3-21. *The character histogram of the word cool generated from the lookup table*

Iterating over the keys in the dictionary forest, we find those keys where all the characters in the histogram match those of the given word by using the following statement:
forest[w].Select (x => x.Key).All(x => hist.Select (h => h.Key).Contains(x)) forest[w] gives us the character histogram. Projecting the keys of this dictionary by using Select (x => x.Key) gives us all the distinct characters. All(x => hist.Select (h => h.Key).Contains(x)) checks whether all these characters are also present in the histogram of the given word.

The last call to All(), forest[w].All (x => hist[x.Key]-forest[w][x.Key] >= 0) checks whether the character frequencies match up for all characters. hist[x.Key] represents the frequency of the character represented by x.Key. forest[w][x.Key] represents the frequency of the character x.Key for the word forest[w].

3-15. Finding All the Subsequences of a Given String

As you learned earlier in this chapter, a *subsequence* is a string that can be formed from a subset of another string, where these characters appear in monotonically increasing indices in the latter string. For example, the word *wine* is a subsequence of the phrase *world is not enough*. Another example is the word *rental* is a subsequence of *ornamental*.

Problem

Write a program to find all the subsequences of the given string.

Solution

Listing 3-15 finds all the sub-sequences of a given word.

Listing 3-15. Finding all sub-sequences of a given word

```
StreamReader sr = new StreamReader ("C:\\T9.txt");
var allWords = Regex.Matches(sr.ReadToEnd(),"[a-z]+").Cast<Match>().Select (m => m.Value).ToList();
sr.Close();
List<string> subsequences = new List<string>();
string bigWord = "awesome";
foreach (string smallWord in allWords)
{
        var q = smallWord
                    .ToCharArray()
                    .Select (x => bigWord
                    .ToCharArray()
                    .ToList()
                    .LastIndexOf(x));

if(q.All (x => x !=-1)
    &&
      q.Take(q.Count () - 1)
       .Select ((x,i) => new {CurrentIndex = x, NextIndex = q.ElementAt(i+1)})
       .All (x => x.NextIndex - x.CurrentIndex > 0))
      {
            subsequences.Add(smallWord);
      }
}
subsequences.Dump("All subsequences");
```

This generates all the subsequences of the word *awesome,* as shown in Figure 3-22.

All subsequences

Figure 3-22. *All the sub-sequences of the word awesome*

How It Works

In this example, the letters of the word *some* appear at monotonically increasing indices in *awesome*. (The letters of *some* appear at indices 4, 5, 6, and 7 in *awesome*.) Thus *some* is a subsequence of *awesome*. The following query finds all the indices of the bigWord word where the letters of the smallWord occur.

```
var q  = smallWord .ToCharArray()
                   .Select (x => bigWord
                   .ToCharArray()
                   .ToList()
                   .LastIndexOf(x));
```

If smallWord is rental and bigWord is ornamental, q will have the indices shown in Figure 3-23.

Indices

▲ IEnumerable<Int32> (6 items) ▶
1
5
6
7
8
9

Figure 3-23. *All the indices of ornamental where the letters of rental occur*

To find the subsequence, it's enough to check for monotonicity of these indices. Also because all characters of the smaller subsequence word have to occur in the bigger word, none of these indices can't be -1. The first statement q.All (x => x !=-1) verifies that statement.

The second statement checks for the monotonicity of these indices. The first part of the second statement is as follows:

```
q.Take(q.Count () - 1)
        .Select ((x,i) => new {CurrentIndex = x, NextIndex = q.ElementAt(i+1)})
```

This code projects a list of key/value pairs, where each key represents the current index at each level and the value represents the next index at each level. So the preceding list of indices gets projected as shown in Figure 3-24.

CurrentIndex ≡	NextIndex ≡
1	5
5	6
6	7
7	8
8	9
27	35

IEnumerable<> (5 items)

Figure 3-24. *Current and next index at each level*

The final call to All(), shown below, checks whether CurrentIndex is less than and not equal to the next level, for all these projected values.

```
All (x => x.NextIndex - x.CurrentIndex > 0)
```

The preceding call will return `true` only when the indices are monotonically increasing.

Here is a negative test case to prove that this code works. The word *saw* is not a sub-sequence of *awesome*. Figure 3-25 shows a table for the current and next index for *saw*.

CurrentIndex ≡	NextIndex ≡
3	0
0	1
3	1

IEnumerable<> (2 items)

Figure 3-25. *The gap (current index) and next index of the word saw*

In this example, the last `All()` call will return `false`, so *saw* can't be a subsequence of *awesome*.

3-16. Squeezing a Paragraph to Fill Tightly

Many text editors support a functionality to fill a paragraph tightly so that the number of words in each line becomes almost the same. This is useful for wrapping text to properly utilize screen area.

Problem

Write a program to wrap a given paragraph of multiple lines so that the lengths of the lines become almost the same.

Solution

This program, shown in Listing 3-16, uses average line length and a LINQ operator to generate a nicely distributed paragraph in which all lines are of almost the same length.

Listing 3-16. Line-wrapping algorithm to equalize line lengths

```
string text =
                @"Almost any text editor provides a fill
                operation. The fill operation transforms raggedy-looking text
                with lines of
                different lengths into nicely formatted text with lines
                nearly the same length.";
text.Dump("Before");

var words = text.Split(new char[]{' ','\r','\n'},StringSplitOptions.RemoveEmptyEntries)
                .Where (t => t.Trim().Length!=0);

var lines = text.Split(new char[]{'\r','\n'},StringSplitOptions.RemoveEmptyEntries);

int max  = lines
                .Select(l => l.Split(new char[]{' '},
                 StringSplitOptions.RemoveEmptyEntries).Count ())
                .OrderByDescending (l => l)
                .First();

max  = max + max / 2;//Maximum width is 1.5 times that of the current maximum width

Enumerable.Range(0,words.Count ()/max + 1)//decide how many lines need to be there.
        .Select(k => words.Skip(k*max).Take(max).Aggregate ((u,v) => u + " " + v))
                .Aggregate ((m,n) => m + Environment.NewLine + n)//provide line breaks
                .Dump("After");
```

This generates the output shown in Figure 3-26.

Before
Almost any text editor provides a fill
      operation. The fill operation transforms raggedy-looking text
           with lines of
           different lengths into nicely formatted text with lines
           nearly the same length.

After
Almost any text editor provides a fill operation. The fill operation transforms
raggedy-looking text with lines of different lengths into nicely formatted text with
lines nearly the same length.

Figure 3-26. *Results before and after the Fill Paragraph routine*

How It Works

The first step to lay lines with even lengths is to determine a decent width for each line. The line with the maximum width is a good starting point. The following code finds the length of the longest line:

```
lines.Select(l => l.Split(new char[]{' '},StringSplitOptions.RemoveEmptyEntries).Count ())
      .OrderByDescending (l => l)
      .First();
```

Using 1.5 times this number should be a good-enough length for the longest line.

The code max = max + max / 2; calculates the maximum line length. The words list contains all the words in the paragraph. Thus words.Length / max + 1 gives the total number of lines required to display the paragraph in the result. Next, the following code creates all the new lines with the required number of words:

```
Select(k => words.Skip(k*max).Take(max).Aggregate ((u,v) => u + " " + v))
```

When k is 0, no word is skipped. At the next stage, when the value of k is increased, that many (k*max) words are skipped. The call to Aggregate() stitches the words together to generate the new line. The final call to Aggregate() inserts the line breaks.

3-17. Printing the Lines of a Song

There are many programming languages, some popular, and some not so popular. Some are considered esoteric; however, that doesn't mean some people don't use them. 99 Bottles of Beer is a web site that challenges people to write a program in any language to generate the lines of the song "99 Bottles of Beer." You can find the lyrics at http://99-bottles-of-beer.net/lyrics.html.

Problem

Write a program to generate the lines of the song "99 Bottles of Beer." Although you can use for loops, please don't; try to do it using LINQ operators instead.

Solution

I wrote the code in Listing 3-17 by using LINQ to generate the song lines. You can find my full solution on the 99 Bottles of Beer web site, at http://99-bottles-of-beer.net/language-csharp-2549.html.

Listing 3-17. Generating the lyrics to "99 Bottles of Beer"

```
using System;
using System.Collections.Generic;
using System.Linq;
using System.Text;

namespace _99Bottlez
{
    class Program
    {
        static void Main(string[] args)
        {
            int countOfBottles = 10;//Number of bottles
            string lineTemplate = @"{X} bottles of beer on the wall, {X} bottles
                            of beer. Take one down and pass it around, {Y}
                            bottles of beer on the wall.";

            string lastLine = @"No more bottles of beer on the wall, no more
                            bottles of beer.Go to the store and buy some
                            more, {X} bottles of beer on the wall.";

            List<string> songLines = new List<string> ();
            Enumerable.Range(1, countOfBottles)
                .Reverse()
                .ToList()
                .ForEach
                (c => songLines.Add(lineTemplate.Replace("{X}",
                c.ToString()).Replace("{Y}", (c-1)!=0?(c - 1).ToString():@" No
                more bottles of beer on the wall.")));

            //Add the last line
            songLines.Add(lastLine.Replace("{X}", countOfBottles.ToString()));

            songLines.ForEach(c => Console.WriteLine(c));
            Console.ReadLine();
        }
    }
}
```

How It Works

The program first generates a list of all line numbers and then reverses the list. Finally, the placeholders in the line template (all but last line) get replaced with the proper numbers and added to the songLines list. The code creates the final line by replacing the placeholders in the last-line template, and appends that to the songLines list. The final lines print the result to the Console.

3-18. Mining Abbreviations and Full Forms from News Articles

Newspaper articles often set abbreviations apart from the rest of the text. Normally, they wrap abbreviations in parentheses. The full form of the abbreviations are typically provided just before the abbreviations appear. For example, a newspaper article might state, "Today United Nations (UN) officials...." If a program can be written to read news articles and mine them for abbreviations and their full forms, making glossaries and indexes would be easy. This program could also be used to automatically tag a news article using abbreviations that appear in the text, making it possible to use an indexcd search to find news articles related to an abbreviation.

Problem

Write a program that reads a news article in the form of plain text and returns all abbreviations and their full forms.

Solution

The following program finds all the abbreviations and their full forms from a given paragraph of a newspaper article. I have made the abbreviations and their expanded forms bold in the sample input in Listing 3-18.

Listing 3-18. Identifying abbreviations and their expanded forms

```
string sentence = @"This is an effort by the World Health Organization (WHO) and
                    Fédération Internationale de Football Association (FIFA) to help
                footballers in poor nations. Associated Press (AP) reports.";
//Add all stop words in this list
List<string> stopWords = new List<string>() {"of", "de"};
foreach(string sw in stopWords)
{
      List<string> matches = Regex
                            .Matches(sentence,sw + " " + "[A-Z][a-z]+")
                            .Cast<Match>()
                            .Select(m => m.Value).ToList();

      foreach (string m in matches)
      {
            sentence = sentence.Replace(m,m.Replace(sw+" ",string.Empty)+"_"+sw);
      }
}
List<string> all = sentence.Split(new char[]{' ',',','!',';','[',']','(',')',
            '-','\'','"','\r','\n'},StringSplitOptions.RemoveEmptyEntries).ToList();
List<string> abbs = all
                    .Where (s => s.ToCharArray().All (x => x>='A' && x<'Z'))
                    .Distinct()
                    .ToList();
```

```
abbs
    .Select (a => new KeyValuePair<int,int>(all.IndexOf(a),a.Length))
    .Select(a => new { Abbreviation = all[a.Key], Expansion =
        Enumerable.Range(a.Key-a.Value,a.Value)

    .Select (e => all[e])
    .Aggregate((f,g) => f.Split('_').Aggregate ((x,y) => y +  " " + x )
                + " " + g.Split('_').Aggregate ((x,y) => y +  " " + x )).Trim()})
    .OrderBy (a => a.Abbreviation).Dump("Abbreviations with Expansions");
```

This program generates the output shown in Figure 3-27. In the table, the first column shows the abbreviation, and the second column shows the expanded form of the abbreviation.

Abbreviations with Expansions

Abbreviation	Expansion
▲ IOrderedEnumerable<> (3 items)	▶
AP	Associated Press
FIFA	Fédération Internationale de Football Association
WHO	World Health Organization

Figure 3-27. *Extracted abbreviations and their expanded forms*

How It Works

The program first loads all the words from the input into a list. Using a regular expression, the program finds the abbreviations within that list and creates a list of them as well. (Of course, those abbreviations are also stored in the first list, because all the words of the given text are stored there.)

The program relies on the length of the abbreviations to backtrack and find the full expanded text for the abbreviation. However, stop words such as *of* or *in* can jeopardize that process, because those words aren't reflected in the abbreviation. For example the abbreviation for "United States of America" is typically USA, not USoA. To fix this potential problem, the example uses a regular expression to locate patterns in which a stop word appears followed by a word with a capital letter. The program transforms this combination to a single word by concatenating the stop word to the following word with a leading underscore. For example, in this example, the phrase of International is transformed to International_of. That may look weird, but the transformation ensures that backtracking will find the complete expanded form of the abbreviation.

Consider this code snippet:

```
abbs
    .Select (a => new KeyValuePair<int,int>(all.IndexOf(a),a.Length))
```

This returns IEnumerable<KeyValuePair<int,int>>, where the first integer represents the index of the abbreviation in the list of all words. The second integer stores the length of all abbreviations as values. This value determines how many words we should check back (backtrack) to find the expansion of the abbreviation.

The following snippet returns as many words as the length of the abbreviation, which are immediately before the abbreviation in the list of all words:

```
Enumerable.Range(a.Key-a.Value,a.Value)
    .Select (e => all[e])
```

a.Key represents the index where the abbreviation is found, and a.Value represents its length. So a.Key - a.Value returns an index which is a.Value ahead of the abbreviation in the list of all words.

The following call to Aggregate deals with the stop word tokens properly:

```
.Aggregate((f,g) => f.Split('_').Aggregate ((x,y) => y + " " + x )
            + " " + g.Split('_').Aggregate ((x,y) => y + " " + x )).Trim()})
```

This call transforms International_of back to of International. It also stitches together the words that form the expanded form of the abbreviation. Finally, the list is sorted alphabetically by abbreviations.

Summary

Congratulations on finishing yet another long chapter. I hope you had fun trying out the examples. Also, you've seen how diverse problems such as human-computer interaction and data-mining tasks can be implemented using LINQ. And you have picked up a few LINQ idioms along the way. These idioms will be useful in later chapters—and beyond this book, when you deal with your own code. The next chapter shows how to refactor code by using LINQ to make it cleaner and more concise.

■ ■ ■

CHAPTER 4

Refactoring with LINQ

When I help my colleagues refactor their loops by using LINQ, they always ask me, "How do you know what LINQ operator to use?" I am sure my colleagues are not alone. This chapter is dedicated to providing detailed examples to help answer that question.

After reading this chapter, you should be able to look at code snippets and know which ones can be replaced with a LINQ query. Think of LINQ operators as similar to Lego blocks. After you know how to use them, you can see and replace a repetitive pattern in your code by gluing together LINQ operators, leading to cleaner, more-intuitive, and thus more maintainable code. Apart from elegance, there is another good reason to transform good old loops into LINQ queries: by doing that, you can make queries run in parallel, using all the cores of the development system by using Parallel LINQ (PLINQ). Parallel queries often run much faster, but remember that LINQ queries aren't inherently faster unless you use parallelism.

4-1. Replacing Loops by Using LINQ Operators

Looping is a basic construct in programming. When someone learns a new programming language, they have to learn the syntax of how to loop through a collection; otherwise, they can't do anything useful. C# has four looping constructs: the for loop, the do-while loop, the while loop, and the foreach loop. C# programmers are familiar with these looping constructs. However, except for the simplest loops, it is often very difficult—if not impossible—to discern a loop's intention simply by looking at it. That's true even of single loops, let alone nested ones. If you have been programming for a while, you will know what I mean.

Several looping constructs appear more often than others in code. Replacing these repeating looping constructs with standard LINQ operators usually results in shorter, more-intuitive code. This section shows how you can replace traditional looping constructs (which sometimes can become ugly quickly) with simpler, smaller, and intuitive LINQ queries. The biggest advantage of using LINQ over looping constructs is that you get to move the code one step closer to the concept. For example, consider the sentence "Check whether any element in the collection matches a given condition." A looping construct doesn't visually reflect the intent of that sentence. But LINQ operators and LINQ queries do.

The recipes in this chapter show looping constructs and the equivalent code using LINQ operators side by side. Each section begins with a LINQ query operator that you can use to simplify the code, followed by the problem statement and a side-by-side comparison of the loop-based and LINQ-based approaches.

A General Strategy to Transform a Loop to a LINQ Query

A loop has three parts: *initialization, condition,* and *loop variable-state-change handler.* If you can rewrite your logic using a foreach loop at each stage, your transformation will become simpler. To do that, follow this three-step process:

1. Identify the range of the loop.

2. Identify the conditional block.

3. Find the appropriate LINQ operator to replace the conditional block.

You'll follow this procedure in the following example.
Suppose you have a loop like this:

```
for(int k = 0 ; k < numbers.Length ; k++)
    if( numbers [ k ] > threshold )
            goodNumbers.Add( numbers [ k ] );
```

In this case, the code loops through an array called numbers, and if the element at a given index is greater than a predefined threshold, it adds that element to goodNumbers.
You could easily rewrite this by using a foreach loop:

```
foreach(var n in numbers)
        if( n > threshold)
            goodNumbers.Add(n)
```

You translate the for loop to foreach because doing so gets rid of all the temporary looping variables. The next step is to identify the LINQ operator that can help you transform the conditional block. In this case, the code simply applies a filter, so the filter operator Where fits the bill. The range of the loop is the range of numbers.
Now reorder these statements. This is closer to the equivalent LINQ statement:

```
goodNumbers.Add(n)
        foreach(var n in numbers)
if(n>threshold)
```

Then do the following:

- Replace the first .Add(n) with = .

- Replace foreach(var n in numbers) with Enumerable.Range(0,numbers.Length).

- Replace if(n > threshold) with Where (n => n > threshold).ToList();.

After making those substitutions, you will have this LINQ script:

```
goodNumbers = Enumerable.Range(0, numbers.Length).Where(n=>n > threshold).ToList();
```

This strategy is applicable for any level of depth of the looping construct that you want to refactor using LINQ.

4-2. The Any Operator

The Any operator returns `true` if there is at least a single element in a collection that matches a given condition.

Problem

Find out whether any number in a collection is greater than 150.

Solution

Use the Any operator to replace a `for` loop.

How It Works

The `for` loop on the left uses a conditional statement in each loop iteration to test the value of each item in the nums collection. To discover that, you have to read the code carefully. In contrast, the refactored LINQ code on the right makes it immediately obvious that the code is checking for any value within the collection greater than 150.

Loop (Imperative Paradigm)	LINQ (Functional Paradigm)

<pre>int[] nums = {14,21,24,51,131,1,11,54};
bool isAny = false;
for(int i=0;i<nums.Length;i++)
{
    if(nums[i]>=150)
    {
        isAny = true;
        break;
    }
}</pre>
	<pre>int[] nums = {14,21,24,51,131,1,11,54};
	bool isAny = nums.Any (n => n >= 150);</pre>

4-3. The All Operator

The `All` operator is useful when you want to check whether all elements in a collection match a given condition.

Problem

Determine whether all elements in a collection are less than 150.

Solution

Use the `All` operator to replace the `for` loop.

How It Works

The `for` loop on the left uses a conditional statement in each loop iteration to test the value of each item in the nums collection. To discover that, you have to read the code carefully. In contrast, the refactored LINQ code on the right makes it immediately obvious that the code is checking for all values of the collection less than 150.

Loop	LINQ

`int[] nums = {14,21,24,51,131,1,11,54};`
`bool isAll = true;`
`for(int i=0;i<nums.Length;i++)`
`{`
`    if(nums[i]<150)`
`    {`
`        isAll = false;`
`        break;`
`    }`
`}`
	`int[] nums  = {14,21,24,51,131,1,11,54};`
	`bool isAll = nums.All (n => n < 150);`

4-4. The Take Operator

The Take operator selects the first specified number of elements from the given collection.

Problem

Extract the first four elements.

Solution

Use the Take operator to replace a for loop that iterates over the first four elements.

How It Works

The for loop on the left loops through the first four elements and puts these numbers in a different array. However, it is evident looking at the LINQ syntax that we want to extract the first four elements.

Loop	LINQ

`int[] nums   = {14,21,24,51,131,1,11,54};`
`int[] first4 = new int[4];`
`for(int i=0;i<4;i++)`
`{`
`    first4[i] = nums[i]; }`
	`int[] nums   = {14,21,24,51,131,1,11,54};`
	`int[] first4 = new int[4];`
	`first4 = nums.Take(4).ToArray();`

4-5. The Skip Operator

The Skip operator picks all except the first k elements elements from a collection.

Problem

Pick all elements of a given integer array except the first four elements.

Solution

Use the `Skip` operator to replace a `for` loop.

How It Works

The `for` loop uses two loop counters to keep track of elements being iterated. However, the LINQ implementation reads like plain English. This also eliminates the need to maintain looping counters.

Loop	LINQ

```int[] nums = {14,21,24,51,131,1,11,54};```
```int[] skip4 = new```
```int[nums.Length - 4];```
```for(int i=4,j=0;i<nums.Length;i++,j++)```
```{```
```   skip4[j] = nums[i];```
```}```
```skip4.Dump();```
	```int[] nums = {14,21,24,51,131,1,11,54};```
	```int[] skip4 = new int[nums.Length - 4];```
	```skip4 = nums.Skip(4).ToArray();```
	```skip4.Dump();```

4-6. The TakeWhile Operator

The `TakeWhile` operator enables you to take elements from a collection as long as a given condition is `true`.

Problem

Pick elements from the start of an unsorted integer array as long as the given condition (the number is less than 50, in this case) is `true`.

Solution

Use the `TakeWhile` operator to replace the `for` loop and branching statement.

How It Works

Imagine `TakeWhile` as shorthand for the looping syntax, where the condition of the nested `if` statement is expressed in the lambda expression `n => n < 50`. The final call to `ToList()` returns a list of integers that are less than 50, taken from the beginning of the array.

Loop	LINQ

```int[] nums = {14,21,24,51,131,1,11,54};```
```List<int> until50 = new```
```   List<int>();```
```for(int i=0;i<nums.Length;i++) {```
```   if(nums[i]<50)```
```   {```
```until50.Add(nums[i]);```
```   }```
```   else```
```   break;```
```}```
```until50.Dump();```
	```int[] nums = {14,21,24,51,131,1,11,54};```
	```List<int> until50 = new List<int>();```
	```until50 = nums.TakeWhile (n => n < 50).ToList();```

4-7. The SkipWhile Operator

SkipWhile skips elements as long as a given condition is true. As soon as the condition becomes false, the operator starts picking values.

Problem

Pick all elements of a given integer array that are not evenly divisible by 7.

Solution

Use the SkipWhile operator to replace a for loop and branching.

How It Works

The condition inside the loop becomes the lambda expression.

Loop	LINQ

```int[] nums = {14,21,24,51,131,1,11,54};```
```List<int> skipWhileDivisibleBy7 = new```
```List<int>();```
```for(int i=0;i<nums.Length;i++)```
```{```
```   if(nums[i] % 7 == 0)```
```   {```
```   continue;```
```   }```
```   else```
```   skipWhileDivisibleBy7.Add(nums[i]);```
```}```
	```int[] nums = {14,21,24,51,131,1,11,54};```
	```List<int> skipWhileDivisibleBy7 =```
	```nums.SkipWhile (n => n % 7 == 0).ToList();```

In the next chapter, you will learn about the TakeUntil() and SkipUntil() operators available in the MoreLINQ project. They are mirrors of the TakeWhile() and SkipWhile() operators.

4-8. The Where Operator

The Where operator finds elements that match a given condition. Think of it as the looping and branching construct all in one. This is one of the most used operators.

Problem

Pick all elements of a given integer array that are greater than 50.

Solution

Use the Where operator to replace a for loop and branching inside the loop.

How It Works

The for loop uses two loop counters to keep track of elements being iterated. However, the LINQ implementation reads like plain English. This eliminates the need to maintain looping counters, and the intent of the code becomes immediately evident.

Loop	LINQ
``int[] nums   = {14,21,24,51,131,1,11,54};
int[] above50 = new int[nums.Length];
int j = 0;
for(int i=0;i<nums.Length;i++)
{
if(nums[i] > 50)
{
above50[j]=nums[i];
j++;
}
}
Array.Resize(ref above50,j);```	```int[] nums = {14,21,24,51,131,1,11,54}; int[]
above50 = nums.Where (n => n > 50).ToArray();```

4-9. The Zip Operator

The Zip operator applies a specified function to the corresponding elements of two sequences to generate a result sequence.

Problem

Print the full names of all family members, including the salutation, first name, and last name.

Solution

Use the Zip operator to replace a for loop.

How It Works

The for loop uses a loop counter to keep track of the current index and prints the values for each array (salutation and name, in this case) as long as there are elements. The LINQ statement does that same thing. The lambda function ((salutation, name) => salutation + " " + name + " Smith") does the work of concatenating parts of the name for each individual person.

Loop	LINQ

string[] salutations =
    {"Mr.", "Mrs.","Master.","Ms."};
 	
string[] names = {"Patrick","Nancy","Jon","Jane"};
 	
List<string> allNames = new
    List<string>();
 	
for(int i=0; i< salutations.Length; i++)
 	
allNames.Add(salutations[i] + " " +
    names[i] + " Smith");
	string[] salutations =
	    {"Mr.", Mrs.","Master.","Ms."};
	
	string[] names = {"Patrick","Nancy","Jon","Jane"};
	
	salutations.Zip(names, (salutation, name)
	    => salutation + " " + name + " Smith")
	    .Dump();

4-10. OrderBy and OrderByDescending Operators

Sorting shouldn't hurt. Use OrderBy and OrderByDescending to sort in order and in descending order, respectively.

Problem

Sort an array of strings based on their length.

Solution

Use the OrderBy operator to replace Comparer logic.

How It Works

The default sorting for string values is alphabetical. So to sort a bunch of strings by their lengths, a comparer must be implemented. But with LINQ, there is no need to create a custom comparer. The key to use for sorting is passed in the form of a lambda expression: in this case, `item => item.Length`.

Loop	LINQ
```public class StringLengthComparer :IComparer<string>{ public int Compare(string x, string y) { return x.Length.CompareTo(y.Length); }}void Main(){ string[] codes ={"abc","bc","a","d","abcd"}; StringLengthComparer slc = newStringLengthComparer(); List<string> codesAsList = codes.ToList(); codesAsList.Sort(slc); codesAsList.Dump(); }```	```string[] codes = {"abc","bc","a","d","abcd"};List<string> codesAsList = codes.OrderBy (item => item.Length).ToList();```

To sort the string in reverse order of their lengths, just change the logic from `x.LengthCompareTo(y.Length)` to `y.Length.CompareTo(x.Length)`. In the LINQ version, using `OrderByDescending()` will do the trick.

4-11. The Distinct Operator

The `Distinct` operator finds unique elements from a given collection.

Problem

Find unique names from the list of a given names.

Solution

Use the `Distinct` operator.

How It Works

The `Distinct` operator has two overloaded versions. The first one uses the default comparer for the type of the collection. The second one expects a custom comparer. In the next chapter, you will learn about the `DistinctBy()` operator, which lets you pass a lambda expression instead of a comparer.

Loop	LINQ
```string[] names = {"Sam","David","Sam","Eric", "Daniel","Sam"}; Array.Sort(names); List<string> distinctNames = new List<string>(); for(int i=0;i<names.Length - 1 ;i++) { if(names[i]!=names[i+1]) distinctNames.Add(names[i]); else { if(distinctNames[distinctNames.Count - 1]!= names[i]) distinctNames.Add(names[i]); } } distinctNames.Dump("Unique names");```	```string[] names = {"Sam","David","Sam","Eric", "Daniel","Sam"}; List<string> distinctNames = names.Distinct(). ToList(); distinctNames.Dump("Unique names");```

4-12. The Union Operator

The Union operator finds the union of two given collections.

Problem

Find the union of a couple of string arrays.

Solution

Use the Union operator.

How It Works

The Union operator has two overloaded versions. The first one uses the default comparer for the type of the collection. The second one expects a custom comparer. For the current example, the default comparer is fine. However, if you need some other custom comparer logic to determine uniqueness, you have to implement a custom comparer.

```
static void Main(string[] args)
{
    string[] names1 = { "Sam", "David", "Sam", "Eric", "Daniel", "Sam" };
    string[] names2 = { "David", "Eric", "Samuel" };

    string[] names = new string[names1.Length + names2.Length];

    for (int i = 0; i < names1.Length; i++)
        names[i] = names1[i];
    for (int i = 0, j = names1.Length; i < names2.Length; i++, j++)
        names[j] = names2[i];
```

```
List<string> unionNames = new List<string>();
Array.Sort(names);

for (int i = 0; i < names.Length - 1 ; i++)
{
    if (names[i] != names[i + 1])
    {
        if (unionNames.Count > 0)
        {
            if (unionNames[unionNames.Count - 1] != names[i])
                unionNames.Add(names[i]);
        }
        else
            unionNames.Add(names[i]);
    }
    else
    {
        if (unionNames[unionNames.Count - 1] != names[i])
            unionNames.Add(names[i]);
    }
}
if (names[names.Length - 1] != names[names.Length - 2])
    unionNames.Add(names[names.Length - 1]);
}
```

The preceding implementation is the most straightforward. You can use a Dictionary to perform the union operation, storing the elements as the key of the dictionary and later producing a list of all keys. However, the argument is, you can save all that and let LINQ handle it by using the LINQ operator Union():

```
unionNames = names1.Union(names2).ToList();
```

4-13. The Intersect Operator

The Intersect operator finds the intersection of two collections.

Problem

Find the intersection of a couple of string arrays.

Solution

Use the Intersect operator.

How It Works

The Intersect operator has two overloaded versions. The first one uses the default comparer for the type of the collection. The second one expects a custom comparer. For the current example, the default comparer is fine. However, if you need some other custom comparer logic to determine uniqueness, you have to implement a custom comparer.

Loop	LINQ
```string[] names1 = {"Sam","David","Sam","Eric", "Daniel","Sam"}; string[] names2 = {"David","Eric","Samuel"}; List<string> commonNames = new List<string>(); for(int i=0;i<names1.Length;i++) { if(Array.FindIndex(names2, m => m == names1[i])!=-1) commonNames.Add(names1[i]); } commonNames.Dump();```	```string[] names1 = {"Sam","David","Sam","Eric", "Daniel","Sam"}; string[] names2 = {"David","Eric","Samuel"}; commonNames = names1.Intersect(names2).ToList(); commonNames.Dump();```

4-14. The Except Operator

The Except operator finds the elements that are exclusively available in one of the given collections.

Problem

Finding names that are exclusively available in one collection and not in another.

Solution

Use the Except operator.

How It Works

The Except operator has two overloaded versions. The first one uses the default comparer for the type of the collection. The second one expects a custom comparer. For the current example, the default comparer is fine. However, if you need some other custom comparer logic to determine uniqueness, you have to implement a custom equality comparer.

Loop	LINQ
```string[] names1 = {"Sam","David","Eric","Daniel"}; string[] names2 = {"David","Eric","Samuel"}; List<string> exclusiveNames = new List<string>(); for(int i=0;i<names1.Length;i++) { if(Array.FindIndex(names2, m => m == names1[i])==-1) exclusiveNames.Add(names1[i]); } exclusiveNames.Dump();```	```string[] names1 = {"Sam","David","Eric","Daniel"}; string[] names2 = {"David","Eric","Samuel"}; List<string> exclusiveNames = new List<string>(); exclusiveNames = names1.Except(names2).ToList();```

4-15. The Concat Operator

The Concat operator concatenates two sequences together, back to back.

Problem

Generate a list of all names (including duplicates, if any) by concatenating two lists of names.

Solution

Use the Concat operator.

How It Works

Concat is useful because it saves you from having to keep track of the size of the array. Using Concat(), you will make sure to avoid one-off errors.

Loop	Linq
``string[] names1 = {"Sam","David","Erik","Daniel"};
string[] names2 = {"David","Erik","Samuel"};
string[] names = new string[names1.Length +
names2.Length];
for (int i = 0; i < names1.Length; i++)
names[i] = names1[i];
for (int i = 0, j = names1.Length; i < names2.
Length; i++, j++)
names[j] = names2[i];```	```string[] names1 = {"Sam","David","Erik","Daniel"};
string[] names2 = {"David","Erik","Samuel"};
string[] names = names1.Concat(names2).
ToArray();```

4-16. The SequenceEqual Operator

The SequenceEqual operator checks whether two sequences have the same element at each index, starting from the 0th index and maintaining the order.

Problem

Check whether two integer arrays are equal.

Solution

Use the SequenceEqual operator.

How It Works

The SequenceEqual operator has two overloaded versions. The first one uses the default comparer for the type of the collection. The second one expects a custom comparer. For the current example, the default comparer is fine. However, if you need some other custom comparer logic to determine uniqueness, you have to implement a custom equality comparer.

Loop	Linq
| ```
public bool IsSequenceEqual(int[] first,int[]
second)
{
    if(first.Length == second.Length)
    {
        for(int i=0;i<first.Length;i++)
            if(first[i]!=second[i])
                return false;
        return true;
    }
    return false;
}
void Main()
{
    int[] codes = {343,2132,12,32143,234};
    int[] expected = {343,12,2132,32143,234};
    IsSequenceEqual(codes,expected).Dump(); }
``` | ```
int[] codes = {343,2132,12,32143,234};
int[] expected = {343,12,2132,32143,234};
codes.SequenceEqual(expected).Dump();
``` |

A different situation arises when we need to check for availability of all elements from a source collection in another collection, disregarding the order of occurrence. SequenceEqual() works only when the elements in both the participating collections appear in the same order. A solution would be to apply OrderBy() calls to both of the participating sequences and then do a SequenceEqual() call. However, the following approach using the All() operator solves that problem without sorting.

Loop	LINQ
| ```
int[] codes = {343,2132,12,32143,234};
int[] expected = {343,12,2132,32143,234};
bool all = false; for(int i=0;i<codes.
Length;i++)
{
  all = expected.Contains(codes[i]);
  if(!all)
      break;
}
``` | ```
int[] codes = {343,2132,12,32143,234}; int[] expected =
{343,12,2132,32143,234};
bool all = codes.All(x => expected.Contains(x)).Dump();
``` |

4-17. The OfType Operator

The OfType operator finds elements of only the given type from a collection that has elements of several types.

Problem

Extract only the string values from an object array that has other types of elements apart from strings.

Solution

Use the OfType operator instead of looping and branching.

How It Works

OfType can be used for sanity checking. For example, let's say you have an object array that is meant to be filled with only strings. Before doing anything with the content of the array, it is good to verify that all the elements of the array are actually strings. To do so, it will be enough to check whether the length of OfType<string>() is the same as the length of the array.

Loop	LINQ
`object[] things = {"Sam",1,DateTime.Today,"Eric"};`	`object[] things = {"Sam",1,DateTime.Today,"Eric"};`
`foreach (var v in things)`	`things.OfType<string>().Dump();`
`if( v.GetType() == typeof(string))`	
`v.Dump();`	

4-18. The Cast Operator

Safe casting isn't hard and shouldn't hurt. The Cast<T>() operator can cast any loosely typed collection to a strongly typed collection of the given type T.

Problem

Create a strongly typed collection from a loosely typed one.

Solution

Use the Cast operator.

How It Works

In the following code snippet, the LINQ code creates IEnumerable<string> from an object array.

Loop	LINQ

```object[] things = {"Sam","Dave","Greg","Travis", "Dan",2};```
 	
```List<string> allStrings = new List<string>();```
 	
```foreach (var v in things)```
```{```
    ```string z = v as string;```
      ```if(z!=null)```
```allStrings.Add(z);```
```}```
	```object[] things = {"Sam","Dave","Greg","Travis", "Dan",2};```
	
	```things.Select (t => t as string)```
	    ```.Where (t => t != null)```
	    ```.Cast<string>()```
	    ```.Dump();```

4-19. The Aggregate Operator

The Aggregate operator joins the elements of a given collection by using a provided lambda function.

Problem

Create a comma-separated list using the names given in a string array.

Solution

Use the Aggregate operator.

How It Works

This works the same way as the comma-quibbling problem code in Chapter 3. The lambda function `(f,s) => f + " " + s` is used to generate the comma-separated list.

Loop	LINQ

```string[] names = {"Greg","Travis","Dan"};```
```for (int k = 0; k< names.Length - 1; k++)```
```Console.Write(names[k]+",");```
```//Printing the last name (one off logic)```
```Console.Write(names[names.Length - 1]);```
	```string[] names = {"Greg","Travis","Dan"};```
	```names.Aggregate((f,s)=>f+","+s).Dump();```

So far, you have seen how to use several LINQ operators to replace traditional loop-based logic, leading to cleaner, intuitive code. In the next section, you will see how operators from a community LINQ project can be used to refactor loops.

4-20. Replacing Nested Loops

Be warned! Replacing nested loops with LINQ standard query operators might look flat, but the complexity doesn't change. However, the point is that by using LINQ operators, the code does look more intuitive.

The most common form of nested loops is a set of two loops. The strategy to replace loops with LINQ is to use projection with SelectMany().

The SelectMany Operator

If we want to print all the characters of all the words for each word in a given array, we can use nested loops or we can replace nested loops with SelectMany(), as shown next. Although this example is trivial, it is deliberately chosen so that you can relate it to one of your own one-to-many situations. You can use this operator to flatten your dictionary-like collections.

```
string[] words = {"dog", "elephant", "fox", "bear"};

List<char> allChars = new List<char>();
foreach(string word in words)
{
    allChars.AddRange(word.ToCharArray());
}

words.SelectMany (w => w.ToCharArray()).Dump();
```

Removing Nested Loops by Using SelectMany

Let's say we have the following nested loop. This simple nested loop just adds two integers together:

```
List<int> fromLoop = new List<int>();
for(int i = 0;i<10;i++)
        for(int j = 0 ; j < 10 ; j ++ )
                fromLoop.Add( i + j);
```

Here is the same loop implemented by using LINQ operators:

```
int[] initialValues = Enumerable.Range(0,10).ToArray();
List<int> fromLINQ = Enumerable.Range(0,10)
                            .SelectMany (e => initialValues.Select (v => v + e )).ToList();

//Finally check whether you have the same values or not.
fromLoop.SequenceEqual(fromLINQ).Dump();
```

This returns true as both the sequences are equal.

Replacing If-Else Blocks Inside a Loop

The philosophy behind replacing a loop-if-else-end-loop block with a bunch of LINQ statements is that *flat is better than nesting.* Let's say you have a loop like this:

```
for(int i = 0;i<4; i++)
{
    if (i%2==0)
    {
        someThings.Insert(0,i);
    }
    else if((2*i+1)%2==0)
    {
        someThings.Add(i);
    }
    else //everything else falls here
    {
        someThings.Add(i);
        someThings.Add(i+1);
    }
}
```

This can be replaced with the following three LINQ statements:

```
List<int> someThings = new List<int>();
Enumerable.Range(0,4).Where(i => i%2==0).ForEach( a => someThings.Insert(0,a));
Enumerable.Range(0,4).Where(i => (2*i+1)%2==0).ForEach( a => someThings.Add(a));
Enumerable.Range(0,4).Where(i => (2*i+1)%2!=0 && i%2!=0).ForEach( a =>
    someThings.AddRange(new int[]{a,a + 1}));
```

The strategy for this approach is simple and can be declared by the following three steps:

- Range (using the Range operator)

- Filter (using the Where operator)

- Perform the action (using the ForEach operator)

The idea is to segregate loops as different Project ➤ Filter ➤ Action blocks and give each block a single responsibility. This way, it will be simpler to refactor when needed.

4-21. Running Code in Parallel Using AsParallel() and AsOrdered() Operators

Making use of all your computing power is simple with LINQ. By using the AsParallel() operator, you can "automagically" make sure that your code runs faster. But be warned, plugging in AsParallel() doesn't always guarantee faster execution time. Sometimes it might take longer to distribute the task to multiple processors, and it can take a longer time running the code in parallel than in sequential mode. AsParallel() splits the input data to multiple groups so the order of the elements in the input doesn't remain intact. If you care about the order of the elements in the result, plug in AsOrdered() right after the AsParallel() call.

Problem

Create a program that finds all the prime numbers from 1 to 10,000—fast.

Solution

The solution is as follows:

```
using System;
using System.Collections.Generic;
using System.Diagnostics;
using System.Linq;
using System.Text;
using System.Threading.Tasks;

namespace RefactoringWithAsParallel
{
    class Program
    {
        static void Main(string[] args)
        {
            Stopwatch w = new Stopwatch();
            w.Start();
            List<int> Qs = new List<int>();
            List<int> Qsp = new List<int>();
            for (int i = 0; i < 2; i++)
                Qs = Enumerable.Range(1, 10000).Where(d => Enumerable.Range(2, d / 2)
                                                    .All(e => d % e != 0)).ToList();
            w.Stop();
            double timeWithoutParallelization = w.Elapsed.TotalMilliseconds;

            Stopwatch w2 = new Stopwatch();
            w2.Start();
            for (int i = 0; i < 2; i++)
                Qsp = Enumerable.Range(1, 10000).AsParallel().Where(d =>
                        Enumerable.Range(2, d / 2)
                        .All(e => d % e != 0)).ToList();
            w2.Stop();
            double timeWithParallelization = w2.Elapsed.TotalMilliseconds;
            double percentageGainInPerformance = (timeWithoutParallelization -
                                                    timeWithParallelization) /
                                                    timeWithoutParallelization;
            bool isSame = Qs.SequenceEqual(Qsp);

        }
    }
}
```

How It Works

Although the algorithm used to check whether the number is prime or not is naïve, that's not the point. The point is that adding AsParallel() makes the code faster. I recommend that you run the program multiple times and check the value of percentageGainInPerformance. For me, that value was roughly between 29% and 45%. However, you will see that isSame is false, because the order of the elements in the result obtained by applying AsParallel() is not the same as that of the input. If you want to guarantee the order, add AsOrdered() right after AsParallel(), as shown next.

```
Qsp = Enumerable.Range(1, 10000).AsParallel().AsOrdered().Where(d => Enumerable.Range(2, d / 2)
                                             .All(e => d % e != 0)).ToList();
```

Note that adding AsOrdered() decreases the performance gain a little. And if you think for a while, that's intuitive. Because after the result is obtained, the program has to order it back as per the order of the elements in the input collection.

Summary

This chapter provided some strategies for refactoring loops with LINQ queries, resulting in cleaner, more-intuitive code. You can make a query run in parallel just by using the AsParallel() operator after the collection, and you can order the result by calling AsOrdered() if the order is important to you. The next chapter takes this concept further to explore using LINQ to help improve readability and maintainability—and even improve code performance—by implementing embedded domain-specific languages (DSLs) for several practical purposes.

CHAPTER 5

Refactoring with MoreLINQ

In the preceding chapter, you saw how LINQ can help replace existing loops. Loop constructs can sometimes range from difficult to impossible to comprehend, especially when nested. This chapter extends the loop-to-LINQ replacement concept by showing how the open source LINQ API called *MoreLINQ* can help you refactor legacy code. By going beyond the core LINQ operators, the MoreLINQ API offers a wide range of operators that you can readily use to replace looping or looping/branching logic. After reading this chapter, you should be able to rewrite such code by using methods found in the MoreLINQ API.

5-1. Getting MoreLINQ

MoreLINQ is a library written by Jon Skeet (see https://twitter.com/jonskeet), which you can find on Google Code (http://code.google.com/p/morelinq/source/browse/).

The following sections show how looping constructs might have been written to solve specific problems, and how the MoreLINQ operators can help you refactor those loops.

5-2. Using the Scan Operator

The Scan operator applies a function cumulatively on a sequence, yielding the result at each stage.

Problem

Find the cumulative sum of a given integer sequence.

Solution

Use the Scan operator instead of using loops. The following table shows a loop solution in the left column, and the equivalent MoreLINQ solution, using Scan, on the right.

Loop	MoreLINQ

```int[] numbers = {1,2,3,4};```
```int[] sums = new int[numbers.Length];```
```for(int i=0;i<numbers.Length;i++)```
```{```
```   for(int j = 0;j<=i;j++)```
```   sums[i]+=numbers[j];```
```}```
```sums.Dump();```
	```int[] numbers = {1,2,3,4};```
	```numbers.Scan((a,b)=>a + b).Dump();```

How It Works

The output of this code is the cumulative sum of the sequence 1,2,3,4, as shown in Figure 5-1.

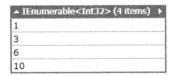

Figure 5-1. *Result of the cumulative sum operation*

At first glance, Scan might look similar to Aggregate. But Aggregate runs the folding function provided on every element of the collection and returns a final value. In contrast, Scan returns the sum of elements up to the current number, for each number, until it reaches the end of the list. So the difference is that the *last* element of the result obtained from a Scan call is the same as the result of an Aggregate call.

5-3. Using the Slice Operator

The Slice operator extracts a slice from a sequence. The first argument to Slice is the starting index, and the second is the run length of the sequence segment to be extracted.

Problem

Extract four elements, starting at the fourth element.

Solution

Use the Slice operator rather than using loops and doing the bookkeeping yourself.

Loop	MoreLINQ
```int[] values = {1,2,3,4,5,6,7,8,9,10};```	```int[] values = {1,2,3,4,5,6,7,8,9,10};```

```
int[] values = {1,2,3,4,5,6,7,8,9,10};
int k = 4;
int start = 3;
int[] slice = new int[k];
for(int i = start,j = 0 ; i< start + k ;i++,j++)
    slice[j] = values[i];
slice.Dump();
```

```
int[] values = {1,2,3,4,5,6,7,8,9,10};
int[] slice = values.Slice(3,4).ToArray();
```

How It Works

You can think of this method as a shortcut to the `Skip(m).Take(n)` idiom, where you simply pass m and n as the arguments to `Slice`.

5-4. Using the Interleave Operator

The `Interleave` operator joins two sequences, taking elements from each sequence alternately.

Problem

Join two integer sequences such that each element in the resultant sequence is taken in turn from one of the source sequences. You can imagine that these integer sequences are formed by the contents of packets arriving over the network, and the processor must pick one element from each sequence, alternating between sequences. Another way to imagine this is as a kind of simple load-balancing strategy.

Solution

Use the `Interleave` operator instead of loops.

Loop	MoreLINQ
```int[] n1 = {1,3,4,5};int[] n2 = { 4,6};int[] total = new int[n1.Length + n2.Length];int first = 0;int second = 0;int index = 0;for(;index< n1.Length+n2.Length;index++){ if(index % 2 == 0) { //Pick element from the first if(first!=n1.Length) { total[index] = n1[first]; first++; } else { if (second != n2.Length) { total[index] = n2[second]; second++; } } }```	```int[] n1 = {1,3,4,5};int[] n2 = { 4,6};int[] total = n1.Interleave(n2) .ToArray();```

(continued)

Loop	MoreLINQ

```
        else
        {
              //Pick element from the second
              if(second!=n2.Length)
              {
                    total[index] = n2[second];
                    second++;
              }
              else
              {
                    if (first != n1.Length)
                    {
                          total[index] = n1[first];
                          first++;
                    }
              }
        }
    }
}
total.Dump();
```

How It Works

In Figure 5-2, the first sequence is longer than the second sequence. The first sequence consists of dark circles, and the second sequence consists of light circles. The resulting sequence created by Interleave takes one element from each source sequence in turn, so the result has one dark circle followed by a light one, and so on. This goes on until the operation reaches the end of the shorter sequence (Sequence #2, in this case), after which the code simply appends elements from the longer sequence until it reaches the end of that sequence as well.

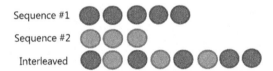

Figure 5-2. *How Interleave() works to generate the interleaved sequence*

5-5. Using the Windowed Operator

The Windowed operator generates content as a collection of collections, creating several intermediate collections for a sliding window of a given size from any given collection.

Problem

Find the moving average from a given sequence in which the moving window size is 2.

Solution

Use the Windowed operator to generate a sequence of sequences instead of using a nested looping construct.

Loop	MoreLINQ

<pre>int[] values = {1,2,3,4,5,6,7,8,9,10,11};
List<List<int>> windowVals = new List<List<int>>();
for(int i=0;i<values.Length-1;i++)
{
   List<int> inner = new List<int>();
   for(int j=i;j<i+2;j++)
     inner.Add(values[j]);
    windowVals.Add(inner);
}
List<double> movingAvgs = new List<double>();
for(int i=0;i<windowVals.Count;i++)
{
     double avg = 0;
     for(int j = 0;j<windowVals[i].Count;j++)
         avg += windowVals[i][j];
     movingAvgs.Add(avg/windowVals[i].Count);
}
movingAvgs.Dump("Moving Averages using loops");</pre>
	<pre>int[] values = {1,2,3,4,5,6,7,8,9,10,11};
	values.Windowed(2)
	     .Select(list => list.Average())
	     .Dump("Moving Averages");</pre>

How It Works

Both the looping example and the `Windowed` example generate the output shown in Figure 5-3.

Moving Averages

▲ IEnumerable<Double> (10 items) ▶
1.5
2.5
3.5
4.5
5.5
6.5
7.5
8.5
9.5
10.5

Figure 5-3. *Moving average of numbers 1 to 11 with two numbers taken at a time*

`Windowed` generates an enumerable of enumerables, in which each enumerable holds the values that result from sliding the window. Figure 5-4 shows how `Windowed` works in more detail. The underline denotes the sliding window.

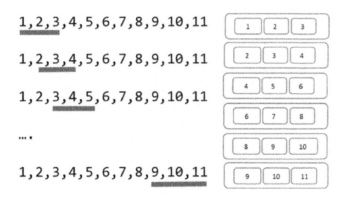

Figure 5-4. *How the sliding window moves and generates intermediate collections*

The call to `Select (list => list.Average())` projects the average of each list generated by `Windowed`.

5-6. Using the Cartesian Operator

The Cartesian operator finds the Cartesian product of a series of collections. As in the other examples in this chapter, this can help you replace vanilla nested loops with more-readable code.

Problem

Find the volumes of all parallelepipeds from a given set of lengths, breadths, and heights.

Solution

Use the Cartesian operator instead of three nested loops.

Loop	MoreLINQ
```int[] lengths = {1,2,3,4,5,6,7};```	```int[] lengths = {1,2,3,4,5,6,7};```

```
int[] lengths = {1,2,3,4,5,6,7};          int[] lengths = {1,2,3,4,5,6,7};
int[] breadths = {1,1,2,3,1,3};           int[] breadths = {1,1,2,3,1,3};
int[] heights = {2,1,3,1,4};              int[] heights = {2,1,3,1,4};
List<int> volumes = new List<int>();      List<int> volumesLINQ = lengths
for(int r = 0;r<lengths.Length; r++)          .Cartesian(breadths, (b,l)=> b * l)
{                                             .Cartesian(heights, (a,b)=> a * b)
    for(int c = 0; c< breadths.Length; c++)   .ToList();
    {                                     volumesLINQ.Take(10).Dump();
        for(int z=0;z<heights.Length;z++)
        {
        volumes.Add(lengths[r]*breadths[c]*heights[z]);
        }
    }
}
```

How It Works

Nested loops are sometimes referred to as *bow-and-arrow patterns*, because they assume a shape similar to a bow and arrow. As shown in the preceding code, you can replace such a bow and arrow pattern with a call to Cartesian. The example on the left in the Solution section above shows applying Cartesian with three nested loops; however, you can use the MoreLINQ Cartesian command to generate Cartesian products nested as deeply as required. Cartesian takes two arguments. The first is an enumerable over which the command will iterate, while the second is a lambda expression that represents the inner calculation. If you have single statements inside the innermost loop, you can translate those loops into a sequence of calls to Cartesian. Figure 5-5 shows the output.

▲ IEnumerable<Int32> (10 items) ▶
2
1
3
1
4
2
1
3
1
4

Figure 5-5. *The first 10 calculated volumes of the set of parallelepipeds*

5-7. Using the Partition Operator

The Partition operator partitions a sequence according to a given number of items.

Problem

Let's say that you have a 10-element array and you want partition the array into three sections such that the first part holds 30 percent of the elements (three, in this case), the middle section holds 60 percent of the elements (six, in this case), and the last part holds 10 percent of the elements (one, in this case).

Solution

Loop	MoreLINQ

```
int[] values = {1,2,3,4,5,6,7,8,9,10};

//We want a List<List<int>>
//with values distributed according to the
//given percentages.
//This means there will need to be three lists
//where the first one will have 30% elements
//second one 60% and the last one 10%.

int[] percentages = {30,60,10};
int[] numbersOfItems =
new int[percentages.Length];
for(int i = 0;i<percentages.Length;i++)
        numbersOfItems[i] = (int) Math.Floor(
(double)values.Length*percentages[i]/100);
List<List<int>> distributions = new
List<List<int>>();
for(int i = 0;i<numbersOfItems.Length;i++)
{
    List<int> innerList = new List<int>();
    if(i==0)
    {
        for(int j=0;j<numbersOfItems[i];j++)
        innerList.Add(values[j]);
    }
    else
    {
        int index = 0;
        for(int k = 0;k<i;k++)
            index+= numbersOfItems[k];
        for (int j = index; j < index +
            numbersOfItems[i];j++ )
            innerList.Add(values[j]);
    }
    distributions.Add(innerList);
}
distributions.Dump("Partitioned as per
percentage");
```

```
int[] values = {1,2,3,4,5,6,7,8,9,10};
int[] percentages = {30,60,10};
List<IEnumerable<int>> distributions = new
List<IEnumerable<int>>();
int[] numbersOfItems = percentages
    .Select (n=> (int) Math.Floor( (double)
values.Length*n/100)).ToArray();
distributions = values.Partition(numbersOfItems)
    .ToList();
distributions.Dump("Partitioned as per
percentage");
```

How It Works

Both versions generate the output shown in Figure 5-6.

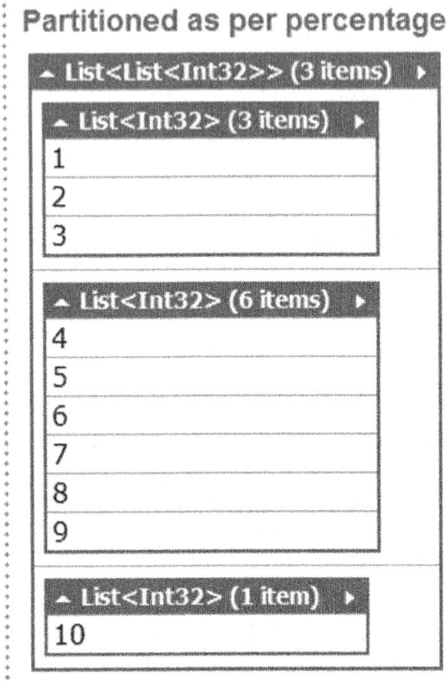

Partitioned as per percentage

```
▲ List<List<Int32>> (3 items)  ▶

  ▲ List<Int32> (3 items)  ▶
  1
  2
  3

  ▲ List<Int32> (6 items)  ▶
  4
  5
  6
  7
  8
  9

  ▲ List<Int32> (1 item)  ▶
  10
```

Figure 5-6. *The result of partitioning an array with the given distribution percentage*

Partition has two overloaded versions. The first version takes a single integer that represents a single size for all the partitions. The other overloaded version takes an IEnumerable<int> whose values represent different sizes for the required partitions. The example first obtains the number of elements required in each partition by calculating that from the given percentages, and stores those values in the numbersOfItems array, which is passed to the second overload of Partition.

5-8. Using the Index Operator

The Index operator returns an enumeration with the index and the value at each index for the given collection.

Problem

Keep track of the index for each character in a given string.

Solution

Loop	MoreLINQ
| ```
string input = "LINQ";
List<KeyValuePair<int,char>> indices = new
List<KeyValuePair<int,char>>();
for(int i = 0; i< input.Length; i++)
{
    indices.Add(new KeyValuePair<int,char>(i,input[i]));
}
indices.Dump();
``` | ```
char[] chars = "LINQ".ToCharArray();
chars.Index().Dump();
``` |

Both of these examples produce the result shown in Figure 5-7. For the looping construct, however, the result is strongly typed to be a List<KeyValuePair<int, char>>.

▲ IEnumerable<KeyValuePair<Int32,Char>> (4 items) ▶	
Key	**Value**
0	L
1	I
2	N
3	Q

Figure 5-7. *The key/value pairs for the word LINQ. The Key columnn shows the index of the letters, while the Value column represents the character values at those indices*

How It Works

Index returns an IEnumerable<int,T> when used on a collection of type T. This operator might not seem so useful, but it can be. For example, in the next section, you will see how Index can help write generic code to remove consecutive duplicates from a given collection, which is a rather common programming task.

5-9. Using the PairWise Operator

The PairWise operator performs an action over two neighboring/consecutive elements of a given collection and returns an enumerable with the result of all such actions performed across the collection. In other words, if you need to perform an operation on each pair of elements, starting from the leftmost element, then PairWise is the operator you need. I won't show the looping code to do this, but you've probably written similar loops before.

Problem

Remove consecutive repeated characters from a string. If you want to experiment further, see if you can use the same method to remove consecutive identical dates.

Solution

The logic for this can be wrapped inside a LINQ extension, as shown here:

```
public static class MyLinqEx
{
        public static IEnumerable<T> RemoveConsecutiveDuplicates<T>(this IEnumerable<T> input)
                                                        where T:IComparable
        {
                var conditions = input.Pairwise((a,b)=>a.Equals(b));
                var dontPickIndices = conditions.Index()
                            .Where (c => c.Value==true)
                            .Select(k => k.Key);
                return Enumerable.Range(0,input.Count())
                        .Where (e => !dontPickIndices.Contains(e))
                        .Select(k => input.ElementAt(k));
        }
}
```

Here is how you can use this operator:

```
void Main()
{
    "LLIIIIINNQQ".ToCharArray().RemoveConsecutiveDuplicates().Dump();
}
```

How It Works

The extension is built around two basic building blocks, Index and PairWise operator. The PairWise operator generates the output in Figure 5-8 by comparing each pair of letters in the input to see whether they're the same.

▲ IEnumerable<Boolean> (9 items) ►
True
False
True
True
True
False
True
False
True

Figure 5-8. *The state of neighborhood similarity of two characters*

Next, the Index operator generates the output shown in Figure 5-9.

▲ IEnumerable<KeyValuePair<Int32,Boolean>> (9 items) ▶	
Key	Value
0	True
1	False
2	True
3	True
4	True
5	False
6	True
7	False
8	True

Figure 5-9. *The indices of neighborhood similarity check result*

By selecting the keys for which the value is true, you would get the indices that have the same characters as those of their next consecutive neighbor. Conversely, by avoiding these indices, you get a list of consecutive nonrepeating characters. The variable dontPickIndices holds the true indices.

5-10. The ForEach Operator

The ForEach operator performs an action on all elements of a given sequence. Without this, the result would need to be projected to a strongly typed list (List<T>) to run an operation on each member, which can lead to performance issues when the list is large.

Problem

Perform an operation on each element in an enumerable.

Solution

Use the ForEach operator instead of looping or converting the enumerable to a strongly typed list.

Loop	MoreLINQ

```int[] numbers = {1,2,8,7,5,6,4,3};```
 ```Action<int> ack = a =>```
 ``` Console.WriteLine(```
 ``` DateTime.Today.AddDays(a)```
 ``` .DayOfWeek);```
 ```foreach (var integer in numbers)```
 ``` ack.Invoke(integer);```
	```int[] numbers = {1,2,8,7,5,6,4,3};```
	 ```Action<int> ack = a => Console.WriteLine```
	 ```(DateTime.Today.AddDays(a).DayOfWeek);```
	 ```numbers.ForEach(ack);```

How It Works

The ForEach operator takes an action that it then invokes on each member of the collection on which ForEach is being invoked.

5-11. Using the MinBy/MaxBy Operator

The MinBy operator finds the value from the given source collection that results in the minimum value of a given function. The LINQ standard query operator Min finds the minimum value of the generated values from the given collection by the given formula.

Problem

Find the value from a set of values that minimizes the given function. Here's an example: Assume you have a list of distances from various cities to a zoo stored in an array—and a tiger has escaped from the zoo. The zoo authorities want to notify people in the city closest to a 10 kilometer radius around the zoo.

Solution

Loop	MoreLINQ

`int[] distances = {23,41,11,34,45};`
`int x = distances[0];`
`for(int i = 0;i<distances.Length;i++)`
`if(distances[i]-10<x-10)`
`x = distances[i];`
`x.Dump();`
	`int[] distances = {23,41,11,34,45};`
	`//The value that minimizes the given function f(x) = x - 10`
	`//in this case distances.`
	`MinBy(a => a - 10).Dump();`
	`//The minimum value of the values projected by the given`
	`formula distances.`
	`Min (a => a - 10).Dump();`

The output of the loop code is 11, while the output of the LINQ code is 11 and then 1. The outputs differ because I added a call to the LINQ Min() operator at the end of the LINQ code to help make the difference between these two operators clear. The extra 1 is the result of the Min() call.

How It Works

The LINQ code generates 11 and then 1 as output. The value 11 minimizes the function f(x) = x – 10, denoted by the lambda expression a => a – 10.

The final call to the LINQ operator Min() generates 1 because that's the minimum value obtained from the projection of all values in the array distance by the function a – 10. By virtue of this internal projection, the values will be {13, 31, 1, 24, 35}. Because 1 is the minimum value in that set, it's the value that Min() returns.

Similar to MinBy(), MoreLINQ offers another operator called MaxBy(), which finds the value that maximizes a given function.

Summary

There are several other operators available in MoreLINQ. However, the ones covered here are the most interesting, and for the most part, are not easily reproducible by combining the standard LINQ operators. However, I recommend you explore the library documentation for yourself. The project has a very good unit test suite, which can help you figure out what the code does.

CHAPTER 6

Creating Domain-Specific Languages

Every domain has a language that helps practitioners communicate their thoughts easily. When a chef instructs a helper to *sauté* vegetables, both parties know what the term means. However, software solutions created for several domains using general-purpose, high-level programming languages such as C# or Java often quickly become difficult to maintain. Even only a few months later, the original authors of these solutions may find it difficult to remember how the code works so they can fix bugs.

Thankfully, you can avoid such problems by creating expressive and succinct internal APIs. These API sets are also called *internal,* or *embedded, domain-specific languages (DSLs)*. You can later extend these to develop an *external DSL* that subject matter experts who do not necessarily have programming experience in a high-level, general-purpose programming language can use. Subject matter experts usually appreciate the opportunity to express themselves with these DSLs. MATLAB is an example of an external DSL, which is unsuitable for general-purpose tasks. In contrast, LINQ is an example of an internal, or embedded, DSL.

In this chapter, the first few sections describe techniques for creating embedded DSLs that blend well with the syntax of the host language (C#, in this case). The later sections show how to use the open source LINQ API to create external DSLs that use the internal DSL created previously. The purpose of this chapter is to illustrate how to apply these techniques to a variety of problem domains for your own purposes.

The next section compares the classic style of coding to using a DSL.

6-1. Feel the Difference

Compare the side-by-side code blocks in Figure 6-1 and try to understand what they do.

```
for(int i = 1;i < 1000; i++)                  Enumerable.Range(1,10000)
{                                                      .Where ( n => n.Digits().Cube().Sum() == n )
    int copy  = i;                                     .Dump("Armstrong Numbers");
    int sum = 0;
    do
    {
        sum += (int) Math.Pow((double)copy % 10, 3 );
        copy = copy / 10;
    }while ( copy != 0);
    if(sum == i)
        i.Dump();
}
```

Figure 6-1. *DSLs can improve the readability of a program*

The loop at the left finds Armstrong numbers between 1 and 1,000. The LINQ query on the right does the same thing. Which one do you think more closely approaches the textual definition of Armstrong numbers? In my opinion, the LINQ query is much cleaner and far more readable than the loop. Some of my colleagues have argued that if they were to start writing code like the LINQ query on the right, they would soon forget how to interpret the loops. You'll have to decide which approach is better. But if you have the war wounds most veteran programmers eventually experience, you will probably agree that code readability counts.

You may have noticed that the Digits() and Cube() methods are not shown in Figure 6-1. DSLs are not magical. Using them will not let you skip the process of implementing the logic. But in this case, the implementations are elsewhere, wrapped in some classes. The next section shows how to create a mini DSL to find numbers such as Armstrong numbers.

6-2. Creating a Simple DSL for Mathematicians

A language is made up of *vocabulary*. A domain-specific language is no different. To create a DSL, you first need to identify the reasonable vocabulary set for that language. The language you'll create in this section is intended to help mathematicians write expressive code to find numbers such as Armstrong numbers.

Problem

Create a set of vocabulary and the grammar that glues those vocabulary terms together.

Solution

You may recall from Chapter 2 that Armstrong numbers and other related numbers are denoted by functions that act on the digits of those numbers. So Digits must be a word in this language. You also want to declare all the functions that can be performed on digits as vocabulary terms, so users (mathematicians) can glue those functions together. So functions such as Sum, Cube, and Factorial have to be declared as vocabulary terms. Since this is going to be a DSL for finding interesting numbers such as Armstrong numbers, I have named it *Armstrong*.

In C#, you can define these vocabulary terms as extension methods. Consider how Microsoft implemented LINQ standard query operators as extension methods of IEnumerable<T>. Can you see a connection?

Add the class code shown in Listing 6-1 to a new LINQPad query tab. Select C# Program from the Language drop-down menu.

Listing 6-1. Caption Here

```
public static class IntEx
{
    public static int Cube(this int number)
    {
        return number * number * number;
    }
    public static int Square(this int number)
    {
        return number * number;
    }
```

```csharp
public static IEnumerable<int> Digits(this int number)
{
    return number.ToString().ToCharArray()
        .Select (n => Convert.ToInt32(n.ToString()));
}
public static IEnumerable<int> ReverseDigits(this int number)
{
    return number.Digits().Reverse();
}
public static IEnumerable<int> EvenDigits(this int number)
{
    return number.ToString().ToCharArray()
        .Where ((m,i) => i%2==0).Select (n => Convert.ToInt32(n.ToString()));
}
public static IEnumerable<int> OddDigits(this int number)
{
    return number.ToString().ToCharArray()
        .Where ((m,i) => i%2!=0).Select (n => Convert.ToInt32(n.ToString()));
}
public static bool Are(this IEnumerable<int> actualDigits, params int[] digits)
{
    return actualDigits.SequenceEqual(digits);
}
public static IEnumerable<int> DigitsAt(this int number, params int[] indices)
{
    var asString = number.ToString();
    return indices.Select (i => Convert.ToInt32(asString[i].ToString()));
}
public static bool AreZero(this IEnumerable<int> digits)
{
    return digits.All (d => d == 0);
}
public static int FormNumber(this IEnumerable<int> digits)
{
    return digits.Select ((d,i) => d * (int)Math.Pow (10,digits.Count()-(i+1)))
                                        .Aggregate ((a,b) => a + b);
}
public static IEnumerable<int> Factorial(this IEnumerable<int> digits)
{
    foreach (var d in digits)
        if (d == 0)
            yield return 1;
        else
            yield return Enumerable.Range(1, d).Aggregate((a, b) => a * b);
}

public static int Product(this IEnumerable<int> digits)
{
    return digits.Aggregate ((f,s) => f*s);
}
```

```
public static IEnumerable<int> Cube(this IEnumerable<int> digits)
{
    return digits.Select (d => d * d * d);
}

public static IEnumerable<int> Square(this IEnumerable<int> digits)
{
    return digits.Select (d => d * d);
}

public static IEnumerable<int> RaiseSelfToSelf(this IEnumerable<int> digits)
{
    return digits.Select (d => (int) Math.Pow(d,d));
}

public static IEnumerable<int> IncrementalPower(this IEnumerable<int> digits)
{
    return digits.Select ((d,i) => (int) Math.Pow(d,i));
}
}
```

Add the following code inside Main():

```
void Main()
{
    Enumerable.Range(1,10000)
            .Where ( n => n.Digits().Cube().Sum() == n )
            .Dump("Armstrong Numbers");
}
```

Running this code results in the output shown in Figure 6-2.

Armstrong Numbers

▲ IEnumerable<Int32> (5 items) ▶
1
153
370
371
407

Figure 6-2. *Armstrong numbers found with the help of the Armstrong DSL*

Some of the extension methods in the IntEx class might look trivial. However, they are important for creating an expressive language. Moreover, these methods are critical when you later want to expose this embedded DSL as an external DSL (outside the host language C#).

Now, let's see how the new language helps define similar numbers. Figure 6-3 shows the definitions of some similar numbers from Wikipedia (en.wikipedia.org/wiki/Narcissistic_number).

- Sum-product numbers (sequence A038369 in OEIS) : $n = \left(\sum_{i=1}^{k} d_i \right) \left(\prod_{i=1}^{k} d_i \right)$, e.g. $144 = (1 + 4 + 4) \times (1 \times 4 \times 4)$.

- Dudeney numbers (sequence A061209 in OEIS) : $n = \left(\sum_{i=1}^{k} d_i \right)^3$, e.g. $512 = (5 + 1 + 2)^3$.

- Factorions (sequence A014080 in OEIS) : $n = \sum_{i=1}^{k} d_i!$, e.g. $145 = 1! + 4! + 5!$.

Figure 6-3. *Definitions for several numbers similar to Armstrong numbers*

Using the newly designed Armstrong embedded DSL, you can find these numbers by writing expressive code, as shown in Listing 6-2. The code segments that use the methods in the DSL appear in bold. Now compare the definitions of these numbers (in Figure 6-3) to the code that finds them in Listing 6-2. This way, this embedded DSL will help users keep their code clean and professional. To run this code in LINQPad, set the Language drop-down menu to C# Statements.

Listing 6-2. Caption Here

```
Enumerable.Range(0,10000)
            .Where (d => d.Digits().Sum().Cube() == d)
            .Dump("Dudeney numbers");
Enumerable.Range(0,10000)
            .Where (d => d.Digits().Factorial().Sum() == d)
            .Dump("Factorions");
Enumerable.Range(0,10000)
            .Where (d => d.Digits().Sum() * d.Digits().Product() == d)
            .Dump("Sum Product numbers");
```

Figure 6-4 shows the result of running the code in Listing 6-2.

Dudeney numbers

▲ IEnumerable<Int32> (5 items) ▶
0
1
512
4913
5832

Factorions

▲ IEnumerable<Int32> (3 items) ▶
1
2
145

Sum Product numbers

▲ IEnumerable<Int32> (4 items) ▶
0
1
135
144

Figure 6-4. *Result of the code written in embedded DSL*

How It Works

Congratulations! You have just created a small embedded DSL. This language has a vocabulary described by using C# extension methods on the integer data type. Table 6-1 lists these methods.

Table 6-1. *Methods in Armstrong*

Function	Purpose
Digits	This returns an IEnumerable<int> with the digits of the given integer.
ReverseDigits	This returns an IEnumerable<int> with the digits of the given integer in reverse order.
EvenDigits	This returns an IEnumerable<int> with just the digits at the even indices of the given integer.
OddDigits	This returns an IEnumerable<int> with just the digits at the odd indices of the given integer.
Cube	There are two versions of this method. The first one operates on a list of digits, and the second one operates on an integer.
Square	Similar to Cube. There are two versions of this method. The first one operates on a list of digits, and the second operates on an integer.
Product	This method returns the product of the digits of the number.
Are	This is a handy synonym for the SequenceEqual method, just to make its purpose a little bit more understandable.

(continued)

Table 6-1. (*continued*)

Function	Purpose
Factorial	This returns the factorials of the digits of the given number.
AreZero	This is a predicate. This returns `true` if all the given digits are zero.
FormNumber	This helper function helps create a number formed from the digits of the given number.
RaiseSelfToSelf	This function returns all the digits raised to the power of themselves.
IncrementalPower	This function returns all the digits raised to the power of their index in the list.

6-3. Testing Armstrong by Using NUnit

Most of the methods shown in the preceding section are simple and easy to understand. However, I thought it would be nice to have a small test suite for these methods to make their usage immediately evident.

Problem

Create a test suite for the methods in Recipe 6-1.

Solution

To create a test suite, I used the NUnit framework. So the first step is to go to the NUnit web site and get the latest appropriate version for you. I used the version available at `http://launchpad.net/nunitv2/trunk/2.6.3/+download/NUnit-2.6.3.msi`.

After you have installed the NUnit framework, follow these steps:

1. Create a Class Library project and copy all the code for Armstrong and name it **Armstrong**.

2. Add another class library project called **ArmstrongTest**. Add NUnit references there along with the Armstrong reference, as shown in Figure 6-5.

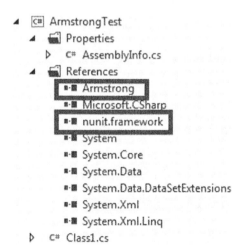

Figure 6-5. *Adding references to NUnit and the Armstrong project to the test project ArmstrongTest*

3. Change the name of the class from Class1.cs to **ArmstrongTest.cs** and add the code in
    Listing 6-3 to that class file.

    Listing 6-3. Caption Here

```
using System;
using System.Collections.Generic;
using System.Linq;
using System.Text;
using System.Threading.Tasks;
using NUnit.Framework;
using Armstrong;

namespace ArmstrongTest
{
    [TestFixture]
    public class ArmstrongTest
    {
        [Test]
        public void TestFormNumber()
        {
            Assert.AreEqual(24, 12345.OddDigits().FormNumber());
            Assert.AreEqual(135, 12345.EvenDigits().FormNumber());
        }
        [Test]
        public void TestDigitsAt()
        {
            Assert.IsTrue(12345.DigitsAt(1, 3).SequenceEqual(new int[] { 2, 4 }));
        }
        [Test]
        public void TestEvenDigits()
        {
            Assert.IsTrue(12345.EvenDigits().SequenceEqual(new int[] { 1, 3, 5 }));
        }
        [Test]
        public void TestOddDigits()
        {
            Assert.IsTrue(12345.OddDigits().SequenceEqual(new int[] { 2, 4 }));
        }
        [Test]
        public void TestFactorial()
        {
            Assert.AreEqual(145, 145.Digits().Factorial().Sum());
        }
        [Test]
        public void TestRaiseToSelf()
        {
            Assert.AreEqual(32, 123.Digits().RaiseSelfToSelf().Sum());
        }
```

```
[Test]
public void TestIncrementalPower()
{
    Assert.AreEqual(12, 123.Digits().IncrementalPower().Sum());
}
[Test]
public void TestProducts()
{
    Assert.AreEqual(6, 123.Digits().Product());
}
[Test]
public void TestDigits()
{
    Assert.IsTrue(1234.Digits().SequenceEqual(new int[]{1, 2, 3, 4}));
}
[Test]
public void TestArmstrongNumber()
{
    Assert.IsTrue(153.Digits().Cube().Sum() == 153);
}
[Test]
public void TestDudeney()
{
    Assert.IsTrue(512.Digits().Sum().Cube() == 512);
}
    }
}
```

■ **Note**   Make sure to add a reference to `Armstrong.dll` to the reference of this test project. Otherwise, it won't compile.

4. After building the test project successfully, open the NUnit GUI to load the tests and run them. To do that, that you must locate `ArmstrongTest.dll`, as shown in Figure 6-6.

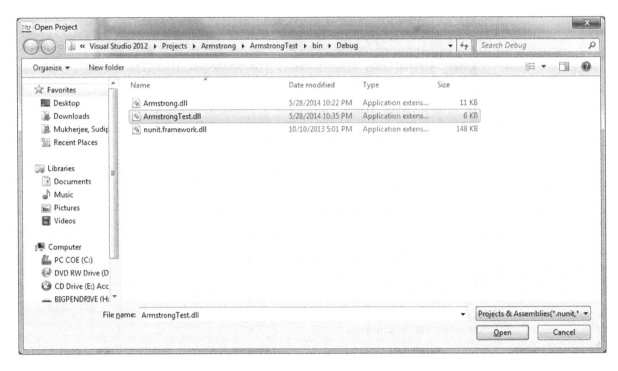

Figure 6-6. *Locate the ArmstrongTest.dll from wherever you have saved the project*

5. When you locate the `ArmstrongTest.dll`, all the tests will load, as shown in Figure 6-7.

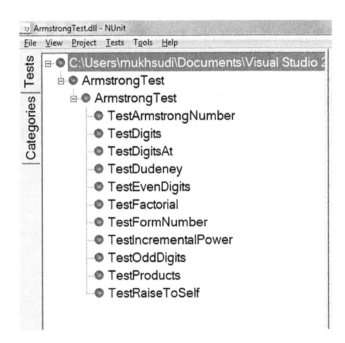

Figure 6-7. *All the Armstrong tests loaded in the NUnit GUI*

6. Click the Run button. Every test should pass, and you should see a green bar.

Feel free to do your own experiments and see how the results differ. In fact, I recommend that you make changes to the tests or to the Armstrong code so it fails some of the tests.

How It Works

The code in this section works by building a series of assertion tests that check the functions in Armstrong.dll, thus verifying that the code works as expected.

6-4. Exposing Armstrong as an External DSL

As designed so far, the Armstrong language is good for boosting developer productivity, but it is still unusable by people who don't code in C# or some other .NET language. For the language to serve its purpose, you need to expose it in a form that accepts free-form input from users and generates the appropriate queries from that input. In this section, you will see how to expose the functionality of the language by using an external English-like language with Armstrong keywords embedded. This will not be hard for users, because the Armstrong keywords match the normal English vocabulary of mathematicians, so they should feel at home using it.

Again, comparing the internal DSL with the typical mathematical vocabulary should help illustrate the difference. Figure 6-8 shows both.

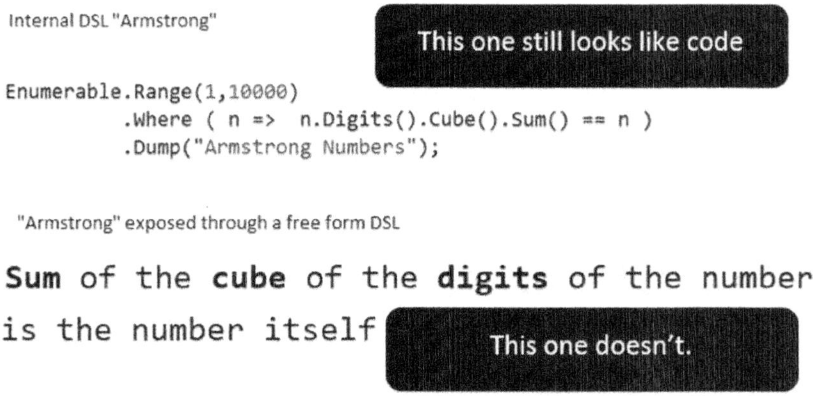

Internal DSL "Armstrong"

This one still looks like code

```
Enumerable.Range(1,10000)
        .Where ( n => n.Digits().Cube().Sum() == n )
        .Dump("Armstrong Numbers");
```

"Armstrong" exposed through a free form DSL

Sum of the **cube** of the **digits** of the number is the number itself

This one doesn't.

Figure 6-8. *The difference between the external and internal representation of Armstrong*

While a C# programmer could write the first version shown in Figure 6-8 by using the internal representation of Armstrong with host language support from C#, a nonprogrammer domain expert (mathematicians, in this case) would likely find the free-flowing form of Armstrong expressed in the lower part of Figure 6-8 far simpler and more intuitive. That's why DSLs are important. I have highlighted the Armstrong tokens in the text phrase in bold.

Problem

Expose Armstrong as a free-flowing, English-like, external DSL.

Solution

The strategy is to generate Armstrong code from an English-like syntax. The generated Armstrong query must be able to run on a range of input variables. To run the generated LINQ statement, you need a LINQ compiler that can take a LINQ statement as a string and run it against a given input range. For this, I have used the open source LINQ compiler available from CodePlex at `http://linqcompiler.codeplex.com/`.

Here are the steps you need to follow:

1. Download the LINQ compiler and place the compiler DLL (`Evaluant.LINQ.Compiler.dll`) in a new folder.

2. In LINQPad, add the `IntEx` class created earlier in this chapter to the query. Change the query type to C# Program. Add the following code in `Main()` and outside of `Main()` as part of the executing class:

```csharp
private static string SanitizeBraces(string generatedStatement)
{
    int gap = generatedStatement.ToCharArray().Count(c => c == '(') -
                    generatedStatement.ToCharArray().Count(c => c == ')');
    if (gap == 0)
        return generatedStatement;
    else
        return generatedStatement + new string(')', gap);
}
private static string GenerateArmStrongStatement(List<string> tokens)
{
    Dictionary<string, string> mapping = new Dictionary<string, string>();
    mapping.Add("*", "*");
    mapping.Add("times", "*");
    mapping.Add("(", ")");
    mapping.Add(")", "(");
    mapping.Add("are-same", ".IsSame()");
    mapping.Add("==", "==");
    mapping.Add("proper-divisors", ".ProperDivisors()");
    mapping.Add("even-digits", ".EvenDigits()");
    mapping.Add("odd-digits", ".OddDigits()");
    mapping.Add("number", "n");
    mapping.Add("square", ".Square()");
    mapping.Add("product", ".Product()");
    mapping.Add("is", "==");
    mapping.Add("!=", "!=");
    mapping.Add("+", "+");
    mapping.Add("-", "-");
    mapping.Add("and", "&&");
    mapping.Add("or", "||");
    mapping.Add("/", "/");
    mapping.Add(">", "<");
    mapping.Add("<", ">");
    mapping.Add("<=", ">=");
    mapping.Add(">=", "<=");
    mapping.Add("divided-by", "/");
    mapping.Add("are", ".Are(");
```

```
        mapping.Add("digits", ".Digits()");
        mapping.Add("reverse-digits",".ReverseDigits()");
        mapping.Add("cube", ".Cube()");
        mapping.Add("factorial", ".Factorial()");
        mapping.Add("sum", ".Sum()");

        //Add all normal LINQ operators
        mapping.Add("average", ".Average()");
        mapping.Add("maximum", ".Max()");
        mapping.Add("minimum", ".Min()");
        mapping.Add("digits-at", ".DigitsAt(");

        StringBuilder armstrongBuilder = new StringBuilder();
        foreach (string to in tokens)
        {
            if (mapping.ContainsKey(to))
                armstrongBuilder.Append(mapping[to]);
            if (to.ToCharArray().All(t => Char.IsNumber(t) || t == '.'))
                armstrongBuilder.Append(to);
        }

        return SanitizeBraces("input.Where ( n => " + armstrongBuilder.ToString() + ")");
}

void Main()
{
    do
    {
        var inputs = Enumerable.Range(1, 10000);
        Console.WriteLine("Armstrong >>");
        string line = Console.ReadLine()
                        .Replace("(", "( ")
                        .Replace(")", " )");
        string statement = GenerateArmStrongStatement(GetTokens(line));

        LinqCompiler lc = new LinqCompiler(statement);
        lc.ExternalAssemblies.Add(typeof(IntEx).Assembly);
        lc.ExternalAssemblies.Add(typeof(MathEx).Assembly);
        lc.AddSource("input", inputs);
        line.Dump("Armstrong Query Expressed in Plain English");
        statement.Dump("Generated LINQ Query");
        lc.Evaluate().Dump("Answers");

    } while (true);
}
```

3. This query uses the LINQ compiler. So you need to point LINQPad to that DLL. To do that, press F4 to load the Query Properties window. Then provide the path to this DLL, as shown in Figure 6-9. In my case, it was available in the C:\ drive. For you, it might be somewhere else.

Figure 6-9. *Add Evaluant LINQ Compiler to LINQPad*

4. Navigate to the Additional Namespaces Imports tab and type **Evaluant.Linq.Compiler**. This tells LINQPad to use the functionality available in the LINQ Compiler project.

Now you are ready to test the "experimental" version of Armstrong. If you run the query from LINQPad, you will see the output shown in Figure 6-10.

Figure 6-10. *LINQPad is waiting on user input*

The black rectangle at the bottom of Figure 6-10 is where you have to type the Armstrong query. Table 6-2 lists a few examples that you can try.

Table 6-2. *Armstrong Statements Illustrating How to Use the External DSL*

Example Armstrong Statement That You Can Type	What It Does
sum of the cube of the digits of the number is the number itself	Finds Armstrong numbers.
cube of the sum of the digits of the number is the number	Finds Dudeney numbers.
sum of the factorial of the digits of the number is the number	Finds factorions.
sum of the odd-digits of the number is 10	Finds all numbers that match this predicate.
sum of the odd-digits of the number is equal to the sum of the even-digits of the number and number >= 200 and number <= 1000	Finds all numbers that match the given condition.
even-digits of the number are the same as that of the odd-digits of the number	Finds all numbers where even and odd digits are the same.
digits of the number are the same as that of the reverse-digits of the number	Finds all numbers that are palindromic. The digits of these numbers read the same both ways.

■ **Tip**   Remember to type queries in lowercase.

Figure 6-11 shows how the interface looked when I started typing the command in the black rectangle provided.

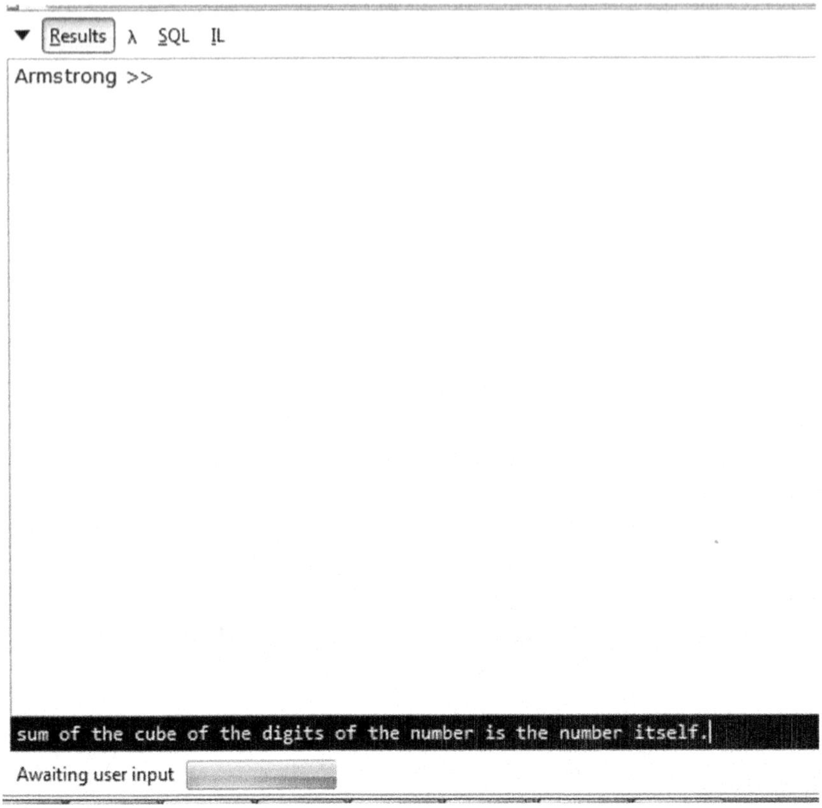
Results
λ
SQL
IL
Armstrong >>
sum of the cube of the digits of the number is the number itself.
Awaiting user input

Figure 6-11. *Typing an Armstrong query in the LINQPad user input box*

Figure 6-12 shows the result after entering the command.

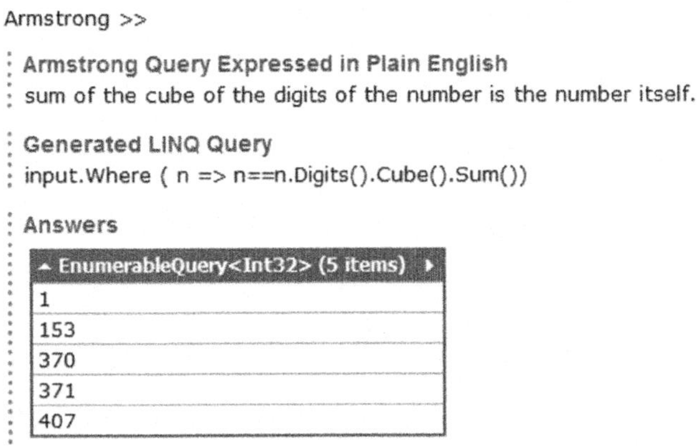
Armstrong >>
Armstrong Query Expressed in Plain English
sum of the cube of the digits of the number is the number itself.
Generated LINQ Query
input.Where (n => n==n.Digits().Cube().Sum())
Answers
EnumerableQuery<Int32> (5 items)
1
153
370
371
407

Figure 6-12. *The result of the Armstrong query (between 1 and 10,000)*

How It Works

The expression entered by a user at the console is parsed. Based on the words that match Armstrong keywords (such as *sum*, *cube*, and *digits*), it generates a LINQ query. Later, the LINQ query is passed to the LINQ compiler, which evaluates the statement.

Note that the keywords in the statement and in the LINQ query appear in reverse order (most of the time). For example, consider the query in Figure 6-11. The keywords *sum*, *cube*, and *digits* occur in sequence in the English-like statement. However, for LINQ to work, these must be glued together in the opposite direction. In other words, the digits of the number have to be extracted first. Then those digits have to be projected, using their cube values, and finally, the cubed digits must be added together by calling sum. In order to achieve this, the code uses a stack. I have put together a small demo of this on YouTube at www.youtube.com/watch?v=x0jbfDq8-Zk.

Here's the take-home lesson from this experiment: After you have a good embedded DSL, it is easy to expose it as an external language. You can write an interpreter like this console to translate that external DSL to your embedded DSL code and then execute it to show results to the users.

6-5. Cloning Handy F# Functions by Using LINQ

LINQ standard query operators are comprehensive enough that you can craft almost any query by using them. However, sometimes the resulting code looks ugly, and that can lead to maintenance nightmares. Although you can already use F# methods in C#, the point of this section is to show you how to use standard LINQ operators to craft any arbitrary operator that other languages (in this case, F#) offer. I have picked ones that are absent conceptually from the LINQ standard set of operators, as shown in Table 6-3.

Table 6-3. *F# Operators Missing from LINQ*

Operator	Purpose
Iterate	Similar to ForEach on IList<T>, this operator iterates over a collection and performs an action.
Exists2	Similar to Any but works on two consecutive elements at a time.
ForAll2	Similar to All but works on two consecutive elements at a time.
Zip3	Combines three collections into a list of tuples of three elements.
FindIndex	Returns the index of the given element in the collection, if found; otherwise, returns -1.
Pairwise	Returns a list of key/value pairs, where the keys represent the first element and the values represent the second element of consecutive-pair collections.
Scan	Generates a sequence of numbers by performing a set of operations.
ScanBack	Same as Scan, but this time the list of operations is read backward.
IntersectMany	Same as Intersect, except this operator works on a list of elements instead of just two.
UnionMany	Same as Union, but this operator works on a list of elements instead of just two.
Partition	Partitions the given collection into two parts. The first part is generated from elements for which the given predicate returns true, and the second part is formed from elements for which the given predicate returns false.
Scan	Generates a series of numbers from a given seed number and a list of functions that depicts the step calculations.
ScanBack	Same as Scan, but in this case the functions are reversed and applied.

Problem

Clone these F# methods so they can be used by any collection in a generic way, using LINQ.

Solution

Change the query type in LINQPad to C# Program, and then add the class FSharpEx shown in Listing 6-4.

Listing 6-4. Caption Here

```
public static class FSharpEx
{
    /// <summary>
    /// This method generates a list of numbers from a given seed number
    /// and a list of functions that are used to generate the next number
    /// one step at a time.
    /// </summary>
    /// <typeparam name="T">The type of the seed and the function arguments</typeparam>
    /// <param name="x0">The seed value</param>
    /// <param name="projectors">The step descriptions in terms of Functions</param>
    /// <returns>A list of generated elements</returns>
    public static IEnumerable<T> Scan<T>(this T x0, IEnumerable<Func<T, T>> projectors)
                                                        where T : IEquatable<T>
    {
        List<T> values = new List<T>();
        values.Add(x0);
        foreach (var f in projectors)
        {
            values.Add(f.Invoke(values.Last()));
        }
        return values.AsEnumerable();
    }

    /// <summary>
    /// This is same as Scan just that the functions provided are used in reverse order
    /// while generating the elements
    /// unlike Scan where the sequence of the functions are used as is.
    /// </summary>
    /// <typeparam name="T">The type of the collection and the seed value</typeparam>
    /// <param name="x0">The seed value</param>
    /// <param name="projectors">The step descriptions</param>
    /// <returns>A list of generated elements</returns>
    public static IEnumerable<T> ScanBack<T>(this T x0, IEnumerable<Func<T, T>> projectors)
                                                    where T : IEquatable<T>
    {
        List<T> values = new List<T>();
        values.Add(x0);
        foreach (var f in projectors.Reverse())
        {
            values.Add(f.Invoke(values.Last()));
        }
        return values.AsEnumerable();
    }
}
```

```csharp
/// <summary>
/// This method partitions the given collection into two parts.
/// The first part contains elements for which the predicate returns true.
/// The other part contains elements for which the predicate returns false.
/// </summary>
/// <typeparam name="T">The type of the collection</typeparam>
/// <param name="collection">The collection</param>
/// <param name="predicate">The predicate.</param>
/// <returns>A tuple with two ranges. The first range has the elements for
/// which the predicate returns true and the second part returns elements
/// for which the predicate returns false.</returns>
public static Tuple<IEnumerable<T>, IEnumerable<T>> Partition<T>(
    this IEnumerable<T> collection, Func<T, bool> predicate)
{

    return new Tuple<IEnumerable<T>, IEnumerable<T>>(
                  collection.Where(c => predicate.Invoke(c)),
                  collection.Where(c => !predicate.Invoke(c)));
}

/// <summary>
/// Applies the given action for all elements of the given collection
/// </summary>
/// <typeparam name="T">The type of the collection</typeparam>
/// <param name="collection">The collection</param>
/// <param name="action">The action to be performed</param>
public static void Iterate<T>(this IEnumerable<T> collection, Action<T> action)
{
    foreach (var v in collection)
        action.Invoke(v);
}

/// <summary>
/// This method wraps three collections into one.
/// </summary>
/// <typeparam name="T1">The type of the first collection</typeparam>
/// <typeparam name="T2">The type of the second collection</typeparam>
/// <typeparam name="T3">The type of the third collection</typeparam>
/// <param name="first">The first collection</param>
/// <param name="second">The second collection</param>
/// <param name="third">The third/last collection</param>
/// <returns>A list of tuples where the items of the tuples are picked from the first,
// second, and third collection,
/// respectively.</returns>
public static IEnumerable<Tuple<T1, T2, T3>> Zip3<T1, T2, T3>(IEnumerable<T1> first,
                                    IEnumerable<T2> second,
                                    IEnumerable<T3> third)
{
    int smallest = (new List<int>() { first.Count(), second.Count(),
    third.Count() }).Min();
    for (int i = 0; i < smallest; i++)
        yield return new Tuple<T1, T2, T3>(first.ElementAt(i), second.ElementAt(i),
        third.ElementAt(i));
}
```

```csharp
/// <summary>
/// Returns the index of the given item in the given collection
/// </summary>
/// <typeparam name="T">The type of the collection</typeparam>
/// <param name="collection">The collection</param>
/// <param name="predicate">The predicate to be used to search the given item</param>
/// <returns>Returns the index of the given element in the collection, else returns -1
/// if not found.</returns>
public static int FindIndex<T>(this IEnumerable<T> collection, Func<T, bool> predicate)
{
    try
    {
        return collection.Select((c, i) => new KeyValuePair<int, bool>(i, predicate.Invoke(c)))
                         .First(c => c.Value == true).Key;
    }
    catch (InvalidOperationException ex)
    {
        return -1;
    }
}

/// <summary>
/// Returns a list of consecutive items as a list of key/value pairs
/// </summary>
/// <typeparam name="T">The type of the input collection</typeparam>
/// <param name="collection">The collection</param>
/// <returns>A list of key/alue pairs</returns>
public static IEnumerable<KeyValuePair<T, T>> Pairwise<T>(
    this IEnumerable<T> collection)
{
    return collection.Zip(collection.Skip(1), (a, b) => new KeyValuePair<T, T>(a, b));
}

/// <summary>
/// Checks whether there is a pair of consecutive entries that matches
/// the given condition
/// </summary>
/// <typeparam name="T">The type of the collection</typeparam>
/// <param name="collection">The collection</param>
/// <param name="predicate">The predicate to use</param>
/// <returns>True if such a pair exists that matches the given predicate pairwise
/// else returns false</returns>
public static bool Exists2<T>(this IEnumerable<T> collection,
    Func<T, T, bool> predicate)
{
    return collection.Zip(collection.Skip(1), (a, b) =>
        predicate.Invoke(a, b)).Any(c => c == true);
}

/// <summary>
/// Checks whether all pairwise items (taken 2 at a time) from the given collection
/// matches the predicate or not
/// </summary>
```

```
/// <typeparam name="T">The type of the collection</typeparam>
/// <param name="collection">The collection</param>
/// <param name="predicate">The predicate to run against all pairwise coupled
/// items.</param>
/// <returns></returns>
public static bool ForAll2<T>(this IEnumerable<T> collection,
    Func<T, T, bool> predicate)
{
    return collection.Zip(collection.Skip(1), (a, b) => predicate.Invoke(a, b))
        .All(c => c == true);
}

/// <summary>
/// Finds intersection of several collections
/// </summary>
/// <typeparam name="T">type of these collections</typeparam>
/// <param name="sets">all collections</param>
/// <returns>A list with all the elements that appear in the intersection of
/// all these collections</returns>
public static IEnumerable<T> IntersectMany<T>(this IEnumerable<IEnumerable<T>> sets)
                                            where T : IComparable
{
    HashSet<T> temp = new HashSet<T>(sets.ElementAt(0));
    sets.ToList().ForEach(z => temp = new HashSet<T>(z.Intersect(temp)));
    return temp;
}

/// <summary>
/// Finds the union of several collections.
/// </summary>
/// <typeparam name="T">The type of these collections</typeparam>
/// <param name="sets">All the collections, not just sets</param>
/// <returns>A collection of elements with all the elements in the total union</returns>
public static IEnumerable<T> UnionMany<T>(this IEnumerable<IEnumerable<T>> sets)
                                          where T : IComparable
{
    HashSet<T> allValues = new HashSet<T>();
    sets.SelectMany(s => s).ToList().ForEach(z => allValues.Add(z));
    return allValues;
}
}
```

Also add the following code in `Main()`:

```
void Main()
{
    int x = 10;
    List<Func<int,int>> steps = new List<Func<int,int>>();
    steps.Add( a => a + 1);
    steps.Add( a => a + 3);
    steps.Add( a => a - 4);
    steps.Add( a => 2*a - 1);
```

```
x.Scan(steps).Dump("Scan");
x.ScanBack(steps).Dump("Scanned Back");
FSharpEx.Zip3(x.Scan(steps),x.ScanBack(steps),x.Scan(steps.Concat(steps.Skip(1))))

    .Dump("Zipped");
x.Scan(steps).Iterate(a => Console.WriteLine("Score is " + a));
int[] series = {1,2,3,4,5,6,7,8,9,10};
//Check whether the given series is in AP
bool isAPSeries = series.Pairwise()
    .Select (s => new {First = s.Key, Second = s.Value,
            Difference = s.Value - s.Key })
    .All (s => s.Difference == series[1]-series[0]);

isAPSeries.Dump("isAP using Pairwise");

series.ForAll2((a,b) => b - a == series[1] - series[0])
      .Dump("isAP using ForAll2");

series.Exists2((a,b) => a + b >= 100 && a + b <= 200)
      .Dump("Is there any such couple of elements");

series.Pairwise().Dump("Items picked Pairwise");

series.Partition(a => a % 2 == 0).Dump("Partitioned");

int[] theseOnes = {1,3,52,2,1};
int[] thatOnes = {4,5,2,1,3,4};
int[] otherOnes = {2,3,1,1,3,14};
FSharpEx.IntersectMany((new List<int[]>(){theseOnes, thatOnes, otherOnes }))
                      .Dump("Intersect Many");
FSharpEx.UnionMany((new List<int[]>(){theseOnes, thatOnes, otherOnes }))
                      .Dump("Union Many");

}
```

When I ran the preceding code, I got the results shown in Figure 6-13. I encourage you to change the values in the collections and observe the effects in the results. I have moved the values to the right in the interest of space.

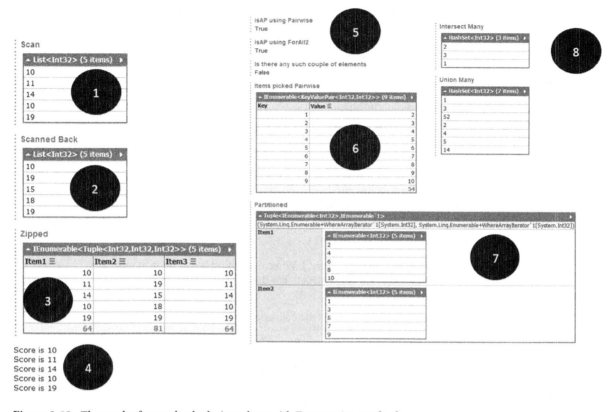

Figure 6-13. *The result of several calculations done with F# extension methods*

How It Works

Because there are so many outputs, I numbered them in Figure 6-13. Here are some explanations of the results.

■ **Tip** The following numbered items correspond to the numbered items in Figure 6-13.

---

1. The rules to increment the given number (10, in this case) are a => a + 1 and so on. So the number changes from 10 to 11 and so on, according to the rules.

2. This case uses the same functions as item 1, but with the order of the functions applied on the seed reversed.

3. Three lists (all are of integer types in this case) are zipped together to form a list of tuples. Notice the result type in the header of the result grid.

4. Because the ForEach operator can be used to perform an action over all the elements of the given collection, there is a requirement to project any collection of <T> to a List<T> just to use this functionality. However, converting any collection to a list is computationally expensive. Therefore, to reduce the projection requirement, you can use the Iteration() operator. The result (in item 4) shows the result of running an iteration over the given collection.

5. The Pairwise() operator returns the elements wrapped into pairs—consecutive pairs, in this case. If you want sorted pairs, you can sort the collection first and then use the Pairwise() operator. In this example, Pairwise() is used to check whether the given sequence on which Pairwise() is called is an arithmetic progression (AP).

   ForAll2() is used to find whether the given sequence is an AP. It would have been sufficient to check whether the values obtained from performing the subtraction between each pair of items is the same as that of the first and second element of the given collection.

6. This grid shows the result of calling Pairwise().

7. This grid shows the result of calling Partition(). When a partition is complete, it returns two sets of values based on the predicate provided. For this example, I have partitioned the given list into even and odd members.

8. This grid shows the intersection and union of the collections.

6-6. Lazily Generating Items from a Recurrence Relation

There are several definitions of recurrence relations. For the purposes of this section, *recurrence relations* are those where the *n*th variable of the sequence is described by the previous elements thus far. For example, the Fibonacci series follows this logic:

```
F[n] = F[n-1] + F[n-2]
```

Therefore, any *n*th item in the Fibonacci series is the sum of the two preceding items.

Finding such numbers using recursion can lead to a stack overflow error. If the sequences are generated lazily—in other words, generated only when elements are required—then a stack overflow error won't occur. To do that, you must store the intermediate results of the recurrence relation in a collection. For example, when Fibonacci numbers get evaluated, the elements identified so far can be stored in a collection. That way, to generate the next number, only the last two items need to be added together. This technique is known as *memoization.*

Problem

Create an embedded DSL that helps with the creation of recurrence relations lazily.

Solution

Paste the following class into LINQPad in a new query. Set the query type to C# Program. Make sure that this class is outside the Main() method.

```csharp
public static class SequenceEx
{
    public static IEnumerable<T> StartWith<T>(params T[] seeds)
    {
        return new List<T>(seeds).AsEnumerable();
    }

    public static IEnumerable<T> ThenFollow<T>(this IEnumerable<T> thisSequence,
        Func<T,T,T> rule) where T:IEquatable<T>
    {
        while(true)
        {
            T last = thisSequence.ElementAt(thisSequence.Count () - 1);
            T lastButOne = thisSequence.ElementAt(thisSequence.Count () - 2);

            thisSequence = thisSequence
                            .Concat((new List<T>()
                            {rule.Invoke(last,lastButOne)}).AsEnumerable());
            yield return rule.Invoke(last,lastButOne);

        }
    }
    public static IEnumerable<T> ThenFollow<T>(this IEnumerable<T> thisSequence, Func<T,T> rule)
        where T:IEquatable<T>
    {
        while(true)
        {
            T last = thisSequence.ElementAt(thisSequence.Count () - 1);

            thisSequence = thisSequence.Concat((new List<T>()
                                    {rule.Invoke(last)}).AsEnumerable());
            yield return rule.Invoke(last);

        }
    }
}
```

Now add the following code in the Main() method:

```csharp
void Main()
{
    Func<long,long,long> A015531Rule = (x,y) =>  4 *x + 5*y;
    Func<long,long,long> fibonacciRule = (x,y) => x + y;
    Func<double,double> arbitraryRule = (x) => 1/(x + 1/x);
    SequenceEx.StartWith<long>(0,1)
                    .ThenFollow(A015531Rule)
                    .Take(5)
                    .Dump("A015531");
```

```
SequenceEx.StartWith<long>(1,1)
                        .ThenFollow(fibonacciRule)
                        .Take(5)
                        .Dump("First few Fibonacci Numbers");

SequenceEx.StartWith(1.0)
                        .ThenFollow(arbitraryRule)
                        .Take(5)
                        .Dump("Arbitrary Sequence");
}
```

When you run it, this code generates the output shown in Figure 6-14.

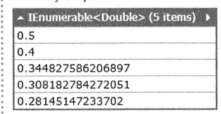

A015531

▲ IEnumerable<Int64> (5 items) ▶
4
21
104
521
2604

First few Fibonacci Numbers

▲ IEnumerable<Int64> (5 items) ▶
2
3
5
8
13

Arbitrary Sequence

▲ IEnumerable<Double> (5 items) ▶
0.5
0.4
0.344827586206897
0.308182784272051
0.28145147233702

Figure 6-14. *Some recurrence relations*

How It Works

The method `Startwith()` generates a list with the seed values. There can be as many seed values as needed, because the values are passed as a params array. Once this initial list of numbers (seed values) is created, the rule can use them to expand the list. The `ThenFollow()` method takes a `Func` that operates on the last (or the last and next-to-last) elements of the collection thus far and returns the new element to be added in the collection. Thus the collection grows lazily. It returns only as many elements as were requested. (This example uses `Take` to find the first five elements in each case.)

If you are wondering why this example is titled A015531, it's because that's the name of an interesting recurrence relation from the On-Line Encyclopedia of Integer Sequences (OEIS). You can see the definition at `https://oeis.org/A015531`.

Summary

This chapter discussed how to use LINQ to design and use domain-specific languages. I kept the examples and the designed DSLs to a bare minimum so you could see the power of DSLs using only a small amount of code. DSLs can make the lives of programmers a lot easier. You may already be thinking of designing your own DSLs for your own problem domains. As a general strategy, remember that the workflow for designing a DSL is to identify the vocabulary first, and then identify the grammar that works well to glue the vocabulary terms together.

This chapter discussed only DSLs that are suited to the functional programming capabilities offered by LINQ. But it's worth noting that other DSLs exist. They're not necessarily functional but are still useful. Consider the Starbucks DSL (`www.fssnip.net/9w`), which lets you find the cost of a cup of coffee. As a useful exercise, try cloning that DSL to C#, using extension methods on integers and doubles.

CHAPTER 7

Static Code Analysis

Programmers always tend to think that code and data are separate. However, for a general-purpose framework such as LINQ, code is also data. By taking advantage of LINQ and .NET Reflection, you can perform a great deal of static code analysis and gain a lot of insight into code. This chapter presents several LINQ scripts that will help you accrue knowledge about your code base.

7-1. Finding Verbose Type Names in the .NET 3.5 Framework

Naming is personal, and naming conventions and the length of names varies between programmers and teams. However, the first step in enforcing naming conventions is knowing what names have been used. For example, if you wanted to find out the longest and shortest names that Microsoft gives to a type in a .NET assembly, you can do that easily by using LINQ.

Problem

Find the most verbose type names in .NET 3.5.

Solution

Enter the following LINQ code in a new LINQPad query. Set the Language drop-down to C# statement(s). Make sure the path in the first line appears on a single line:

```
Directory.GetFiles(@"C:\Program Files\Reference Assemblies\
    Microsoft\Framework\v3.5","*.dll")
    .SelectMany (d => Assembly.LoadFrom(d).GetTypes())
    .Where (a => a.IsClass && a.IsPublic)
        .Select (a =>new { Namespace = a.Namespace,
                           Name = a.Name,
                           Length = a.Name.Length}))
    .ToLookup (d => d.Length)
    .OrderByDescending (d => d.Key)
    .Select (d => d.ElementAt(0) )
    .Take(20)
    .Dump("Top 20 most verbose types in .NET 3.5");
```

This code produces the output shown in Figure 7-1.

Top 20 most verbose types in .NET 3.5

▲ IEnumerable<> (20 items)		▶
Namespace	**Name**	**Length ☰**
System.Workflow.Activities	WorkflowServiceAttributesDynamicPropertyValidator	49
System.ServiceModel.Configuration	ExtendedWorkflowRuntimeServiceElementCollection	47
System.Web.UI.Design	UpdateProgressAssociatedUpdatePanelIDConverter	46
System.ComponentModel.DataAnnotations	AssociatedMetadataTypeTypeDescriptionProvider	45
System.Data.Linq	ForeignKeyReferenceAlreadyHasValueException	43
System.Data.Objects.DataClasses	EdmRelationshipNavigationPropertyAttribute	42
System.ServiceModel.Channels	JavascriptCallbackResponseMessageProperty	41
System.Web.UI.WebControls	EntityDataSourceContextCreatingEventArgs	40
System.Web.UI.WebControls	EntityDataSourceContextCreatedEventArgs	39
System.AddIn.Hosting	AddInSegmentDirectoryNotFoundException	38
Microsoft.VisualC.StlClr.Generic	ConstContainerBidirectionalIterator`1	37
Microsoft.VisualC.StlClr.Generic	ConstContainerRandomAccessIterator`1	36
Microsoft.VisualC.StlClr.Generic	ConstReverseBidirectionalIterator`1	35
Microsoft.VisualC.StlClr.Generic	ConstReverseRandomAccessIterator`1	34
Microsoft.Build.BuildEngine	InvalidToolsetDefinitionException	33
Microsoft.Build.Framework	ExternalProjectFinishedEventArgs	32
Microsoft.Build.Framework	ExternalProjectStartedEventArgs	31
Microsoft.VisualC.StlClr.Generic	ReverseBidirectionalIterator`1	30
Microsoft.Build.Framework	CriticalBuildMessageEventArgs	29
Microsoft.Build.BuildEngine	ConfigurableForwardingLogger	28
		755

Figure 7-1. *The top 20 longest type names in the .NET 3.5 framework*

■ **Note**   This example and others in this chapter assume that Windows is installed on the root of your C:\ drive; if not, you will need to modify the path appropriately.

How It Works

The first SelectMany() call returns an IEnumerable<Type>. This list of types includes all the types for the entire .NET 3.5 framework. The Where() clause filters out everything except public classes. The next call to Select() creates a custom projection with three attributes (Namespace, Name, and Length) that apply to the name of the type. Later these are projected using ToLookup() as a lookup table. For each key of the lookup table, the code takes the first entry and projects it by using the call to Select (d => d.ElementAt(0)). This example shows 20 such items.

7-2. Finding the Number of Overloads for a Method

Sometimes you can refactor function overloading by using .NET generics. Other times, function overloads are exactly what you need. But the decision depends on the function algorithm. Therefore, before deciding to refactor, knowing how many overloads a method has can be crucial.

Problem

Find the number of overloads that each LINQ standard operator has.

Solution

Enter the following code into a new LINQPad query, selecting C# Statement(s) from the Language drop-down. Note that you will need to change the path in the first line if the framework is installed in a nonstandard location on your computer.

■ **Note**   Make sure that the entire path C:\Program Files\Reference Assemblies\Microsoft\Framework\v3.5 in the following code appears on a single line; otherwise, the example won't work.

```
Directory.GetFiles(@"C:\Program Files\Reference Assemblies\
    Microsoft\Framework\v3.5","*.dll")
    .SelectMany (d => Assembly.LoadFrom(d).GetTypes()
    .SelectMany (a => a.GetMethods()))
        .Where (d => d.IsPublic
            && d.DeclaringType.Namespace=="System.Linq"
            && !d.Name.StartsWith("get_")
            && !d.Name.StartsWith("set_"))
        .ToLookup (d => d.Name)
        .Select (d => new { MethodName = d.Key,
            Overloads = d.Count ()})
            //Overloads = 1 doesn't make sense.
            .Where (d => d.Overloads>=2)
            .OrderByDescending (d => d.Overloads)
            .Take(10)//Show only the top 10 entries
            .Dump();
```

This code produces the output shown in Figure 7-2.

MethodName	Overloads ≡
Sum	60
Average	60
Min	46
Max	46
GroupBy	24
GetEnumerator	15
Where	13
Select	13
SelectMany	12
Aggregate	11
	300

▲ IEnumerable<> (10 items) ▶

Figure 7-2. Partial result of the number of overloads for all methods in System.Linq

How It Works

This example shows nested SelectMany() calls, which find all the methods of all the types available in the System.Linq namespace.

The first SelectMany() call returns a list of the public methods from all the types. Then the Where() clause filters out methods that don't belong to the System.Linq namespace or that are getter/setter functions for properties, leaving only public methods from the System.Linq namespace.

Next, this list is used to create a lookup table in which the key of the table is the name of the method. Later it projects the lookup table values. The key of the lookup table is the name of the method, and the total number of entries for each key is the number of overloads. These results are projected using the following call to Select:

```
.Select (d => new { MethodName = d.Key, Overloads = d.Count ()})
```

When the value of Overloads is 1, the method doesn't have any overloads. The Where() clause filters out these values. Finally, the results are sorted by the number of overloads in descending order.

To save space, I have limited the result to just the top ten values. You can see the complete results by commenting out the Take() call. The result is quite interesting. Who would have thought that Sum()—the method to perform summation on a given collection of items—would have 60 overloads?

7-3. Finding the Size of a Namespace

The *size* of a namespace is defined by the number of types it contains. The greater the number of types a namespace includes, the greater its conceptual load. In other words, it will take longer to discover what a namespace is useful for if it contains a lot of types. During refactoring, such information can be crucial.

Problem

Find the number of types in a namespace.

Solution

Enter the following code in LINQPad. Set the Language drop-down to C# Statement(s).

```
//Find conceptual load for all namespaces in .NET 3.5
//Conceptual load is the total number of public types in the namespace

Directory.GetFiles(@"C:\Program Files\Reference Assemblies\
    Microsoft\Framework\v3.5","*.dll")
    .SelectMany (d => Assembly.LoadFrom(d).GetTypes()
        .Where (a => a.IsClass && a.IsPublic))
    .ToLookup (d => d.Namespace)
    .ToDictionary (d => d.Key, d => d.Count ())
    .OrderByDescending (d => d.Value )
    .Take(10)//Only the first 10 elements are shown
    .Dump();
```

The preceding code produces the output shown in Figure 7-3.

▲ IEnumerable<KeyValuePair<String,Int32>> (10 items) ▶	
Key	Value ≡
System.Data.Common.CommandTrees	64
System.Web.UI.WebControls	56
System.Data.Metadata.Edm	43
Microsoft.Build.Framework	42
System.Web.UI	39
System.Linq.Expressions	38
System.Web.DynamicData	37
System.ComponentModel.DataAnnotations	35
Microsoft.Build.BuildEngine	32
System.Net.PeerToPeer.Collaboration	28
	414

Figure 7-3. The number of types available in various namespaces

How It Works

The first SelectMany() call returns all the public types available in the .NET 3.5 framework. Don't be surprised if it contains some types and namespaces you may never have seen. The truth is that few people have ever seen the entire list of .NET types. Don't worry about all the names.

The call to ToLookup() creates a lookup table with the keys as the namespaces. Figure 7-4 shows a partial view of that lookup table. Here's the code I used to get that partial view:

```
Directory.GetFiles(@"C:\Program Files\Reference Assemblies\
    Microsoft\Framework\v3.5","*.dll")
    .SelectMany (d => Assembly.LoadFrom(d).GetTypes()
        .Where (a => a.IsClass && a.IsPublic))
    .ToLookup (d => d.Namespace)
    .OrderBy (d => d.Count () )
    .Take(4)
    .Dump();
```

Figure 7-4. Showing a partial view of the lookup table

As you can see, the value of each key of the lookup table is an object of type IGrouping<string, Type>. So .ToDictionary (d => d.Key, d => d.Count ()) creates a dictionary in which the keys are the same as those of the lookup table. The dictionary values are the count of types available in that list.

Finally, the code sorts the dictionary entries by the number of types they contain, in descending order. This example shows only the first ten such entries. To show the complete results, remove the Take() call.

7-4. Finding the Code-to-Comment (C# Style) Ratio

Commenting code is necessary because even the original authors of programs can find it difficult to understand what a particular portion of code does after some time has passed. While refactoring, it is beneficial to know the *code-to-comment ratio* for the code to be refactored. The ratio helps identify code that isn't sufficiently commented.

Problem

Write a LINQ script to find the code-to-comment ratio of a C# code. Assume that there are no C-style comments (/* ... */) in the code.

Solution

Enter the following code in a LINQPad query tab. Set the Language drop-down to C# Statement(s).

```
string code = @"//This is a test
    int x = 10;//set x to 10
    //increase x by one
    x++;
    var rad = Radius(x);//Find radius";

var lookup = code.Split(new string[]{Environment.NewLine,";"}
    ,StringSplitOptions.RemoveEmptyEntries)
    .Select (line => line.Trim())
    .Select (line =>
    new
    {
        Line = line,
        IsComment = line.StartsWith("//")
    })
    .ToLookup (line => line.IsComment);

lookup.Select (entry =>
    new
    {
        Component = entry.Key==true?"Comment":"Code",
        Percentage = 100*Math.Round((double)entry.Count()/
        (double)lookup.SelectMany (l => l).Count(),2)
    })
    .Dump("Code to Comment Ratio");
```

This produces the output shown in Figure 7-5.

Code to Comment Ratio

Component	Percentage ≡
Comment	57
Code	43
	100

▲ IEnumerable<> (2 items) ▶

Figure 7-5. Code-to-comment ratio for a sample code snippet

How It Works

As the first step, this script tokenizes the entire code snippet, resulting in multiple lines. Each line that starts with // is assumed to be a comment line; otherwise, the code assumes it's a code line. The second Select() call, shown here

```
.Select (line =>
new
{
    Line = line,
    IsComment = line.StartsWith("//")
})
```

creates a projection of anonymous type with two attributes: Line and IsComment. A lookup table is created from this projection in which the key is the value of IsComment. Because IsComment is a Boolean field, there will be only two entries in the lookup table. Figure 7-6 shows the lookup table for this example.

▲ Lookup<Boolean,> (2 items) ▶

Key= True

▲ IGrouping<Boolean,> (4 items) ▶

Line	IsComment
//This is a test	True
//set x to 10	True
//incrase x by unity	True
//Find radius	True

Key= False

▲ IGrouping<Boolean,> (3 items) ▶

Line	IsComment
int x = 10	False
x++	False
var rad = Radius(x)	False

Figure 7-6. Lookup table showing code vs. comment splits

As you can see in Figure 7-6, there are four comment entries and three code entries, making a total of seven lines of code. So the percentage of code lines is 400/7, or roughly 57 percent.

The code (double)lookup.SelectMany (l => l).Count() finds the total number of lines in the code snippet.

7-5. Finding the Size of Types

The *size* of a type can be expressed as the number of public methods it exposes. The greater the number of public methods, the greater the size. Generally, best practice is to avoid types with a large number of methods. Therefore, being able to determine the size of public types in a framework is a good starting point for refactoring.

Problem

Write a LINQ script to find the size of all public types in .NET 3.5.

Solution

Enter the following LINQ script into a new LINQPad query:

```
Directory.GetFiles(@"C:\Program Files\Reference Assemblies\
    Microsoft\Framework\v3.5","*.dll")
    .SelectMany (d => Assembly.LoadFrom(d).GetTypes()
        .Where (a => a.IsClass && a.IsPublic)
            .Select ( s =>
            new
            {
                TypeName =  s.FullName,
                MethodCount = s.GetMethods()
                .Count(m => m.IsPublic
                    && !m.Name.StartsWith("get_")
                    && !m.Name.StartsWith("set_"))})
            .OrderByDescending (d => d.MethodCount)
            .Take(10)
            .Dump();
```

The preceding code produces the output shown in Figure 7-7.

TypeName	MethodCount
System.Linq.Expressions.Expression	316
System.Linq.ParallelEnumerable	207
System.Linq.Enumerable	179
System.Data.Objects.SqlClient.SqlFunctions	144
System.Linq.Queryable	127
System.Data.Spatial.DbSpatialServices	127
System.Data.Common.CommandTrees.ExpressionBuilder.DbExpressionBuilder	121
System.Xml.Linq.XElement	113
System.Data.Objects.EntityFunctions	97
System.Data.TypedTableBase`1	92
	1523

Figure 7-7. Size of public types in .NET 3.5

How It Works

The first call, to SelectMany(), returns an IEnumerable of all the public classes. The second call, to Select(), projects this result as an IEnumerable of an anonymous type that has two attributes: the type name, and the number of public methods that aren't property getters or setters. Note that names of property getter methods start with get_ and set_, respectively.

Finally, the code sorts the projected list in descending order based on the number of methods (MethodCount). For brevity, I have used the Take() operator to pick only the first ten elements.

7-6. Generating Documentation Automatically

Sometimes you get to use libraries that don't come with explicit documentation. LINQ can help you generate documentation on-the-fly.

Problem

Write a LINQ script to generate documentation automatically from the DLL and the corresponding XML file.

Solution

Write the following query in a LINQPad query tab:

▮ **Note**   You need to add the MoreLINQ DLL and namespace to LINQPad to run this script.

```
public string GetSummary(string total, string methodName)
{
        string search = methodName;
        string summary = total.Substring(
            total.IndexOf(search)+search.Length);
        summary = summary.Substring(
        summary.IndexOf("<summary>")+"<summary>".Length);
        summary = summary.Substring(0,summary.IndexOf("</summary"));
        return summary;
}
void Main()
{
        string moreLINQdll = @"C:\MoreLINQ\MoreLINQ.dll";
        string xmlFilePath = @"C:\MoreLINQ\MoreLinq.xml";
        StreamReader sr = new StreamReader (xmlFilePath);
        string total = sr.ReadToEnd();
        sr.Close();
        total = total
            .Replace("<c>",string.Empty).Replace("</c>",string.Empty)
            .Replace("&lt;","<").Replace("&gt;",">");
        var allMethods = Assembly
            .LoadFrom(moreLINQdll)
            .GetTypes()
```

```
        .Where (a => a.IsPublic )
        .ToList()
        .Select(t => new KeyValuePair<string,
                List<KeyValuePair<string,string>>>
                (t.Name,t.GetMethods()
                        .Where (x => x.IsPublic
                                && (!x.Name.StartsWith("get_")
                                && !x.Name.StartsWith("set_")
                                && !x.Name.StartsWith("GetHashCode")
                                && !x.Name.StartsWith("ToString")
                                && !x.Name.StartsWith("Equals")
                                && !x.Name.StartsWith("CompareTo")
                                && !x.Name.StartsWith("GetType")))
                        .Select (x => new
                                KeyValuePair<string,string>
                                (x.Name, GetSummary(
                                        total,t.Name+"."+x.Name)))
                                .DistinctBy(z => z.Key)
                                .ToList()))
            .First()
            .Dump();
}
```

This generates the output shown in Figure 7-8.

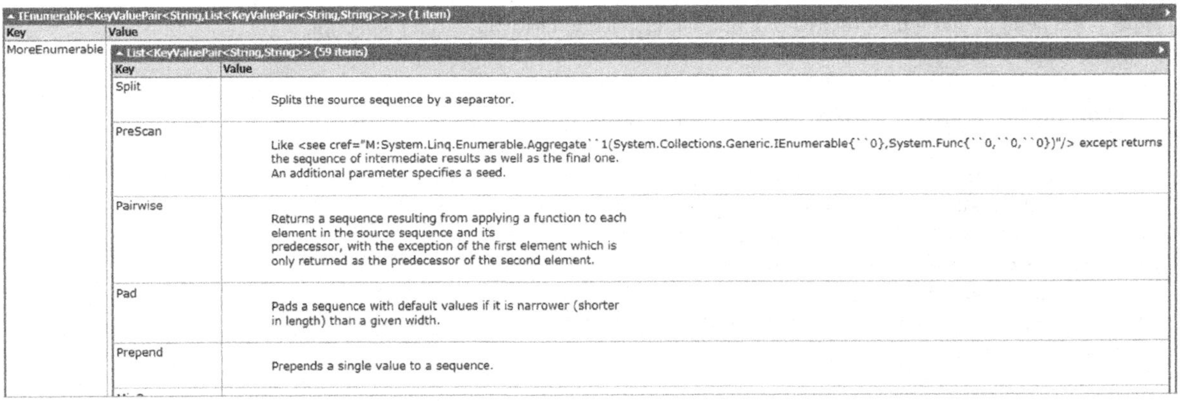

Figure 7-8. *Partial documentation of MoreLINQ methods*

How It Works

Because every class will include the methods of the Object class, you can get rid of those methods. Also, you want to ignore class properties along with their getter and setter methods.

The call to Where() does that:

```
.Where (x => x.IsPublic &&
        (!x.Name.StartsWith("get_")
        && !x.Name.StartsWith("set_")
        && !x.Name.StartsWith("GetHashCode")
```

```
&& !x.Name.StartsWith("ToString")
&& !x.Name.StartsWith("Equals")
&& !x.Name.StartsWith("CompareTo")
&& !x.Name.StartsWith("GetType")))
```

At the heart of this script is the following data structure:

```
KeyValuePair<string,List<KeyValuePair<string,string>>>
```

This nested KeyValuePair structure holds all the methods (including overloads) of all the public classes available in the explicitly loaded assembly. The key of the outer KeyValuePair denotes the public class name, while the keys of the inner key/value pair represent the names of the methods. The values of the inner key/value pair represent the summary of the method. The summary is extracted from the XML documentation that was written by the library developers.

There can be many entries of the same type. This script uses the DistinctBy operator from MoreLINQ to remove duplicates by class name.

For this example, I chose to show only the documentation for the first type in the library. To get the documentation for all the types in a library (which is generally what you will want), remove the call to First().

7-7. Finding Inheritance Relationships

One best practice guideline is to avoid classes with deep inheritance relationships. Therefore, it's useful to be able to explore the inheritance relationships within a given framework.

Problem

Write a LINQ script to find out the inheritance relationship between several classes in the given framework.

Solution

Write the following code in a new LINQPad query tab. As usual, the path must appear without the following:

```
Directory.GetFiles(@"C:\Program Files\Reference Assemblies\
    Microsoft\Framework\v3.5","*.dll")
    .SelectMany (d => Assembly.LoadFrom(d).GetTypes().Where
        (a => a.IsPublic && a.IsClass)
    .Select (a => new { Parent =  a.BaseType, Name = a.Name}))
        .Where (d => d.Parent!=null)
        .Select (a => new { Parent = a.Parent.Name , Name = a.Name})
            .ToLookup (a => a.Parent )
            .Take(10)
            .Dump();
```

The preceding code generates the output shown in Figure 7-9.

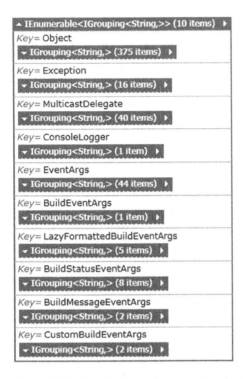

Figure 7-9. *Showing inheritance relationships between several types in the .NET framework*

How It Works

BaseType returns the type from which the current type inherits. Therefore, the name property of BaseType returns the name of the parent class. The code creates the lookup table by using the parent class as the key and its children as the values.

7-8. Locating Complex Methods

Creating methods that require lots of parameters is generally a bad idea. The rule of thumb is that methods with seven parameters (plus or minus two) are generally too complex to use and understand easily. Such methods scream for refactoring.

Problem

Write a LINQ script to discover methods that require a large number of input parameters.

Solution

Write the following code in a new LINQPad query:

```
//Locate highly complex methods with lots of arguments
Directory.GetFiles(@"C:\Program Files\Reference Assemblies\
    Microsoft\Framework\v3.5","*.dll")
    .SelectMany (d => Assembly.LoadFrom(d).GetTypes()
        .SelectMany (a => a.GetMethods()))
        .Where (d => !d.Name.StartsWith("get_")
                && !d.Name.StartsWith("set_"))
        .Select (d => new { MethodName = d.Name,
            NameSpace = d.DeclaringType.Namespace,
            Class = d.DeclaringType.FullName,
            NumberOfParameters = d.GetParameters().Count()} )
                .Where (d => d.NameSpace=="System.Linq")
                .OrderByDescending (d => d.NumberOfParameters )
                .Take(20)
                .Dump();
```

The preceding code generates the output shown in Figure 7-10.

MethodName	NameSpace	Class	NumberOfParameters
Join	System.Linq	System.Linq.Queryable	6
GroupJoin	System.Linq	System.Linq.Queryable	6
Join	System.Linq	System.Linq.Enumerable	6
GroupJoin	System.Linq	System.Linq.Enumerable	6
Join	System.Linq	System.Linq.ParallelEnumerable	6
Join	System.Linq	System.Linq.ParallelEnumerable	6
GroupJoin	System.Linq	System.Linq.ParallelEnumerable	6
GroupJoin	System.Linq	System.Linq.ParallelEnumerable	6
Join	System.Linq	System.Linq.Queryable	5
GroupJoin	System.Linq	System.Linq.Queryable	5
GroupBy	System.Linq	System.Linq.Queryable	5
Join	System.Linq	System.Linq.Enumerable	5
GroupJoin	System.Linq	System.Linq.Enumerable	5
GroupBy	System.Linq	System.Linq.Enumerable	5
Join	System.Linq	System.Linq.ParallelEnumerable	5
Join	System.Linq	System.Linq.ParallelEnumerable	5
GroupJoin	System.Linq	System.Linq.ParallelEnumerable	5
GroupJoin	System.Linq	System.Linq.ParallelEnumerable	5
GroupBy	System.Linq	System.Linq.ParallelEnumerable	5
Aggregate	System.Linq	System.Linq.ParallelEnumerable	5
			108

Figure 7-10. *The top 20 methods sorted by the number of arguments they take*

How It Works

The explanation for this example is similar to its predecessors. The code first makes a projection, and then sorts it in descending order based on the number of parameters, providing a list of the most complex methods in each namespace. To save space, I have limited the output to only 20 methods. To see the full list, remove the Take(20) call.

Summary

In this chapter, you've seen several examples of how you can use LINQ to Reflection to quickly find details and gain insights into a code base. These examples should help illustrate that you can use LINQ to query essentially any data. Code is usually considered separate from data, but by using LINQ, you can treat code itself as data. Besides showing how to use LINQ to Reflection, the examples in this chapter exemplify several idiomatic LINQ usages—for example, projecting followed by creation of a lookup. The next chapter follows up on the idea of LINQ as a general-purpose tool to perform scripting-like exploratory data analysis.

■ ■ ■

CHAPTER 8

Exploratory Data Analysis

Generalization is an extremely powerful concept when applied correctly. For example, in MATLAB even the most trivial addition is performed as a matrix addition. Data comes in many formats. Mostly these formats are not ready for analysis, so programmers, researchers, and data scientists often need to write a lot of data-wrangling code to get the data into a useful form. However, LINQ has changed the way programmers interact with data. LINQ works on the generalization that data is a list—of something. For example, you can think of a database table as a list of rows, an XML file as a list of nodes, a CSV file as a list of comma-delimited string arrays, and so on.

Exploratory data analysis typically starts with a set of questions and then tries to obtain answers by examining the available data. Sometimes this is done just by finding statistics, but other times plotting data helps find trends or compare values.

In some of the examples in this chapter, you will see data visualizations that represent the findings in a concise manner. This approach often leads to insights that go beyond the initial answers to questions. You will see examples of using LINQ to analyze data and find such insights. For each problem presented here, a few questions will be posed, and then you'll see example LINQ queries that can find the answers to those questions. Along the way, you should pick up some useful LINQ idioms that I hope are general enough to apply to your own data analysis problems. Anonymous types and anonymous methods will play a major role in most of the queries in this chapter.

8-1. Analyzing the Titanic Survivors Dataset

The Titanic dataset is a CSV file containing the list of passengers and their survival status. The dataset contains the following information:

Field Name	Description
PassengerId	The ID of the passenger. This is an integer.
Survived	A Boolean field that has the value 1 or 0; 1 means the passenger survived.
PClass	The class of the passenger: first, second, or third.
Name	Name of the passenger.
Sex	Gender of the passenger.
Age	Age of the passenger.
Sibsp	Count of sibling or spouse of the passenger onboard.
Parch	Count of parent or child of the passenger onboard.
Ticket	Ticket number of the passenger.

(continued)

Field Name	Description
Fare	The fare paid by the passenger .
Cabin	Cabin number of the passenger.
Embarked	Which port the passenger boarded from: S—Southampton C—Cherbourg Q—Queenstown

Problem

The question I posed for this dataset is, "What's the chance of survival for passengers in each class, grouped by gender?"

Solution

To begin, you need to load the Titanic dataset from the CSV file to an in-memory collection. Because the dataset has names wrapped in double quotes, I had to use regular expressions.

Open a new LINQPad tab and write the code in Listing 8-1. Change the value of the Language box drop-down to C# Statements.

Listing 8-1. Finding Titanic passenger survival rates

```
string text = File.ReadAllText(@"C:\titanic.csv");

Regex.Matches(text,"\"[A-Za-z ., ()'-/]+\"").Cast<Match>()
    .Select (m => m.Value)
    .ToList()
    .ForEach( z => text = text.Replace(z, z.Replace(",","[__COMMA__]")));

text.Split(new char[]{'\r','\n'},StringSplitOptions.RemoveEmptyEntries)
    .Skip(1)//Skip the column header row of the CSV file
    .Select (t => t.Split(','))
    .Select (t => new
    {
        PassengerId = t[0],
            Survived = t[1]=="1"?"Yes":"No",
            Pclass = t[2],
        Name = t[3].Replace("[__COMMA__]",","),
            Sex = t[4],
            Age = t[5].Length !=0 ? Convert.ToDouble(t[5]):-1,
            SibSp = t[6],
            Parch = t[7],
            Ticket = t[8],
            Fare = Convert.ToDouble(t[9]),
            Cabin = t[10],
            Embarked = t[11]
    })//At this point the CSV is loaded as a collection of an anonymous type
```

```
.Select (f => new   Tuple<string,double,string,string,double>
              (f.Pclass,Math.Round(f.Fare,2),f.Survived,f.Sex,f.Age))
.ToLookup (f => f.Item1)
.OrderByDescending (f => f.Key)
.ToDictionary(f => f.Key, f=> new KeyValuePair<double,double>
              (100*((double)f.Count (x => x.Item4 == "female" && x.Item3 == "Yes")/
              (double)f.Count(j => j.Item4=="female")),
              100*((double)f.Count (x => x.Item4 == "male" && x.Item3 == "Yes")/
              (double)f.Count(j => j.Item4=="male"))))
.Select (f => new { PClass = f.Key,
              FemaleSurvivalRate = Math.Round(f.Value.Key,3) ,
              MaleSurvivalRate = Math.Round(f.Value.Value,3)} )
.OrderByDescending (f => f.FemaleSurvivalRate )
.Dump("Survivor Percentage per class");
```

This produces the output shown in Figure 8-1.

Survivor Percentage per class

PClass	FemaleSurvivalRate	MaleSurvivalRate
1	96.809	36.885
2	92.105	15.741
3	50	13.545
	238.914	66.171

Figure 8-1. *Survivor percentage per class*

LINQPad has a cool feature that draws a horizontal bar chart. As you click the bar icons visible in the top row, LINQPad draws the bar charts as shown in Figure 8-2.

Survivor Percentage per class

PClass	FemaleSurvivalRate	MaleSurvivalRate
1	96.809	36.885
2	92.105	15.741
3	50	13.545
	238.914	66.171

Figure 8-2. *Bar charts for survivor percentage for each passenger class*

How It Works

At first, the code masks commas within names with a special string [__COMMA__] so that splitting the values in any given row at the commas later in the process doesn't affect the field values. Then the code parses the CSV, splitting each row (except the first row, which contains the header) at the commas, thus generating a list of values. These values then get assigned to properties of an anonymous type. Each anonymous type instance represents one row of the CSV file. The column header names become properties of the anonymous type.

Next, the collection of this anonymous type is projected with five fields—class, fare, survival status, sex, and age—by using the following code:

```
Select (f => new Tuple<string,double,string,string,double>
            (f.Pclass,Math.Round(f.Fare,2),f.Survived,f.Sex,f.Age))
```

The code then creates a lookup table in which the key represents the passenger classes. Later it creates a dictionary from this lookup table: the dictionary keys are the passenger classes, and the values are key/value pairs of doubles that represent the survival percentages of females and males, respectively, for the associated passenger class. The keys of the key/value pair represent the female survival percentages, while the values represent the male survival percentages.

The final call to Select()

```
Select (f => new { PClass = f.Key,
                   FemaleSurvivalRate = Math.Round(f.Value.Key,3) ,
                   MaleSurvivalRate = Math.Round(f.Value.Value,3)} )
```

projects these dictionary values in a meaningful way, with three columns: PClass, FemaleSurvivalRate, and MaleSurvivalRate. This result is then sorted in descending order by FemaleSurvivalRate. As expected, the result shows that passengers in the higher classes were more likely to survive.

Problem

Another question you could pose using this data is, "What's the survival percentage grouped by the following age ranges?"

- 0–2: Infants

- 2–6: Toddlers

- 6–12: Kids

- 13–19: Teenagers

- 20–30: Young adults

- 30–35: Early thirties

- 36–40: Late thirties

- 40–50: Middle-aged

- 50–60: Old

- 60+: Retired

Solution

To answer the question, you need a way to create the age groups by using the age value. The anonymous function shown in Listing 8-2 does that.

Listing 8-2. Creating age range groups

```
Func<double,string> AgeGroup =
                    x => x!=-1 && x<2?"Infants"
                  :x>=2 && x<6 ? "Toddlers"
                  :x >= 6 && x<13 ?"Kids"
                  :x>=13 && x<=19?"Teenagers"
                  :x>=20 && x<30? "Young Adults"
                  :x>=30 && x<=35? "Early thirties"
                  :x>=36 && x<40? "Late thirties"
                  :x>=40 && x<=50? "Middle Aged"
                  :x>=51 && x<60 ? "Old"
                  :"Retired";
```

The data contains a few rows where the age value is missing, so for those rows I have assigned the value of -1. This way, the analysis will skip the rows where the age is missing. Otherwise, the result would be wrong.

As in the previous problem, you also want to project the CSV to a collection of an anonymous type. For the sake of avoiding duplicated code, I won't repeat that code here. So everything up to the comment //At this point the CSV is loaded as a collection of the anonymous type in Listing 8-1 shown previously is identical in this solution too. After that, the projection in Listing 8-3 does the job.

Listing 8-3. Calculating survivor percentages by age range

```
.Select( x =>
              new
              {
                  Sex = x.Sex,
                  Age = x.Age,
                  Embarked = x.Embarked,
                  AgeGroup = AgeGroup(x.Age),
                  Survived = x.Survived
              })
.ToLookup (x => x.AgeGroup)
.ToDictionary (x => x.Key, x => new KeyValuePair<double,double>
 (100*((double)x.Count (z => z.Sex == "female" && z.Survived == "Yes")/(double)x.Count()),
 100*((double)x.Count (z => z.Sex == "male" && z.Survived  == "Yes")/(double)x.Count())))
.Select(x =>
        new
        {
            AgeGroup = x.Key,
            FemaleSurvival = Math.Round(x.Value.Key,2),
            MaleSurvival = Math.Round(x.Value.Value,2)
        }
      )
.OrderByDescending( x=> x.FemaleSurvival)
.Dump("Agewise survival percentages");
```

Figure 8-3 shows the output sorted by female survival percentage in descending order for each age group.

Agewise survival percentages

AgeGroup	FemaleSurvival ≡	MaleSurvival ≡
Toddlers	40	23.33
Teenagers	35.79	5.26
Old	31.58	7.89
Early thirties	30.97	14.16
Infants	28.57	57.14
Late thirties	27.78	12.96
Middle Aged	26.26	13.13
Young Adults	23.64	11.36
Retired	19.7	9.36
Kids	12	24
	276.29	178.59

▲ IOrderedEnumerable<> (10 items)

Figure 8-3. *Survivors in different age groups*

How It Works

The anonymous function AgeGroup returns the age group for each row, given the integer value of the age. For example, if the age value is 14, AgeGroup returns Teenagers. Next, the code creates a lookup table in which the keys represent the age groups. ToDictionary() transforms the lookup table to a dictionary with keys that still represent the age groups, but with values that are key/value pairs of doubles. The first double represents the survival percentage of female passengers in that age group, and the second double represents the percentage of male passengers who survived in that age group.

However, up to this point in the code, all these values are internal; thus it is hard to make sense of the data. Therefore, a Select() call projects this data as an IEnumerable of an anonymous type with three attributes: AgeGroup, FemaleSurvival, and MaleSurvival; the last two are percentages.

Finally, to find out which age range of female passengers was most likely to survive, the result is sorted by the FemaleSurvival column in descending order.

8-2. Converting SurveyMonkey Results to CSV

Last year during my company's official outing, a colleague of mine tasked with handling the logistics created a survey on the popular free survey web site SurveyMonkey. He had to arrange for buses for people to travel from our office to the resort where the day's outing was planned. However, he wanted to be sure of the number of people who would need the bus service before striking a deal with our travel vendor.

Unfortunately, after the survey was complete, he found the data unusable: it wasn't in CSV format, which meant that running any kind of analysis was difficult. I wrote a converter to get the data into CSV format, but that converter wasn't generic; it would work only for his particular survey. It later occurred to me that such conversions are a common issue. Therefore, in writing this chapter, I created a parser that can translate any SurveyMonkey results to CSV file format. The headers of the CSV file will be the questions used for the survey.

Problem

Write a parser that can parse SurveyMonkey results and return a CSV file.

Solution

SurveyMonkey results aren't CSV files, so the first step is to get the data into CSV format. Listing 8-4 shows the code.

Listing 8-4. Turning SurveyMonkey results into CSV format

```
//Parsing Survey Monkey Results
string result = @"Will you come by bus
                                No
                                Name
                                Sam
                                Phone number
                                1234
                                Will you come by bus
                                Yes
                                Name
                                Ram
                                Phone number
                                3213
                                Will you come by bus
                                Yes
                                Name
                                Raul
                                Phone number
                                4245";

string[] questions = {"Will you come by bus","Name","Phone number"};
var allResponses = result.Split(questions,StringSplitOptions.RemoveEmptyEntries)
    .Select (r => r.Trim());
int numberOfResponses = allResponses.Count ()/questions.Length;

string csv =
//Headers
questions
        .Select (q => "\"" +  q + "\"" )
                .Aggregate ((h1,h2) => h1 + "," + h2 ) +
//Insert Newline
Environment.NewLine  +
//Rows
Enumerable.Range(0,numberOfResponses)
        .Select (e => allResponses.Skip(e*questions.Length).Take(questions.Length))
                .Select (e => Enumerable.Range(0,questions.Length)
                                    .Select (en => e.ElementAt(en) ))
                .Select (e => e.Select (x =>  "\"" +  x + "\"")
                                    .Aggregate ((m,n) => m + "," + n  ))
                .Aggregate ((a,b)  =>  a + Environment.NewLine + b);

csv.Dump("CSV representation");
```

This generates the output shown in Figure 8-4.

```
CSV representation
"Will you come by bus","Name","Phone number"
"No","Sam","1234"
"Yes","Ram","3213"
"Yes","Raul","4245"
```

Figure 8-4. *SurveyMonkey result converted to CSV format*

If you save the preceding content in a text (.csv) file and then open it in Microsoft Excel, it shows up formatted as shown in Figure 8-5.

	A	B	C
1	Will you come by bus	Name	Phone number
2	No	Sam	1234
3	Yes	Ram	3213
4	Yes	Raul	4245

Figure 8-5. *SurveyMonkey converted result shown in Excel*

How It Works

Splitting the result by the questions leaves only the answers, which appear in the same order as the questions. The total number of responders is equal to the total number of answers divided by the number of questions. Each such set of answers represents one row.

The code allResponses.Skip(e*questions.Length).Take(questions.Length) returns a list of elements that are answers to the current question. At the first run, the value of e is zero. So the number of elements picked from the start is equal to the number of questions. At each iteration, the value of e increases by one. Thus an appropriate number of responses are ignored and the latest answer set is picked up to form the current row.

Skip() followed by Take() is a common idiom to progressively advance the scanning window of any algorithm that picks some elements, skipping a few from the beginning of a given collection.

As you can see, this code is almost completely generic: to run it against data from a different survey, you just need to change the values in the questions array, and you will be finished.

8-3. Analyzing Trends in Baby Names

Baby names always capture the imagination of new parents. Even though I have already named my son, I still find the trend analysis of baby names a fascinating topic. At one point, I found a list of baby names along with a measure for popularity. The data was a CSV file, which had the following fields:

Field	Description
Year	The information in the current row is for this year. The range of the years is 1880 to 2008.
Name	The name of the baby.
Percent	A measure of popularity.
Sex	Gender of the baby.

Problem

Looking at this dataset, I posed couple of questions that would help make sense of the data:

1. What are the top ten boys' and girls' names?

2. How has the popularity of a name changed over the course of the years?

3. What are the top ten most popular boy and girl names for each decade?

Solution

Go to a new LINQPad tab and add the query shown in Listing 8-5.

Listing 8-5. Determining name popularity

```
var babyNames = File.ReadAllLines(@"C:\Personal\TableAPI\baby-names.csv")
     .Select (f => f.Split(','))
     .Skip(1) //Skip the header row
     .Select
         (
             a =>
                 new
                 {
                   Year = Convert.ToInt32(a[0]),
                   Name = a[1].Trim(new char[]{'"',' '}),
                   Percentage = Convert.ToDouble(a[2]),
                   Sex = a[3].Trim(new char[]{'"',' '})
                 }
         );

babyNames
         .Where (n => n.Sex == "boy") // This analysis is being done for baby boy names.
         .ToLookup (n => n.Name)
         .ToDictionary (n => n.Key )
         .Select (n =>
                     new {
                         Name = n.Key,
                         Popularity =  n.Value
                         .Select (v => new { Year = v.Year,
                                               PopularityPercentage = v.Percentage})
                         .ToList()
                     })

         .OrderByDescending (n => n.Popularity.Select (p => p.PopularityPercentage )
                             .Average ())
         .Take(10) //Show top 10 names as per the average popularity
         .Dump("Popularity of top 10 baby \"boy\" names over the years");
```

Figure 8-6 shows the overall result structure. I have collapsed the entries for each name.

Popularity of top 10 baby "boy" names over the years

Name	Popularity
John	▼ List<> (129 items) ▶
James	▼ List<> (129 items) ▶
William	▼ List<> (129 items) ▶
Robert	▼ List<> (129 items) ▶
Charles	▼ List<> (129 items) ▶
Michael	▼ List<> (129 items) ▶
Joseph	▼ List<> (129 items) ▶
David	▼ List<> (129 items) ▶
George	▼ List<> (129 items) ▶
Thomas	▼ List<> (129 items) ▶

▲ IEnumerable<> (10 items) ▶

Figure 8-6. *The top ten baby boy names between 1880 and 2008*

Figure 8-7 shows a partial view of the 129 items for the name *John*.

Popularity of top 10 baby "boy" names over the years

Name	Popularity	
John	▲ List<> (129 items) ▶	
	Year ≡	PopularityPercentage ≡
	1880	0.081541
	1881	0.080975
	1882	0.078314
	1883	0.079066
	1884	0.076476
	1885	0.075517
	1886	0.07582
	1887	0.074181
	1888	0.071186
	1889	0.071804
	1890	0.071034
	1891	0.070292
	1892	0.068759
	1893	0.066495
	1894	0.065961
	1895	0.065699
	1896	0.063051

▲ IEnumerable<> (10 items) ▶

Figure 8-7. *The decreasing popularity of the name John over time*

Although these results show the top baby names between 1880 and 2008, the format makes it hard to compare the popularity of one name to another. Also it is hard to figure out when a particular name started to become more popular than other names at that time.

I could have found these insights immediately if the data were plotted, as you'll see. For the example, I've used Highcharts—a popular JavaScript-based data-visualization engine. You can download it from highcharts.com.

After downloading Highcharts, you can explore all the chart types it supports, but this example uses only the area-inverted chart. Open the file index.html located under the examples/area-inverted/ folder. You will see that you provide data to this chart in JSON format:

```
series: [{
            name: 'John',
            data: [3, 4, 3, 5, 4, 10, 12]
        }, {
            name: 'Jane',
            data: [1, 3, 4, 3, 3, 5, 4]
        }]
```

In the previous sections, you saw how to get the data for each name. That makes it easy to generate data in JSON format so you can chart name popularity. Add the following code after the Take(10) call in the previous code snippet:

```
.Select (n => "{" + String.Format(@"
                name: '{0}',
                data: [{1}]
            ",n.Name,n.Popularity.Select (p => p.PopularityPercentage.ToString())
                                    .Aggregate ((p,q) => p + "," + q ))+"}")
.Aggregate ((m,n) => m + "," + n )
```

This generates all the series using all the names and their associated popularity percentages for all the years in the range. Copy this generated string representing the series and replace the series section in the existing file. Change the name of the file to something you prefer so you don't lose the original example.

The y axis of the chart needs to show the years, so edit the categories to reflect that change. Here is a partial list of categories:

```
categories:
['1880','1881','1882','1883','1884','1885','1886','1887','1888','1889','1890','1891','1892',
'1893','1894','1895','1896','1897','1898','1899','1900','1901','1902','1903','1904','1905',
'1906','1907','1908','1909','1910','1911','1912','1913','1914','1915','1916','1917','1918',
'1919','1920','1921','1922','1923','1924','1925','1926','1927','1928','1929','1930','1931'...
'1990','1991','1992','1993','1994','1995','1996','1997','1998','1999','2000','2001','2002',
'2003','2004','2005','2006','2007','2008']
```

The final remaining task is to change the chart title to **Baby Name Popularity from 1880 to 2008** and the x-axis caption to **Baby Name Popularity**. After completing those changes, open the new file in your browser. You will see something similar to Figure 8-8.

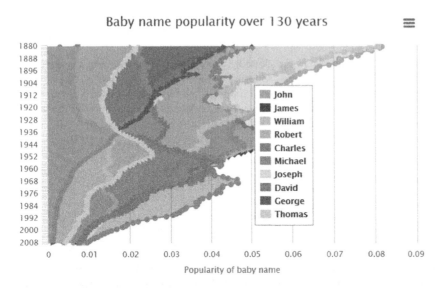

Figure 8-8. *Popularity of baby boy names over time*

You can see the color version of this visualization at https://twitter.com/samthecoder/status/502471431519608832/photo/1.

I did the same experiment with baby *girl* names and found the trends shown in Figure 8-9.

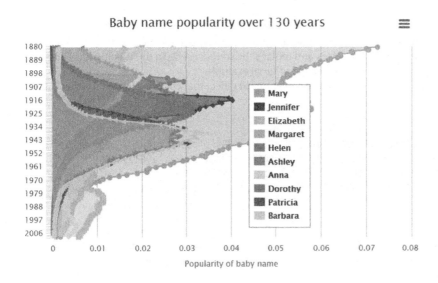

Figure 8-9. *Popularity of baby girl names over time*

The color visualization is here: https://twitter.com/samthecoder/status/502472516342784000/photo/1.

By looking at the charts, I can say with confidence that *John* and *Mary* have been by far the most popular names in the last 130 years.

How It Works

The CSV file is first loaded into a collection of an anonymous type representing each row of the data. Each row has four columns: Year, Name, Popularity Percentage, and Sex. The first Skip() call skips the CSV headers, while the next Select() call generates a list of an anonymous type that represents the CSV as an in-memory collection.

The filter Where (n => n.Sex == "boy") filters out baby girl names, leaving only baby boy names in the collection. Next the code creates a lookup table with each name using .ToLookup (n => n.Name). This lookup table is converted to a dictionary where the keys of the dictionary represent baby boy names and the values represent the list of years and the percentage popularity of the name in that year. Figure 8-7 shows one such entry from this dictionary.

Finally, the dictionary entries are sorted based on the average popularity of the names, in descending order, ensuring that the most popular names appear at the top. The top ten entries are selected to discover the top ten most popular baby boy names.

To do this analysis for baby girl names, you need to change only the Where clause to filter out the baby boy names instead.

8-4. Analyzing Stock Values

Data about stock prices of many companies are available from Yahoo Finance. If you want to know historical stock prices for Google, you can find them at http://finance.yahoo.com/q/hp?s=GOOG. The word *GOOG* is the ticker symbol for Google. For Microsoft, it is *MSFT*; for Apple, it is *AAPL*.

If you visit this page, you will see a table showing the historical values for the company for which the symbol is provided. Below the table is a CSV file available for download. If you copy the link to the CSV file, it looks like this:

```
http://real-chart.finance.yahoo.com/table.csv?s=
GOOG&d=7&e=22&f=2014&g=d&a=2&b=27&c=2014&ignore=.csv
```

Note that the query string in the link has the symbol s=GOOG. So if you wanted to download historical stock prices for Microsoft, you would change the ticker symbol to MSFT, resulting in the following query string:

```
http://real-chart.finance.yahoo.com/table.csv?s=
MSFT&d=7&e=22&f=2014&g=d&a=2&b=27&c=2014&ignore=.csv
```

Problem

Given a list of ticker symbols, create a program to load the historical stock values for those companies.

Solution

The code in Listing 8-6 uses the historical values from the Yahoo CSV files mentioned above.

Listing 8-6. Loading historical values for specified stock symbols

```
string[] symbols =  {"AAPL","GOOG","MSFT"};
WebClient wc = new WebClient();
//This structure will hold the stock values
List<Tuple<string,DateTime,double,double,double,double,double,Tuple<double>>> mapping
    = new List<Tuple<string,DateTime,double,double,double,double,double,Tuple<double>>>();
foreach (var symbol in symbols)
{
        File.Delete("temp.csv");
```

```
        wc.DownloadFile(
        String.Format(
//Make sure the following URL string appears in a single line. Otherwise, the program won't work
@"http://realchart.finance.yahoo.com/table.csv?s={0}&d=7&e=19&f=2014&g=d&a=2&b=13&c=1986&ignore=
    .csv",symbol),"temp.csv");

mapping.AddRange(File.ReadAllLines(@"temp.csv")
        .Skip(1)//Skip the header
        .Select( l =>
        {
            var toks = l.Split(',');
            return new Tuple<string,DateTime,double,double,double,double,double,Tuple<double>>
            (
             symbol,
             DateTime.Parse(toks[0]),
             Convert.ToDouble(toks[1]),
             Convert.ToDouble(toks[2]),
             Convert.ToDouble(toks[3]),
             Convert.ToDouble(toks[4]),
             Convert.ToDouble(toks[5]),
             //The last element must be a Tuple again.
             new Tuple<double>(Convert.ToDouble(toks[6])));
        }));

}
var stocks = mapping.Select (m =>
                        new
                        {
                          Symbol = m.Item1,
                          Date = m.Item2,
                          Open = m.Item3,
                          High = m.Item4,
                          Low = m.Item5,
                          Close = m.Item6,
                          Volume = m.Item7,
                          AdjClose = m.Rest.Item1
                        })
                        .ToLookup (m => m.Symbol)
                        .SelectMany (m => m.Take(7));

stocks.Dump("Stock values for last month");
```

Figure 8-10 shows a partial result of this query.

Stock values for last month

Symbol	Date	Open	High	Low	Close	Volume	AdjClose
AAPL	8/19/2014 12:00:00 AM	99.41	100.68	99.32	100.53	69274700	100.53
AAPL	8/18/2014 12:00:00 AM	98.49	99.37	97.98	99.16	47572000	99.16
AAPL	8/15/2014 12:00:00 AM	97.9	98.19	96.86	97.98	48951000	97.98
AAPL	8/14/2014 12:00:00 AM	97.33	97.57	96.8	97.5	28116000	97.5
AAPL	8/13/2014 12:00:00 AM	96.15	97.24	96.04	97.24	31916000	97.24
AAPL	8/12/2014 12:00:00 AM	96.04	96.88	95.61	95.97	33795000	95.97
AAPL	8/11/2014 12:00:00 AM	95.27	96.08	94.84	95.99	36585000	95.99
GOOG	8/19/2014 12:00:00 AM	585	587.34	584	586.86	976000	586.86
GOOG	8/18/2014 12:00:00 AM	576.11	584.51	576	582.16	1280600	582.16
GOOG	8/15/2014 12:00:00 AM	577.86	579.38	570.52	573.48	1515000	573.48
GOOG	8/14/2014 12:00:00 AM	576.18	577.9	570.88	574.65	982800	574.65
GOOG	8/13/2014 12:00:00 AM	567.31	575	565.75	574.78	1435300	574.78
GOOG	8/12/2014 12:00:00 AM	564.52	565.9	560.88	562.73	1537800	562.73
GOOG	8/11/2014 12:00:00 AM	569.99	570.49	566	567.88	1211400	567.88
MSFT	8/19/2014 12:00:00 AM	44.97	45.34	44.83	45.33	28115600	45.33
MSFT	8/18/2014 12:00:00 AM	44.94	45.11	44.68	45.11	26891100	44.83
MSFT	8/15/2014 12:00:00 AM	44.58	44.9	44.4	44.79	41611300	44.51
MSFT	8/14/2014 12:00:00 AM	44.08	44.42	44.01	44.27	19313200	44
MSFT	8/13/2014 12:00:00 AM	43.68	44.18	43.52	44.08	22889500	43.81

Figure 8-10. *Values of stock prices for some companies during a week*

___

■ **Note**   This code uses the WebClient class from the System.Net namespace, so you must add a reference to that DLL and add that namespace in LINQPad to get this code to work.

___

How It Works

This example demonstrates the special case of tuple creation. For a tuple with eight or more elements, the last element must be a tuple again. This element is denoted as Rest for the outer tuple, and its elements are accessed the usual way, as Rest.Item1 and so on.

Tuples are great for representing rows of CSV/database tables. However, one problem with using a tuple is that you can't name its properties. It is difficult to understand the intent of code such as something.Item1, where something is a tuple. But by projecting a list of tuples by using Select(), you can create easy-to-understand code. This code employs two Select() calls. This is an idiom you'll find frequently in LINQ code.

The second Select() call gives proper names to the tuple items.

After projecting the CSV as a list of anonymous objects, the code creates a lookup table using the symbol as the key. Because there are three symbols in this example, there will be three keys. So when SelectMany() is called with the argument 7, the call takes 7 from each of the entries in the lookup table values, resulting in 21 rows. If necessary, you can dump the lookup table to visualize what's happening. That's a big benefit of using LINQPad. You can even save these internal views of your code for future references.

8-5. Analyzing Git Logs

Contributors around the world participate in open source projects and contribute their code. It is interesting to see how these projects evolve, using code contributions from people who don't even know each other. Git maintains logs of all the commits that have happened. Figure 8-11 shows a snapshot of a Git log for the jQuery project.

```
commit 269a27c70204c7d233eac3cd91a383e9b5759a2f
Author: Timmy Willison <timmywillisn@gmail.com>
Date:   Thu Jul 17 11:15:19 2014 -0700

    Build: update source map options for the new grunt jshint

commit c869a1ef8a031342e817a2c063179a787ff57239
Author: Timmy Willison <timmywillisn@gmail.com>
Date:   Thu Jul 17 10:25:59 2014 -0700

    Build: update grunt-jscs-checker and pass with the new rules

commit 8e3a0ceafa2c7c78902d0eab07d21b793deb5366
Author: Timmy Willison <timmywillisn@gmail.com>
Date:   Thu Jul 17 10:24:37 2014 -0700

    Build: update node dependencies barring jscs

commit 8356948ed4ee13af218af74c56c8a91ee9523828
Author: Timmy Willison <timmywillisn@gmail.com>
Date:   Thu Jul 17 09:03:29 2014 -0700

    Build: update front-end dependencies
```

Figure 8-11. *A portion of the JQuery Git log*

Problem

Here are couple of data analysis tasks that make sense for any project that uses Git, either publicly or on a private server. I will start with the simpler task:

Develop a leaderboard that shows the top contributors, sorted by number of commits in descending order. (Sometimes developers commit more often than they would prefer because of missing files and such. But for this example, I have assumed that all commits are genuine and not the result of fixing an earlier faulty commit.)

Solution

Save the JQuery Git log to a text file, jquerygitlogs.txt. Then write the query in Listing 8-7 in a new LINQPad tab. This query finds the leaders who contributed more than their peers for JQuery. This also includes the project founder.

Listing 8-7. Creating a Jquery Git leaderboard

```
string log = File.ReadAllText("C:\\jquerygitlogs.txt");
string[] commits = Regex.Matches(log,"commit [a-zA-Z0-9]{40}")
                                .Cast<Match>()
                                .Select (m => m.Value)
                                .ToArray();
string[] authors = Regex.Matches(log,"Author: [a-zA-Z0-9-. @<>']+")
                                .Cast<Match>()
                                .Select (m => m.Value)
                                .ToArray();
string[] dates = Regex.Matches(log,"Date: [a-zA-Z0-9-:+ ]+")
                                .Cast<Match>()
                                .Select (m => m.Value)
                                .ToArray();

List<Tuple<string,string,string>> details = new List<Tuple<string,string,string>>();
Enumerable.Range(0,5000).ToList().ForEach( k => details.Add(new
Tuple<string,string,string>(commits[k],authors[k],dates[k])));
```

```
details.Select (d =>
            new {
                  Author = d.Item2.Substring(d.Item2.IndexOf(':')+1),
                  Date = DateTime.ParseExact(
                     d.Item3.Substring(d.Item3.IndexOf(' ')).Trim(),
                      "ddd MMM d HH:mm:ss yyyy zzz",CultureInfo.InvariantCulture),
                   Location = d.Item3.EndsWith("-0700")?"USA/Canada":"Elsewhere"
               }
           )
       .ToLookup (d => d.Author)
       .Select (d => new { Author = d.Key, CommitCount = d.Count()})
       .OrderByDescending (d => d.CommitCount )
       .Take(10)
       .Dump("JQuery Leaderboard");
```

This produces the output shown in Figure 8-12. This result correctly shows *John Resig* at the top, because he is the main author of the JQuery library and has committed significantly more than other core team members.

JQuery Leaderboard

▲ IEnumerable<> (10 items)	
Author	**CommitCount** ≡
John Resig <jeresig@gmail.com>	879
Dave Methvin <dave.methvin@gmail.com>	524
jeresig <jeresig@gmail.com>	503
jaubourg <j@ubourg.net>	279
Rick Waldron <waldron.rick@gmail.com>	246
Timmy Willison <timmywillisn@gmail.com>	222
Brandon Aaron <brandon.aaron@gmail.com>	219
Ariel Flesler <aflesler@gmail.com>	200
Richard Gibson <richard.gibson@gmail.com>	177
timmywil <timmywillisn@gmail.com>	149
	3398

Figure 8-12. *JQuery leaderboard*

How It Works

The leaderboard is created from a projection that holds data about the authors. I created a list of author names, the date when each commit was performed, and the author's location. You can determine the rough location by examining the GMT offset. I haven't used these variables; however, I encourage you to experiment with the information. One possible task is to identify how many contributions have been made from various continents.

Returning to the explanation at hand, the list of authors (which is basically a list of anonymous types representing author names, locations, and commit dates) is used to generate a lookup table where the index is the author names. So there will be as many keys in the table as there are distinct author names in the log file. The values of this lookup table show all the commits performed by the author whose name is being used as the key of the lookup table. You can dump this table to see what's happing visually.

Later these values from the lookup table are used to generate a different projection with author names and the total number of commits each author performed. Finally, this is sorted by the number of commits in descending order. Taking the top ten such entries results in the leaderboard.

Problem

Another, slightly more complex problem is to show a timeline of how the JQuery project has grown by monitoring commits.

Solution

For this, I decided to use the Highcharts line-time series chart. This chart is zoomable, which is convenient. In a new LINQPad query tab, write the query in Listing 8-8 to generate and save the number of commits done per day.

Listing 8-8. Creating a Jquery timeline by monitoring Git commits

```
string log = File.ReadAllText("C:\\jquerygitlogs.txt");
string[] commits = Regex.Matches(log,"commit [a-zA-Z0-9]{40}")
                                .Cast<Match>()
                                .Select (m => m.Value)
                                .ToArray();
string[] authors = Regex.Matches(log,"Author: [a-zA-Z0-9-. @<>']+")
                                .Cast<Match>()
                                .Select (m => m.Value)
                                .ToArray();
string[] dates = Regex.Matches(log,"Date: [a-zA-Z0-9-:+ ]+")
                                .Cast<Match>()
                                .Select (m => m.Value)
                                .ToArray();
//There can be the word "commit" followed by a valid SHA ID of the commit inside a commit
//To bypass these we need to take the minimum length of all these three arrays.
var length = (new List<int>(){commits.Length, authors.Length, dates.Length}).Min();

List<Tuple<string,string,string>> details = new List<Tuple<string,string,string>>();
Enumerable.Range(0,length).ToList().ForEach( k => details.Add(new Tuple<string,string,string>(commit
s[k],authors[k],dates[k])));

var logs = details.Select (d =>
                        new
                            {
                                Author = d.Item2.Substring(d.Item2.IndexOf(':')+1),
                                Date = DateTime.ParseExact(
                                    d.Item3.Substring(d.Item3.IndexOf(' ')).Trim(),
                                    "ddd MMM d HH:mm:ss yyyy zzz",
                                    CultureInfo.InvariantCulture)
                            });

DateTime startDate = logs.OrderBy (l => l.Date).First ().Date.Date;
DateTime endDate = logs.OrderBy (l => l.Date).Last().Date.Date;

startDate.Dump("Start Date");
var logMap = logs.ToLookup (l => l.Date.Date)
                .ToDictionary (l =>  l.Key, l => l.Count());
```

```
List<int> commitCounts = new List<int>();
for(;startDate!=endDate;startDate = startDate.AddDays(1))
{
        if(logMap.ContainsKey(startDate))
            commitCounts.Add(logMap[startDate]);
        else
            commitCounts.Add(0);
}
StreamWriter sw = new StreamWriter("C:\\dataJQuery.txt");
sw.WriteLine(commitCounts.Select (c => c.ToString()).Aggregate ((m,n) => m + "," + n));
sw.Close();
```

This generates the following output:

```
5644
3/22/2006 12:00:00 AM
```

The output shows that there have been 5,644 commits, and that the first commit was performed on March 22, 2006. In addition to this output, the query saves the number of commits made per day in the file dataJQuery.txt. Open the file, and you will see the data shown in Figure 8-13.

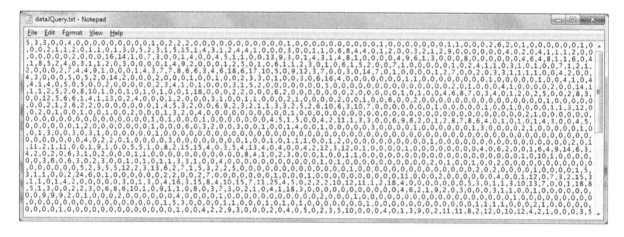

Figure 8-13. *The number of commits done per day in the JQuery project*

Copy the entire content of this file. Go to the example\line-time-series\ folder in the Highcharts example directory. Copy the file index.htm and paste it in the same directory. Open the copied file in your favorite text editor or in Visual Studio. Locate the string data: [and replace everything between the braces that appear right after data:. In other words, replace the data with the generated content that you copied earlier.

Right before data: you'll see the following line:

```
pointStart: Date.UTC(2006, 0, 01)
```

Replace this line with the following:

```
pointStart: Date.UTC(2006, 2, 22)
```

This line marks the starting point of the zoomable timeline that gets rendered. The parameters UTC takes are the year, an integer between 0–11 representing the month, and an integer between 1–31 representing the day of the month. Because the first commit of the JQuery was done on March 22, 2006, the date as per UTC is 2006, 2, 22.

Finally, change the chart title and axis titles, as follows:

Existing Text	Replace With
text: 'USD to EUR exchange rate from 2006 through 2008'	text: 'JQuery Growth from 2006 through 2014'
name: 'USD to EUR'	'Commits'
text: 'Exchange rate'	text: 'Contributions'

At this stage, you are all set to see the visualization. Open the modified HTML file in your favorite browser. Figure 8-14 shows how it rendered in Mozilla Firefox.

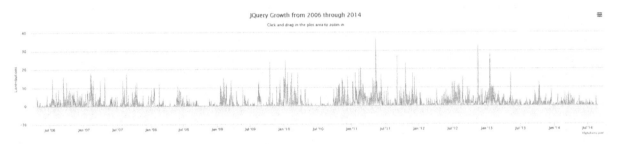

Figure 8-14. *JQuery commit pattern from inception until 2014 (the time this chapter was written)*

How It Works

I have created a video of the visualization. You can see it at www.youtube.com/watch?v=i6s8hcIciUM.

The code works by identifying the dates between which commits have happened. The dictionary logMap keeps track of all the commits that have been pushed to JQuery on a particular date. If a date isn't found as a key of logMap, no commit was made on that date. Using a loop, the list commitCounts is populated such that the first entry of this list stores the number of commits performed on the day the JQuery project started, and so on for all other dates. Finally, the series is dumped as a CSV file in dataJQuery.txt.

8-6. Analyzing Movie Ratings

MovieLens is a defunct dataset containing various types of movies along with recorded ratings. This dataset is good for testing movie recommendation engines. However, it is also just sheer fun to perform some exploratory analysis on this data. In doing so, I found some startling myth-buster information that I hadn't known before. For example, one myth is that women like romantic movies more than men. I found the reality to be the opposite.

You can get the MovieLens files from http://grouplens.org/datasets/movielens/. There are several files in the ml-100k.zip file. For this example, I have used only the following files:

u.Item: I renamed this file to movies.txt. (This has details about movies.)

u.User: I renamed this file to users.txt. (This has demographic information about users.)

u.Data: I renamed this file to movieRatings.txt. (This has rating information about movies.)

I recommend that you read the ReadMe.txt file available from the grouplens.org link previously provided so you understand the layout of the data being parsed for each file.

Problem

Here are the questions I tried to answer with the analysis:

1. How many movies were made in each category?

2. What types of movies (by category) do men and women like?

3. What are the genre preferences of men and women?

Solution

To obtain the answer to the first question, create a new C# statement query in LINQPad and write the code in Listing 8-9.

Listing 8-9. Analyzing Movie Categories

```
string[] allStrings = File.ReadAllText(@"C:\Personal\TableAPI\movies.txt")
                          .Split(new string[]{"|","\r","\n"},StringSplitOptions.None);

var movies =
Enumerable.Range(0,allStrings.Length/24)
          .ToList()
          .Select ( s  => allStrings.Skip(s*24).Take(24))
          .Select (s =>
          {
          return new
          {
                  ID = s.ElementAt(0),
                  Title = s.ElementAt(1),
                  ReleaseDate = s.ElementAt(2).Trim(),
                  IMDBURL = s.ElementAt(4),
                  IsAction = s.ElementAt(5)=="1"?true:false,
                  IsAdventure = s.ElementAt(6)=="1"?true:false,
                  IsAnimation = s.ElementAt(7)=="1"?true:false,
                  IsChildrens = s.ElementAt(8)=="1"?true:false,
                  IsComedy = s.ElementAt(9)=="1"?true:false,
                  IsCrime = s.ElementAt(10)=="1"?true:false,
                  IsDocumentary = s.ElementAt(11)=="1"?true:false,
                  IsDrama = s.ElementAt(12)=="1"?true:false,
                  IsFantasy = s.ElementAt(13)=="1"?true:false,
                  IsFilm_Noir = s.ElementAt(14)=="1"?true:false,
                  IsHorror = s.ElementAt(15)=="1"?true:false,
                  IsMusical = s.ElementAt(16)=="1"?true:false,
                  IsMystery = s.ElementAt(17)=="1"?true:false,
                  IsRomance = s.ElementAt(18)=="1"?true:false,
                  IsSci_Fi = s.ElementAt(19)=="1"?true:false,
                  IsThriller = s.ElementAt(20)=="1"?true:false,
                  IsWar = s.ElementAt(21)=="1"?true:false,
                  IsWestern = s.ElementAt(22)=="1"?true:false
          };
  });
```

```
Dictionary<string,int> moviesPerCategory = new Dictionary<string,int>();

foreach (var movie in movies)
{
  movie
      .GetType()
      .GetProperties()
      .Select (m => new KeyValuePair<string,object>(m.Name, m.GetValue(movie)))
      .Skip(4)//Skipping ID,Title,ReleaseDate and IMDBURL field
      .Where (f => Convert.ToBoolean(f.Value)==true)
      .Select (f => f.Key.Substring(2))
      .ToList()
      .ForEach( k =>
        {
            if(!moviesPerCategory.ContainsKey(k))
                moviesPerCategory.Add(k,1);
            else
                moviesPerCategory[k]++;
        });
}
int totalMovieCount = moviesPerCategory.Select( t => t.Value).Sum();
moviesPerCategory.Select (pc =>
                new {
                    Category = pc.Key,
                    Count = pc.Value,
                    Percentage = (100*Math.Round((double)pc.Value/(double)totalMovieCount,2))
                })
                .OrderByDescending (movie => movie.Percentage)
                .Dump("Movie Categories");
```

Running this code results in the output shown in Figure 8-15. I have enabled charting. It is clear from this result that during the early '90s (the time when this dataset was created), Fantasy movies were in great demand. One in every four movies made was a Fantasy movie.

Movie Categories

Category	Count	Percentage	
▲ IOrderedEnumerable<> (18 items)			►
Fantasy	725		25
Crime	505		18
Adventure	251		9
War	251		9
Sci_Fi	247		9
Animation	135		5
Comedy	122		4
Documentary	109		4
Thriller	101		4
Musical	92		3
Western	71		2
Mystery	56		2
Drama	50		2
Romance	61		2
Childrens	42		1
Film_Noir	22		1
Horror	24		1
Action	2		0
	2866		101

Figure 8-15. *SPercentage of movies made of each genre*

How It Works

The variable movies is an anonymous type collection representing each movie. Each public property, such as IsRomance holds a Boolean determining whether the movie belongs in that genre. An individual movie can be associated with multiple genres. The goal in this example was to find out the number of movies made in each genre. To represent this data, I needed a dictionary in which the keys were the movie genres and the values the number of such movies. The dictionary moviesPerCategory holds this information.

The way this dictionary gets populated is particularly interesting. The loop that iterates over the movies collection uses reflection to determine the type of the anonymous type, and then lists all the public properties that represent the genres. The names of these properties are used as the keys of the moviesPerCategory dictionary. The call to Substring() drops the initial two letters Is for each of the properties.

To obtain the percentage of movies made in each genre, you need to know the total number of movies made. That value is saved in totalMovieCount. Finally, the dictionary entries are projected to show the genre of the movie, total number of movies made in that genre, and the percentage of movies made in that genre. This result is then shown sorted by the percentage of movies made in descending order.

You can build on the code so far to find the answer for the second question: What types of movies (by category) do men and women like?

To find the answer, create the query in Listing 8-10 in LINQPad.

Listing 8-10. Discovering what movies men and women like

```
string[] allStrings = File.ReadAllText(@"C:\movies.txt")
                        .Split(new string[]{"|","\r","\n"},StringSplitOptions.None);
var movies =
Enumerable.Range(0,allStrings.Length/24)
        .ToList().Select ( s  => allStrings.Skip(s*24).Take(24))
        .Select (s =>
        {
        return new
      {
                ID = s.ElementAt(0),
                Title = s.ElementAt(1),
                ReleaseDate = s.ElementAt(2),
                IMDBURL = s.ElementAt(4),
                IsAction = s.ElementAt(5)=="1"?true:false,
                IsAdventure = s.ElementAt(6)=="1"?true:false,
                IsAnimation = s.ElementAt(7)=="1"?true:false,
                IsChildrens = s.ElementAt(8)=="1"?true:false,
                IsComedy = s.ElementAt(9)=="1"?true:false,
                IsCrime = s.ElementAt(10)=="1"?true:false,
                IsDocumentary = s.ElementAt(11)=="1"?true:false,
                IsDrama = s.ElementAt(12)=="1"?true:false,
                IsFantasy = s.ElementAt(13)=="1"?true:false,
                IsFilm_Noir = s.ElementAt(14)=="1"?true:false,
                IsHorror = s.ElementAt(15)=="1"?true:false,
                IsMusical = s.ElementAt(16)=="1"?true:false,
                IsMystery = s.ElementAt(17)=="1"?true:false,
                IsRomance = s.ElementAt(18)=="1"?true:false,
                IsSci_Fi = s.ElementAt(19)=="1"?true:false,
                IsThriller = s.ElementAt(20)=="1"?true:false,
                IsWar = s.ElementAt(21)=="1"?true:false,
                IsWestern = s.ElementAt(22)=="1"?true:false
            };
        })
.ToLookup (s => s.ID);

//Loading users in a collection
var users  = File.ReadAllText(@"C:\users.txt")
                        .Split(new char[]{'\r','\n'},StringSplitOptions.RemoveEmptyEntries)
                        .Select (f => f.Split('|'))
                        .Select (f => new { ID = f[0], Age = f[1], Sex = f[2],
                            Profession = f[3], ZIP  = f[4]} )
                        .ToLookup(f => f.ID);

//Loading movie ratings
var movieRatingTokens = File.ReadAllText(@"C:\Personal\TableAPI\movieRatings.txt")
            .Split(new char[]{' ','\t','\r','\n'},StringSplitOptions.RemoveEmptyEntries);

var movieRatings = Enumerable.Range(0,movieRatingTokens.Length/4)
                                        .Select( k => movieRatingTokens.Skip(4*k).Take(4))
```

```
.Select (k => new { UserID = k.ElementAt(0), MovieID = k.ElementAt(1), Rating =
        Convert.ToInt32( k.ElementAt(2)), TimeStamp = k.ElementAt(3)
} )
 .Select (k =>
        {
                var currentUser = users[k.UserID].First();
                var movie  = movies[ k.MovieID].First();
                        return new { Age = currentUser.Age, Sex = currentUser.Sex,
                Movie = movie.Title, Rating = k.Rating ,
                IsAdenture = movie.IsAdventure,
                IsAnimation = movie.IsAnimation,
                IsChildrens = movie.IsChildrens,
                IsComedy = movie.IsComedy,
                IsCrime = movie.IsCrime,
                IsDocumentary = movie.IsDocumentary,
                IsDrama = movie.IsDrama,
                IsFantasy = movie.IsFantasy,
                IsFilm_Noir = movie.IsFilm_Noir,
                IsHorror = movie.IsHorror,
                IsMusical = movie.IsMusical,
                IsMystery = movie.IsMystery,
                IsRomance = movie.IsRomance,
                IsSci_Fi = movie.IsSci_Fi,
                IsThriller = movie.IsThriller,
                IsWar = movie.IsWar,
                IsWestern = movie.IsWestern
            };
} );

Dictionary<string,Dictionary<string,int>> genderBias = new
    Dictionary<string,Dictionary<string,int>>();
genderBias.Add("M",new Dictionary<string,int>());
genderBias.Add("F",new Dictionary<string,int>());
foreach (var mr in movieRatings)
{
        string strRep = mr.ToString();
        string key = strRep.Contains("Sex = M")?"M":"F";

        var matches = Regex.Matches(strRep,"Is[A-Za-z_ ]+= True")
                        .Cast<Match>()
                                        .Select (m => m.Value)
                                        .Select (m => m.Substring(2,m.IndexOf('=')-2)
                                        .Trim());

        foreach (var m in matches)
        if(!genderBias[key].ContainsKey(m))
                genderBias[key].Add(m,1);
        else
                genderBias[key][m]++;

}
```

```
var pieData = genderBias.ToDictionary (b =>  b.Key,
                             b => b.Value
                                    .Select
                  (
                    v =>
                    new
                    {
                             Key = v.Key ,
                          Liking = (double)v.Value/(double)(b.Value
                                   .Select (va => va.Value).Sum ())
                    }
                                    )
                  .OrderByDescending (v => v.Liking )
                  .ToDictionary (v => v.Key))
                     .Select (b => b.Key + "->" + b.Value.Select (v => "['" +
                          v.Key + "'," + 100 * Math.Round( v.Value.Liking,2) +"]")
                  .Aggregate ((m,n) => m + "," + n));

Console.WriteLine(pieData);
```

This generates the following output:

```
▲ IEnumerable<String> (2 items)
M->['Fantasy',18],['Crime',14],['Adenture',13],['War',11],['Sci_Fi',9],['Animation',7],['Thriller',6],['Western',5],['Documentary',4],['Comedy',3],['Musical',3],['Romance',2],['Mystery',2],['Childrens',2],['Horror',1],['Film_Noir',1],['Drama',0]
F->['Fantasy',21],['Crime',15],['Sci_Fi',11],['Adenture',10],['War',10],['Animation',6],['Thriller',5],['Comedy',4],['Western',4],['Documentary',3],['Mystery',3],['Romance',2],['Musical',2],['Childrens',2],['Horror',1],['Film_Noir',1],['Drama',0]
```

Using this data, you can draw a couple of pie charts showing the genre preferences of men and women. Highcharts has a pie chart folder. Copy the file you find there, and then make the following changes to the copied file:

Change This	To This
['Firefox', 45.0],	The first row M->['Fantasy',18]... etc. of the result obtained
['IE', 26.8],	
{	
name: 'Chrome',	
y: 12.8,	
sliced: true,	
selected: true	
},	
['Safari', 8.5],	
['Opera', 6.2],	
['Others', 0.7]	
'Browser market shares at a specific website, 2014'	'What kind of movies do men like?'
name: 'Browser share'	name: 'Movie Likings'

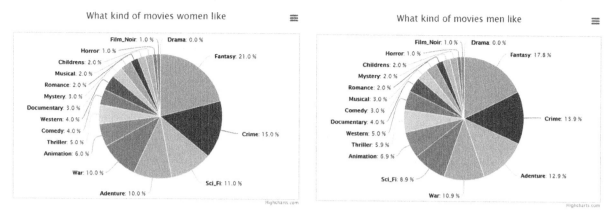

Figure 8-16. *Showing movie genre preferences of men and women*

Now, when you open the modified file in a browser, you will see a pie chart showing men's movie preferences. The two pie charts in Figure 8-16 show the results for both men and women.

8-7. Identifying Flowers by Using Machine Learning

Classification is a common problem in machine learning. There are several *supervised learning algorithms* (http://en.wikipedia.org/wiki/Supervised_learning) for determining the class of a given element. One of the most commonly used supervised learning algorithms is *k*–Nearest Neighbors (*k*-NN). In this example, you will see how to use LINQ to implement *k*-NN () to identify the species of an iris flower.

■ **Note**   See http://en.wikipedia.org/wiki/K-nearest_neighbors_algorithm for an explanation of the *k*–Nearest Neighbors algorithm.

Problem

The iris multivariate dataset (downloadable from http://en.wikipedia.org/wiki/Iris_flower_data_set) contains data about three varieties of iris flowers. The task is to identify the species of the iris flower from the given dataset by using the *k*-NN algorithm. You can download the dataset from http://aima.cs.berkeley.edu/data/iris.csv.

Solution

Enter the following as a new query in LINQPad:

```
//Nearest Neighbor
var trainingSet = File.ReadAllText(@"C:\iris.csv")
                            .Split(new char[]{'\r','\n'},StringSplitOptions.RemoveEmptyEntries)
                .Select ( f => f.Split(','))
                .Skip(1)
                .Select (f =>
```

```
                          new
                           {
                                 SepalLength = Convert.ToDouble( f[0]),
                                 SepalWidth = Convert.ToDouble(f[1]),
                                 PetalLength = Convert.ToDouble(f[2]),
                                 PetalWidth = Convert.ToDouble(f[3]),
                              Name = f[4]
                           })
                    //RandomSubset is a method from MoreLINQ.
                    // So you have to reference that
                    //in LINQPad to use this method. Refer to Chapter 5.
                    .RandomSubset(100);

//Test data
double sepalLength = 5.5;
double sepalWidth  = 2.6;
double petalLength = 4;
double petalWidth = 1.2;

int k = 5;
//Euclidean distance function
Func<double,double,double,double,double,double,double,double,double> Distance =
     (sl1,sl2,sw1,sw2,pl1,pl2,pw1,pw2)  => Math.Sqrt(Math.Pow(sl1-sl2,2)
                                          + Math.Pow(sw1-sw2,2)
                                          + Math.Pow(pl1-pl2,2)
                                          + Math.Pow(pw1-pw2,2));

//Figure out what flower it is.
trainingSet
      .Select (s => -
         new
           {
              Name = s.Name,
              DistanceFromTestData =
              Distance(sepalLength,s.SepalLength,sepalWidth,s.SepalWidth,
              petalLength, s.PetalLength, petalWidth, s.PetalWidth)
           })
      .OrderBy (s => s.DistanceFromTestData )
      //Take the first "k" elements
      .Take(k)
      //Create a lookup with the "Name"
      .ToLookup (s => s.Name)
      //Sort the elements as per the descending order of number of elements in that class
      .OrderByDescending (s => s.Count())
      //Pick the first one--with the highest count
      .First ()
      //Pick its class
      .Key
      .Dump("I think the flower is");
```

This generates the following output:

```
I think the flower is
Iris-versicolor
```

How It Works

At the heart of this query is the Euclidian distance function, represented by the method `Distance`.

The `Distance` method determines the distance between each point in the training set and the point in question—the target point. Then this projected result, along with the distance from the test point, is sorted by the distance, and the first k entries are picked. This projection is then used to create a lookup table with the `Name` property, which is the class or tag of that entry. The count of values for each tag/key in the lookup table is the number of the nearest neighbors whose tag is represented by the associated key. So the key with the highest number of values is probably the best guess for the class/tag of the given test point. I recommend you change the value of k to something big, such as 25, and dump the lookup table in LINQPad to see what's happening visually.

Summary

Congratulations! You've covered a lot of ground in this chapter. The goal of this chapter was to show you how to perform several data processing tasks by using LINQ in a functional way. Along the way, you should have also picked up how to use some of the most frequent LINQ idioms, including `Skip()` followed by `Take()`, `Select()` followed by `ToLookup()` and `ToDictionary()`, and so on. I urge you to experiment with these examples, pose other questions for yourself, and see how you can obtain the answers for those questions by using the techniques you have seen so far in this book.

CHAPTER 9

Interacting with the File System

You can use LINQ as you would a scripting programming language to perform several types of file system analytics operations. For .NET developers, LINQ can be as useful as PowerShell—in fact, sometimes even better, because when using LINQ, developers can still leverage all the other benefits that the host language has to offer (C# in this case).

In this chapter, you will see recipes that illustrate how you can use LINQ to perform various file operations, including the following:

- Comparing CSV files
- Finding the total size of a set of files in a directory
- Simulating some common LINUX commands
- Finding duplicate files, duplicate file names, and zero-length files

9-1. Comparing Two CSV Files

Most file diff utilities work on matching files on a line-by-line basis. However, this scheme doesn't work for CSV file comparison. Two CSV files are the same if their rows are the same—irrespective of the order in which the rows appear. The same is true for columns. If two CSV files have the same columns, even if the columns appear in a different sequence, the files can be considered to have the same column headers.

Problem

Write a general-purpose function to check whether two CSV files are the same or different.

Solution

Listing 9-1 provides an admirably short, yet still complete solution.

Listing 9-1. Determine whether two CSV files are the same.

```
Func<string,IEnumerable<string>> GetHeaders =
    (fileName) => File.ReadAllLines(fileName)
        .First()
        .Split(new char[]{','},StringSplitOptions.None);
```

```
Func<string,IEnumerable<string>> GetBody   =
    (fileName) => File.ReadAllLines(fileName)
        .Skip(1)
        .Where (f => f.Trim().Length!=0);
Func<string,string,bool> IsSameCSV =
    (firstFile,secondFile) =>
        //Match column headers
        GetHeaders(firstFile)
            .All (x => GetHeaders(secondFile).Contains(x))
        //Match the body
        && GetBody(firstFile)
            .All (x => GetBody(secondFile).Contains(x));
```

When this code is run using the two CSV files shown in Figure 9-1, the function IsSameCSV returns true.

	A	B	C
1	Name	Age	Course
2	Jen	21	Ruby
3	Sam	22	C#

1	Name	Age	Course
2	Sam	22	C#
3	Jen	21	Ruby

Figure 9-1. *Showing two same CSV files*

How It Works

Comparing two CSV files requires comparing both the headers and the rows. When the header order and row order are the same, the problem is trivial, but the task becomes more complicated when the headers and/or the rows appear in a different order in one file than in the other. Therefore, when comparing two CSV files, you must make sure that you're comparing only the values in the lines—irrespective of the order in which the lines appear.

■ **Note**   When referring to the order of lines, the code still assumes that the header line is the first line in the file (which is reasonable, because that is part of the CSV specification).

The methods GetHeaders() and GetBody() return the headers (columns) and the body (rows) of the CSV file, respectively. Note that the GetBody() method skips the header line, by calling Skip(1).

IsSameCSV takes two file names as arguments, and returns true if the headers and body of these two CSV files are the same. It compares the headers and bodies separately. The following code compares the headers, but you can see from the "Solution" section that the code to compare the bodies follows exactly the same logic.

```
GetHeaders(firstFile)
    .All (x => GetHeaders(secondFile).Contains(x))
```

9-2. Finding the Total File Size in a Directory

Finding the total size of the files in each of a set of directories and showing that in megabytes or gigabytes is an important component of understanding disk space consumption. To find the total size of a directory, you must recursively calculate the size of all the files in each subdirectory of that directory.

Problem

Write a LINQ script that lists the size (measured in megabytes) of all the directories and files inside a given directory.

Solution

Listing 9-2 shows a complete solution.

Listing 9-2. Calculate the total size of files in a directory.

```
Directory.GetFiles(@"C:\Users\mukhsudi\Downloads","*.*",
                   SearchOption.AllDirectories)
    .Select (d => new FileInfo(d))
    .Select (d => new { Directory = d.DirectoryName,
        FileSize = d.Length} )
    .ToLookup (d => d.Directory )
    .Select (d => new { Directory  = d.Key, TotalSizeInMB =
    Math.Round(d.Select (x => x.FileSize).Sum () /
        Math.Pow(1024.0,2),2)})
    .OrderByDescending (d => d.TotalSizeInMB)
    .Dump();
```

■ **Note**   You will need to edit the path in the following code to be a valid directory on your computer.

How It Works

Calling GetFiles with SearchOption.AllDirectories returns the full name of all the files in all the subdirectories of the specified directory. The operating system represents the size of files in bytes. You can retrieve the file's size from its Length property. Dividing it by 1024 raised to the power of 2 gives you the size of the file in megabytes. Because a directory/folder can contain many files, d.Select(x => x.FileSize) returns a collection of file sizes measured in megabytes. The final call to Sum() finds the total size of the files in the specified directory.

9-3. Cloning LINUX Head and Tail Commands

Listing the first few or the last few lines of a file is a common task. Linux includes the commands head and tail to do this; however, the Windows command prompt doesn't include any equivalent commands. Using LINQ, you can easily brew up your own version of head and tail.

Problem

Write a program to clone the Linux head and tail commands for Windows.

Solution

Listing 9-3 creates clones of the LINUX head and tail commands.

Listing 9-3. Clone the Linux head and tail commands

```
Func<IEnumerable<string>,int,IEnumerable<string>> TakeLast =
    (list, count) => list.Skip(list.Count()-count);
//Cloning head
Func<string,int,IEnumerable<string>> Head = (fileName, lineCount)=>
    File.ReadAllLines(fileName).Take(lineCount);
//Cloning tail
Func<string,int,IEnumerable<string>> Tail = (fileName, lineCount)=>
    TakeLast(File.ReadAllLines(fileName),lineCount);

Head("C:\\conf.txt",4).Dump();
Tail("C:\\conf.txt",4).Dump();
```

Figure 9-2 shows the content of the conf.txt file.

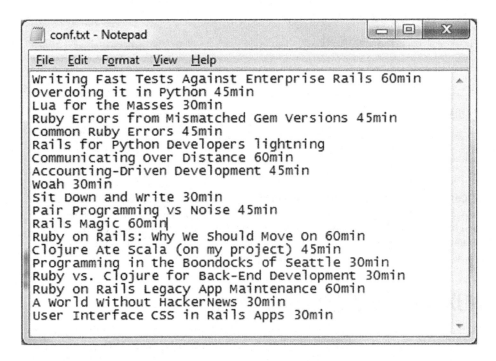

Figure 9-2. *Content of the conf.txt file*

The output of the code is shown in Figure 9-3.

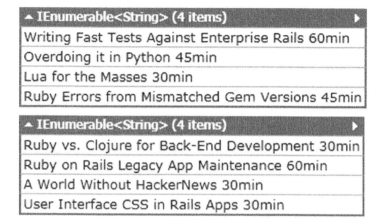

Figure 9-3. *Output of the cloned Linux head and tail commands*

How It Works

Showing the first few lines from a text file is the same as taking the first few lines from the file. The Take() operator, which you've encountered numerous times earlier in this book, works perfectly in this context. On the other hand, showing the last few rows of the file is the same as skipping the total number of lines minus the number of lines you want to show, and then showing those last few lines. The TakeLast() method does exactly that.

9-4. Locating Files with the Same Name (Possible Duplicates)

Sometimes the same file gets copied to multiple destinations. From a file management perspective, it's important to be able to find such duplicate files and delete all the unneeded copies. The first step in doing that is to locate all files that have the same name.

■ **Caution**   Just because two files have the same name doesn't necessarily mean that they're duplicates. For example, two very different software installations might use the file name license.txt. But the content of the two files is likely to be different.

Problem

Write a LINQ script to find files residing in different directories with the same name.

Solution

Listing 9-4 shows how to find identically named files in different directories.

Listing 9-4. Find files of the same name.

```
//Locating duplicate files
Directory.GetFiles(@"C:\Users\mukhsudi\Downloads",
                "*.*",SearchOption.AllDirectories)
            .Select (d => new FileInfo(d))
            .Select (d => new {FileName = d.Name,
                    Directory = d.DirectoryName})
            .ToLookup (d => d.FileName)
            .Where (d => d.Count ()>=2)
            .Dump();
```

How It Works

The code first finds the files and maps their directories. Next, it creates a lookup table using the file name as the key. The result is that for any file whose name is duplicated elsewhere in some other folder/directory, there will be at least two entries for that particular key. These duplicate entries are found by the filter .Where (d => d.Count ()>=2).

9-5. Finding Exact-Duplicate Files

This is an extension of the preceding recipe. Sometimes people rename duplicate files without changing the contents. Unfortunately, that means the same file—but with different names—may exist in several different folders. The code from the previous recipe finds only duplicate names, not duplicate files. This recipe finds exact file duplicates—even if the file names are different.

Problem

Write a LINQ script to find duplicate files with different names, even if the duplicate files reside in different folders.

Solution

This solution, shown in Listing 9-5, complements the previous solution by finding files with identical content, even if the file names are different.

Listing 9-5. Find files with identical content

```
//Locating exact-duplicate files
Directory.GetFiles(@"C:\Program Files"
                ,"*.*",SearchOption.AllDirectories)
        .Where (d => d.EndsWith(".txt"))
        .Select (d => new { FileName = d,
                ContentHash = File.ReadAllText(d).GetHashCode()})
        .ToLookup (d => d.ContentHash)
        .Where (d => d.Count ()>=2)
        .Dump();
```

■ **Note**   The code below will raise an error if you do not have sufficient rights to access all the files in the specified directory.

How It Works

Locating exact-duplicate files is an expensive process, because to determine whether the content of two files is identical, you need to read the files, create a hashcode, and then compare hashcodes. Unlike the previous example, this example creates the lookup table using the hashcodes of the files as the lookup table key. If the result contains two or more elements for any given hashcode key, then those files are exact duplicates.

9-6. Organizing Downloads Automatically

If you're like me, you probably download a lot of files—and then forget about them. Over time, it becomes a pain to organize all these files in proper directories. Using a LINQ script, you can bring order to this chaos.

Problem

The problem here is to manage downloaded files by placing them in specific directories organized by file type and keyword.

Solution

Listing 9-6 organizes downloaded files by keyword and file type, storing them in appropriate directories.

Listing 9-6. Programmatically organize downloaded files.

```
string[] keywords = {"Roslyn","Rx","LINQ","F#"};
string[] videoFormats = {".mp4",".mpg",".mpeg",".flv"};
string[] slides = {".pptx",".ppt"};
string[] articles = {".pdf",".doc",".docx"};
string[] blogs = {".html",".htm"};

Directory.GetFiles(@"C:\Users\mukhsudi\Downloads")
.ToLookup (d => keywords.FirstOrDefault(x => d.Contains(x)))
.Where (d => d.Key != null )
.Select (d =>
         new
           {
             Key = d.Key,
             //Find all the videos for the given keyword
             Videos = d.Where (x => videoFormats
                              .Any (f => x.EndsWith(f))),
             //Find all the articles
              Articles = d.Where (x => articles
                               .Any (f => x.EndsWith(f)))
```

```
        //I omitted Slides and Blogs because those will be similar.

            })
.ToList()
.ForEach(z =>
        {
                Directory.CreateDirectory(z.Key + " Videos");
                z.Videos
                 .ToList()
                .ForEach(f =>
                 File.Copy(f,Path.Combine(z.Key + " Videos",
                            new FileInfo(f).Name)));
                Directory.CreateDirectory(z.Key + " Articles");
                z.Articles.ToList().ForEach(f =>
                File.Copy(f,Path.Combine(z.Key + " Articles",
                            new FileInfo(f).Name)));
});
```

How It Works

At the heart of this solution are the lists of keywords that determine how you want to classify your files. Each list contains several types of files that you want to store in separate directories. In this case, the file type lists are as follows:

```
string[] videoFormats = {".mp4",".mpg",".mpeg",".flv"};
string[] slides = {".pptx",".ppt"};
string[] articles = {".pdf",".doc",".docx"};
string[] blogs = {".html",".htm"};
```

These arrays determine the various file types in each different category. For example, if a file's extension is either pptx or ppt, it's a presentation file. I want to keep these files in a folder called XYZ Slides, where XYZ is a placeholder for the keywords defined in the first line—in this case, Roslyn, C#, LINQ and F#. The goal is that if the file name contains one of the keywords, for example, LINQ, and has a .pptx extension, then that file will be copied into a LINQ Slides folder. The idea is the same for all the other keywords and for all the other extensions.

The first call to ToLookup() tries to find matching keywords from the files. It stores the keywords and the file names in a lookup table. For file names that don't contain any of the specified keywords, the key returned is null. The next Where() call filters out those files. Finally, the Select() call projects the list of the files with the file name—the videos and articles associated with the current keyword.

At the end, the call to ForEach copies all the files into their appropriate destination folders.

9-7. Finding Files Modified Last Week

While doing forensic analysis on a file system, you often need to know when a file was last accessed. Using LINQ and the FileSystem APIs, it's easy to find all files modified within the last week.

Problem

Find all files in a directory that were modified during the past week.

Solution

Listing 9-7 finds all the files modified within the previous week.

Listing 9-7. Find modified files within a date/time range

```
Directory.GetFiles(@"C:\Program Files","*.*",SearchOption.AllDirectories)
            .Select (d => new FileInfo(d))
            .OrderByDescending (d => d.LastWriteTime)
            .Select (d => new {Name = d.FullName ,
                   LastModifiedTime = d.LastWriteTime})
            .Where (d => d.LastModifiedTime.AddDays(7)
                       .CompareTo(DateTime.Today)>=0 )
            .Dump("Files modified during last week");
```

■ **Note**   The code below will raise an error if you do not have sufficient rights to access all the files in the specified directory.

How It Works

Whenever a file is modified, the last write time changes. Thus you can use the last write time to determine when a file was last changed. Knowing that, you can find all files where the last write time is within seven days of the current date, using the filter call shown here:

```
.Where (d => d.LastModifiedTime.AddDays(7)
                       .CompareTo(DateTime.Today)>=0 )
```

9-8. Locating Dead Files (Files with Zero Bytes)

A *dead file* is a file that has nothing in it. These files are far more common than you might think in your file system.

Problem

Locate dead files in your file system.

Solution

This short solution, shown in Listing 9-8, finds dead files in a specified directory and all its subdirectories.

Listing 9-8. Find zero-length files in a directory tree

```
Directory.GetFiles(@"C:\Program Files","*.*",SearchOption.AllDirectories)
        .Select (d => new FileInfo(d))
        .Where (d => d.Length == 0)
        .Dump("Dead Files");
```

■ **Note**   The code below will raise an error if you do not have sufficient rights to access all the files in the specified directory.

How It Works

Files with nothing in them are generally not useful. You can find these files by checking whether the Length property of the file is zero. GetFiles() returns a string array containing the names of the files, and then Select() projects this list as an IEnumerable of FileInfo.

APPENDIX A

Lean LINQ Tips

LINQ allows users to query any data source in a unified way. However, even with the LINQ standard query operators, used to create these queries, it's easy to misuse these operators unless you have a solid understanding of how they work internally. Such misuse leads to inefficient queries that are slower—in some cases much slower—than the equivalent properly tuned query.

For example, .NET 4.0 offers implicit typing, in which the compiler figures out the intended data type of a query result at runtime. That's convenient, so developers tend to be comfortable projecting the result to a strongly typed collection like List<T> via the projection operators ToList() and such. But such conversions and projections are computationally expensive and offer little benefit. People may also use the convenient range methods such as ForEach() that List<T>) exposes. Again, these provide no benefits; in fact, they simply contribute to the performance issues.

This appendix contains a list of tips (or in some cases "micro-tips," if you will) that you can use to tune your queries to yield results faster.

Tip 1

Avoid projection such as ToList() or ToArray(), when possible They make the program slow.

Explanation

ToList(), and ToArray() project a list to a newly created list. These projections also force the list values to be evaluated, which is not helpful because that negates the benefits of lazy evaluation and deferred execution that LINQ offers.

Tip 2

Combine multiple Where clauses into a single Where clause unless they are done on separate lists.

Explanation

For each Where clause, you must loop through the collection once. Therefore, the looping process will occur as many times as there are Where loops on any given list. So while refactoring multiple nested if statements together in a Where clause, try putting all of the clauses together.

Tip 3

Use the `TrueForAll()` method available on the `IList<T>` implementation instead of `All()`.

Explanation

For long-running operations and cross-collection membership checks, `All<T>()` offers worse performance than `TrueForAll`. `TrueForAll()` uses a `for` loop, whereas `All<T>()` uses a `foreach` loop.

Tip 4

Use `OrderBy()` and `OrderByDescending()` wherever you can instead of the native `Sort()` implementations for lists.

Explanation

To use `Sort()`, you have to project the collection as a `List<T>()`. Moreover, `Sort()` is an in-place implementation. This way, using `Sort()` the original collection will be corrupted.

Tip 5

Avoid membership lookup using `Contains()` on any native container within lambda expressions.

Explanation

With the exception of `HashSet<T>`, collections are not optimized for membership lookup. Therefore, using `Contains()` inside a lambda means it will have to loop over the entire collection to find the membership status. This makes the query slower.

Tip 6

Use public property `Count` in the Boolean expression list `Object.Count > 0` instead of `Any()`.

Explanation

The `Count` property is updated whenever a new entry gets added to the collection. Therefore, using `Count > 0` to determine whether the collection contains any elements is faster than calling `Any()`, which has to loop through the collection and update a local variable with the count, as long as the collection remains iterable. Thus, `Any()` is slower.

Tip 7

Avoid using ElementAt() on containers that support native array-based indexing.

Explanation

For collections that aren't IList based, ElementAt() loops through the collection to find the element at the specified index, which takes time. So when you need to repeatedly use indexing over the collection, projecting it to an array by using ToArray() once is more efficient than using ElementAt().

Tip 8

Don't use ElementAt() on dictionaries. It's not guaranteed to return what you think it should.

Explanation

Dictionaries are implemented by using binary search trees, which by nature are nonlinear data structures. So, by default, integer indexing is not available for dictionaries. In general, if you need integer indexing over a dictionary, it's time to rethink the design. For example, you might be better off using a List<KeyValuePair<T,U>> type.

Tip 9

Prefer exception handling over ElementAtOrDefault(), FirstOrDefault(), or SingleOrDefault().

Explanation

ElementAtOrDefault() and the other methods in this tip throw exceptions when no element is found at the specified index or when no element is found that matches the given criterion. So don't rely on these methods to deal with exceptions—it won't happen. The default versions give you the default values of the type of the collection.

Tip 10

For IList-based containers that support native indexing, don't use First() or Last(). Instead, use [0] and [Count-1].

Explanation

Integer indexing over an array or an IList implementation is the fastest performance you can get in terms of indexing over a generic collection in .NET. In contrast, Last() loops through the entire collection as long as it remains iterable. However, whenever a new element is added to a collection, the Count property gets updated. Thus Count - 1 gets evaluated in constant time, regardless of the size of the collection. Therefore, retrieving the last element using [Count - 1] is usually faster than using Last(). The exception is when you are using the overload of Last() that takes a predicate. In that case, the execution time is essentially the same.

Tip 11

Use IEnumerable<T> as much as possible in public APIs.

Explanation

Because the entire LINQ API is based on the IEnumerable<T> type, if you take advantage of that by exposing IEnumerable<T> in your public APIs, consumers of your API can immediately take full advantage of everything that LINQ has to offer—most important, deferred execution. In LINQ, unless you're using a projection operator (such as ToList() and so forth), a query doesn't get executed immediately. However, when you expose strongly typed collections, any queries performed against your collections must be evaluated immediately, which leads to slower performance.

Tip 12

Consider using home-grown mathematical routines over Sum(), and Average(). Typically, these are about three times slower than their loop-based cousins.

Explanation

Sum(), and Average() use foreach loops internally. In addition, they check for null references. These are slower than a home-grown solution that uses a straight for loop. When you need to find a sum or average, particularly repeatedly, resist the temptation to use the built-in methods and write your own, using a for loop.

Tip 13

Create your own ForEach(Action<T>) that can work on an IEnumerable<T> instance.

Explanation

By doing that, you save the time required to convert the collection to an IList<T> implementation. If you recall, you can use the ForEach operator from MoreLINQ, as discussed in Chapter 5.

Tip 14

Prefer Select<T>() over Cast<T>().

Explanation

Projecting is essentially casting with some sidebars to hold on to when things go wrong (think "exceptions"). Cast<T> throws an exception when it can't cast the collection to the type specified. However, if you use Select<T>(), you gain complete control on how the casting happens and what to do when an exception occurs.

Tip 15

For any container that supports a public `Count` property, prefer `<instance of container>.Count == 0` over `Any()`.

Explanation

As explained in earlier tips, calling the `Count` property is a constant-time operation, whereas `Any()` iterates over the collection. Thus the first version is much faster.

Tip 16

Don't use `Aggregate` over a long list. Use a straight `for` loop instead.

Explanation

At each step, `Aggregate` has to determine whether it's reached the edge of the collection. This makes it slower than a straight `for` loop, where programmers are responsible for handling the number of elements and edge conditions.

Tip 17

Don't use `FirstOrDefault` in a loop. It can be terribly slow when called repeatedly (such as in a loop).

Explanation

`FirstOrDefault` loops from the beginning to the end to find an element that matches a specified predicate condition. Therefore, when placed inside a loop, it results in quadratic time increases.

APPENDIX B

███

Taming Streaming Data with Rx.NET

Developers now have access to more streaming data than ever before. Much of this data originates from sensors connected to the Internet. These sensors continually post the data they collect.

For example, a high-profile gym asks users to swipe their smart membership cards at an RFID reader placed at the entrance. As soon as members do this, an event fires (assume the name of the event is `MemberEnteredGym`). Subscribers can register for the event, and are notified immediately. However, that's nothing new. What's new is that this event will be fired every time a member swipes his or her card. And there may be thousands or millions of members around the world, each generating an event each time they enter their gym. Suddenly, you have a pool of events, or an *event stream*.

There are two inherent characteristics of a .NET event. First, events don't offer composability. If you have a stream of `MemberEnteredGym` events and you want to filter that stream for unauthenticated or fraudulent accesses, your only option is to write the code inside the event handler of a particular subscriber. Unfortunately, that means creating composable solutions using LINQ is not possible.

Moreover, .NET events aren't first-class citizens in the .NET ecosystem. For example, you can pass an integer around to functions. You can even pass a function around to other functions (provided you declared it with `Func<>` as a variable). But you can't pass around a .NET event, such as a `MouseMove` event from a Windows Forms class.

When you move your mouse over a form, the form generates `MouseMove` events. However, if you create a traditional event, you can't pass around `MouseMove` event arguments that hold data about where the mouse has been so far.

Rx.NET is a framework that offers the ability to translate such events to an `Observable` collection of event arguments that interested parties can subscribe to. Rx.NET piggybanks on the composable nature of LINQ and is built on a push-based architecture rather than the pull-based concepts of `IEnumerable`.

Push and pull have an excellent real-life use-case analogy these days. For example, assume you go to a busy restaurant for your Sunday brunch. You place your order and then wait for your meal to appear. After a while, when your order still hasn't shown up, you get a little restless. Perhaps you inquire about its status at the counter or ask your waiter. Asking is the same as polling, or *pulling*. On the other hand, some restaurants now give their customers an RFID-enabled vibrator when they place their orders. When the order is ready for pickup, the device receives a signal. That way, users know that their order is ready for pickup. This is a *pushing* scheme. The source (in this case the restaurant) is notifying the targets (the people who placed orders).

Figure B-1 captures this expression nicely in general terms.

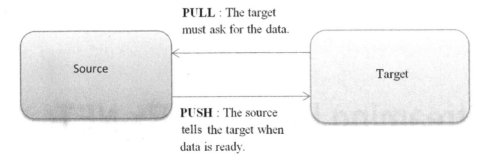

Figure B-1. *The intent of push and pull operations in a .NET eventing context*

In the Interactive model, shown in Figure B-2, the consumers of the enumerations ask for the next element available by calling MoveNext() on the iterator. However, in the reactive world, the source (also known as the *Observable*) returns the value as it is generated by calling OnNext(). The Reactive model also has two more methods, called OnError() and OnCompleted(). These methods fire when an error occurs (like exceptions) or when the sequence doesn't have any more elements.

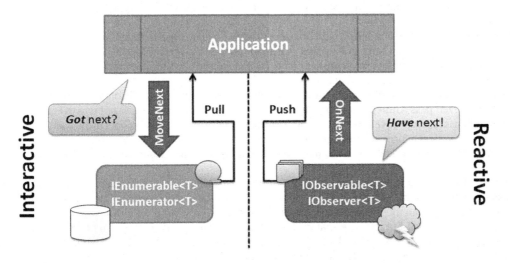

Figure B-2. *Bart De Smet's depiction of the Interactive and Reactive paradigm*

Figure B-3 shows a comparison between using IObserver and IEnumerator.

```
...public interface IEnumerator          public interface IObserver<in T>
{                                         {
    ...object Current { get; }                ...void OnCompleted();
                                              ...void OnError(Exception error);
    ...bool MoveNext();                       ...void OnNext(T value);
    ...void Reset();                      }
}
```

Figure B-3. *Side-by-side comparison of the main interfaces of Reactive and Interactive paradigm*

A Brief Explanation of the Interfaces

IEnumerator is the basis of a pull-based world, where client code polls for the next element by calling the enumerator's MoveNext() method. Any of three conditions can occur during this activity. First, if everything works as expected, the client code will obtain the next element T after MoveNext(), by evaluating Current. Second, there may be no more items in the collection to be iterated. This is same as successful completion of the iteration, and the code must handle that condition. Third, an error can occur during this process—again, the client code must handle that condition.

Put another way, calling MoveNext can result in a T, a void signaling completion, or an Exception signaling an error. These three situations are mirrored in a push-based world by the OnNext(), OnCompleted(), and OnError() methods of the IObserver<> interface. There is a good video by Bart De Smet at http://channel9.msdn.com/Shows/Going+Deep/Bart-De-Smet-Observations-on-IQbservable-The-Dual-of-IQueryable that explains these concepts. I recommend you watch that video.

In the rest of this chapter, you'll see how to use Rx.NET to tame oncoming event streams. The Observable class has a number of extension methods for processing the event stream. Some are ported from the IEnumerable class but have been made usable for Observables as extension methods. For example, Range() is one such extension method. Some of these methods are also explained in this chapter.

Getting Rx.NET

You can download Rx.NET from http://msdn.microsoft.com/en-in/data/gg577610.

Rx.NET is being made available for several platforms, including Windows Phone.

Using Rx.NET in LINQPad

LINQPad is the one of the coolest tools out there for .NET developers. We are all grateful to Joseph Albahari for creating it. One special LINQPad feature can even help you understand Rx.NET better.

To configure LINQPad to use Rx.NET, you need to add references for the following assemblies:

- System.Reactive.Core.dll

- System.Reactive.Interfaces.dll

- System.Reactive.Linq.dll

■ **Note** Every example in this chapter uses version 2.2.5 of all these assemblies. By the time this book is published, there may be another stable version available—-but it's also possible that some of the methods I've used might be deprecated. So to follow the examples, I recommend getting version 2.2.5. For your own experiments, you should download any more recent versions.

Press F4 in LINQPad and you'll see the dialog box to add the DLLs. After adding them, the list should look like Figure B-4. Make sure to click the Set as Default for New Queries button.

Figure B-4. *The list of Rx.NET references in LINQPad*

This will make sure that you get Rx.NET extension methods and classes on all the new LINQPad tabs that you open. Next, click the Additional Namespace Imports tab and add the following namespaces, as shown in Figure B-5.

Figure B-5. *Showing additional namespaces to include for using Rx.NET*

Click the Set as Default for New Queries" button in this tab as well.

Finally, click OK to save your settings and exit.

Now that you are ready to use LINQPad with Rx.NET, it's a good time to mention the special feature that LINQPad offers. You can use LINQPad's Dump() method to dump Observables to the output. As long as they are being evaluated, the Dump() result header will remain green; however, when the evaluation completes—in other words, when the Observable raises the OnCompleted() event—the Dump() result header turns blue (green and blue are LINQPad's default colors). I found this transition to be extremely helpful while running Rx.NET queries.

Also, you can terminate evaluation of any long-running Observable by pressing Ctrl+Shift+F5. This message also appears at the bottom right of LINQPad.

Now use the following query to make sure you are ready to run Rx queries in LINQPad.

Open a new LINQPad window and paste in the following query. Change the Language drop-down value to C# Statements.

```
Observable.Interval(TimeSpan.FromSeconds(1))
        .Take(10)
        .Dump("Slow stream");

Observable.Interval(TimeSpan.FromSeconds(0.5))
        .Take(10)
        .Dump("Fast stream");
```

This should generate the outputs shown in Figure B-6. I've shown only three here, all captured at different times: the first dump, one in the middle, and one at the end. The operation is best captured through a video, so I recorded my result and posted it at https://www.youtube.com/watch?v=mYinKlHET5s&feature=youtu.be.

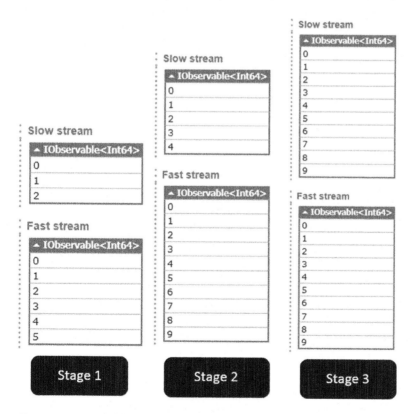

Figure B-6. *Special feature of LINQPad*

Creating Observables and Subscribing

The Observable class offers several extension methods to create Observables. It's unlikely that you would ever need to implement the interfaces to create Observables in your own class.

Here are some of the extension methods used most frequently to generate Observables:

- Range
- Repeat
- Never
- Throw (throws an Exception)
- Interval
- Generate
- ToObservable

The following sections describe how to use these methods to generate and subscribe to Observables.

Range

The Range() method creates an Observable with values in the given range. This is conceptually the same as creating a range with an Enumerable class.

■ **Note**   Set the Language drop-down to C# Statement for all the code in this chapter unless instructed otherwise.

Add the following code in a new LINQPad tab:

```
var range  = Observable.Range(1,10);
range.Take(4).Dump();
```

When you run the query, it generates the output shown in Figure B-7.

▲ IObservable<Int32>
1
2
3
4

Figure B-7. *Showing first four values of the Observable collection created with Range()*

Notice that the type of the output is IObservable<int>.

Repeat

The Repeat method does just what you probably expect—it repeats the given value. For example, if you want an infinite Observable of the value 42, you can write it like this:

```
Observable.Repeat(42).Dump();
```

Because this will run as long as you want it to, you need to resort to a deferred execution model, which you can do by plugging a Take() call at the end, like this:

```
Observable.Repeat(42).Take(10).Dump();
```

This will return an Observable with 42 repeated ten times.

Never

The Never method is almost the same as the Enumerable.Empty method. Empty produces an empty Enumerable, while Never produces an empty Observable. It will never produce any value. Never can't determine the type of the Observable, so you must provide the value as a generic type, as shown here:

```
Observable.Never<int>().Dump();
```

Interval

The Interval() method lets you create an Observable that produces an element at a given frequency. You can provide the frequency as a Timespan. Here's an example:

```
var times = Observable.Interval(TimeSpan.FromSeconds(2)).Take(10);
times.Dump();
```

This generates ten values—one every 2 seconds.

Generate

Using Generate, you can generate arbitrary Observable collections. The method takes four arguments:

- A seed value.
- A functor that returns a Boolean and determines how long the Observable should run. Generate continues to generate data as long as this returns true.
- A delegate that tells Generate how to update the seed value to the next one.
- A projection strategy—how you want to project the data.

Here is an example showing how to use Generate to generate Fibonacci numbers:

```
KeyValuePair<int,int> seed = new KeyValuePair<int,int>(0,1);

Observable.Generate(
        //Start with this seed value
        seed
        // Run it eternally
        ,x=>true
        //Here is how to step through to go to the next one
        ,x => new KeyValuePair<int,int>(x.Value,x.Key+x.Value)
        //Return the "Key" of the key value pair.
        ,x => x.Key)
    .Take(10)
    .Dump("First 10 Fibonacci numbers");
```

This is one of the best implementations of generating Fibonacci numbers because it uses only one KeyValuePair to store the last-calculated Fibonacci number, which is a very effective way to implement memoization. Observables don't have to remember the values that have been generated so far.

You can see the output in Figure B-8.

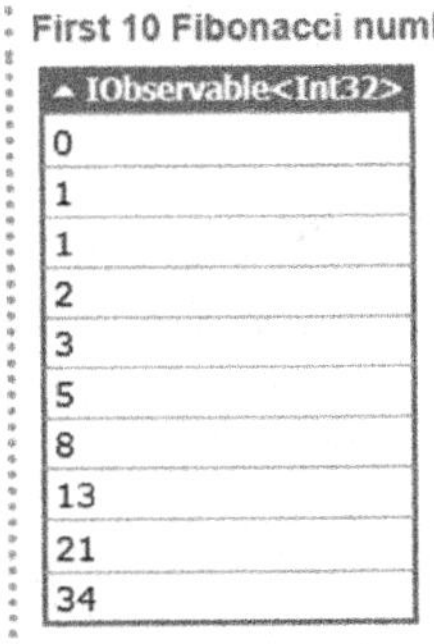

First 10 Fibonacci numbers

▲ IObservable<Int32>
0
1
1
2
3
5
8
13
21
34

Figure B-8. *Fibonacci numbers calculated using the Generate method*

An earlier version of Rx.NET had a member called GenerateWithTime that could produce values at a given frequency supplied in the form of a TimeSpan. However that method is no longer available. You can still generate values at a certain frequency. Just replace the line

```
x => x.Key
```

with

```
,x => {Thread.Sleep(TimeSpan.FromMilliseconds(500));return x.Key;})
```

Now you have an Observable that churns out the next Fibonacci number every half a second. Such techniques can be extremely useful in simulations. For example, suppose you were writing a car-parking simulation and the model you are using assumes that every half-second the number of cars appearing is the same as the next Fibonacci number.

ToObservable

ToObservable converts Enumerables to Observables. This method comes in very handy while trying to write unit tests for Observables.

Here's a simple example that takes an array of integers and returns the corresponding Observable:

```
(new int[]{1,2,3}).ToObservable().Dump();
```

Creating Observables from .NET Events

Most of the time in real-life applications, your Observable collections are generated from .NET events. To convert a .NET event to an event stream, you can use the Observable.FromEventPattern method.

Open a new LINQPad window and add the following code:

```
Form myForm = new Form();
 myForm.Show();
 var moves = Observable.FromEventPattern<MouseEventArgs>
                        (myForm,"MouseMove")
                        .Select( p => p.EventArgs.Location);

 var bisector = moves.Where(p => p.X == p.Y);
 bisector.Dump("You are on the bisector at");
```

■ **Note**   To run this code, you need to add System.Windows.Forms.dll to the references and then click Additional Namespaces. Click the Pick from Assemblies link, then click System.Windows.Forms.dll and select System.Windows.Forms from the Namespaces list.

Running the code creates a Windows form. When you move your mouse over the form, LINQPad will show the co-ordinates of the mouse pointer whenever it crosses the form's *bisector*—a slanted line running from upper left to bottom right.

Figure B-9 shows some typical output.

You are on the bisector at

IObservable<Point>		
IsEmpty	**X ≡**	**Y ≡**
False	94	94
False	83	83
False	65	65
False	68	68

Figure B-9. *Points where the mouse crossed the form's bisector*

Again, this is an example best shown through video. I recorded my experiment with LINQPad for this example and posted it at https://www.youtube.com/watch?v=4FTkRF7aYLo. If you're not running the example, the video will be helpful. Observables are generated, so there is a very real sense of time involved, and the concepts are difficult to grasp solely by reading.

Subscribe

The Subscribe method subscribes to an event. Subscribe requires at least one parameter to print the result generated from the Observable collection. You will find examples of this method used later in this chapter.

Combining Observable Collections

In real-life applications, you often get Observable collections from more than one source and need to combine them to get a single Observable collection. Fortunately, there are several useful extension methods to do just that:

- Concat
- Merge
- Amb
- Zip

Concat

Concat plugs in two or more Observables, one *after* the other.

The image in Figure B-10 is a marble diagram showing how Concat works. A marble diagram shows the values from several Observables as colored marbles.

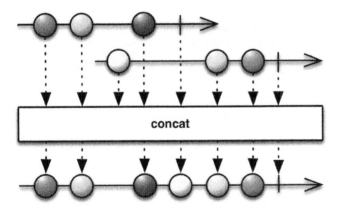

Figure B-10. *Marble digram for Concat*

Paste the following code into LINQPad to see how Concat works:

```
var range1 = Observable.Range(11,5).Select(x => (long)x);
var inte1 = Observable.Interval(TimeSpan.FromSeconds(.5)).Take(5);

range1.Concat(inte1).Dump();
```

Running this code produces the output shown in Figure B-11

▲ IObservable<Int64>
11
12
13
14
15
0
1
2
3
4

Figure B-11. *A Concat result.*

Merge

The Merge method combines two Observable collections as depicted in the marble diagram in Figure B-12 The X in the first line represents an exception; in other words, the first Observable collection threw an exception.

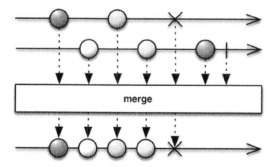

Figure B-12. *Marble diagram for the Merge method*

Add the following code to LINQPad in a new tab and change the Language drop-down to C# Program.

```
void Main()
{
        var slow = GetSomeTokens().ToObservable();
        var fast = GetSomeTokensFast().ToObservable();
        Observable.Merge(slow,fast).Dump();
}
public IEnumerable<string> GetSomeTokensFast()
{
        string[] names = {"A","B","C","D","E","F","G"};
        for(int i = 0;i<names.Length;i++)
        {
                Thread.Sleep(new Random().Next(500));
                yield return names[i];
        }
}


public IEnumerable<string> GetSomeTokens()
{
        string[] names = {"Af","fB","fD","fE","fF","fG"};
        for(int i = 0;i<names.Length;i++)
        {
                Thread.Sleep(new Random().Next(1000));
                yield return names[i];
        }
}
```

This generates the output you would expect, as shown in Figure B-13.

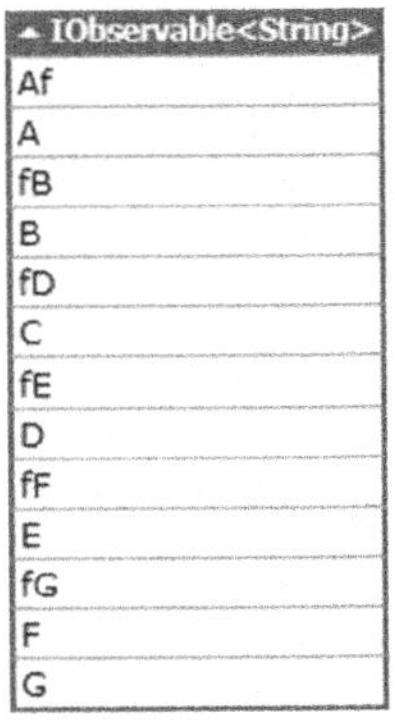

▲ IObservable<String>
Af
A
fB
B
fD
C
fE
D
fF
E
fG
F
G

Figure B-13. *The result of Merge*

Amb

The Amb method lets you pick the Observable that reacts faster and completely ignores the other sources. Amb is short for *ambiguous*. As shown in Figure B-14, this method can generate a different result each time it is used.

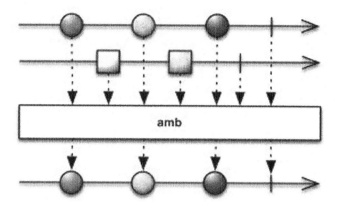

Figure B-14. *Marble diagram for Amb*

To explore how Amb works, just change the method in the preceding example from Merge to Amb. You will get the output shown in Figure B-15.

▲ IObservable<String>
Af
fB
fD
fE
fF
fG

Figure B-15. *The output from* Amb()

Zip

The Zip() method works the same as it does for Enumerables. The example used for Amb and Merge is just as useful for showing how Zip works. Just change the call in the first line to use Zip rather than Merge or Amb:

```
Observable.Zip(slow,fast).Dump();
```

Note that the Zip operation yields a value at each index only after the slowest Observable is done churning out the values.

Zip generates the output shown in Figure B-16.

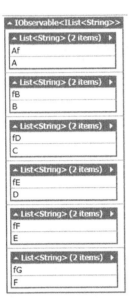

Figure B-16. *The result of Zip applied on two* Observables

Here is a common scenario in which you might want to use Zip. Let's say you have two servers that are sending e-book prices. You want to show readers the cheapest price. Typically, you would have to wait until both servers have sent all the data, so it's quite difficult to do traditionally.

Here's a simulation of this example. Paste the following code into LINQPad as a new C# statement query:

```
var ebookPricesOne = Observable.Interval(TimeSpan.FromSeconds(1))
                    .Select( x => new Random().NextDouble()*10)
                    .Take(4);
var ebookPricesTwo = Observable.Interval(TimeSpan.FromSeconds(.5))
                    .Select( x => new Random().NextDouble()*10)
                    .Take(4);

ebookPricesOne.Dump("First Service");
ebookPricesTwo.Dump("Second Service");

Observable.Zip(ebookPricesOne, ebookPricesTwo)
        .Select(x => x.First() <= x.Last ( )? x.First ():x.Last ( ))
        .Dump("Cheapest e-book prices");
```

Running this code will produce a result similar to that shown in Figure B-17. Every time you run it, the code generates a different output, because it works with random numbers. However the overall effect remains same.

First Service

▲ IObservable<Double>
0.13
7.53
4.92
2.31

Second Service

▲ IObservable<Double>
3.23
3.72
4.21
9.48

Cheapest e-book prices

▲ IObservable<Double>
0.13
3.72
4.21
2.31

Figure B-17. *The result of Zip() to find out the cheapest e-book price*

Partitioning Observables

Streaming data is generally serviced with multiple servers. However, generating data load for all these servers can be difficult. In other words, generating the right amount of data for each buffer for sending it to the assigned server can be difficult. Buffer and Window are the two functions that help make this easy. They are conceptually similar, but Buffer returns an IObservable<IList<T>> while Window returns an IObservable<IObservable<T>>.

Window

Window returns several windows with nonoverlapping values from the source collection:

```
var times = Observable.Interval(TimeSpan.FromSeconds(2))
                      .Take(10);
times.Window(2).Dump();
```

The output of this code is shown in Figure B-18.

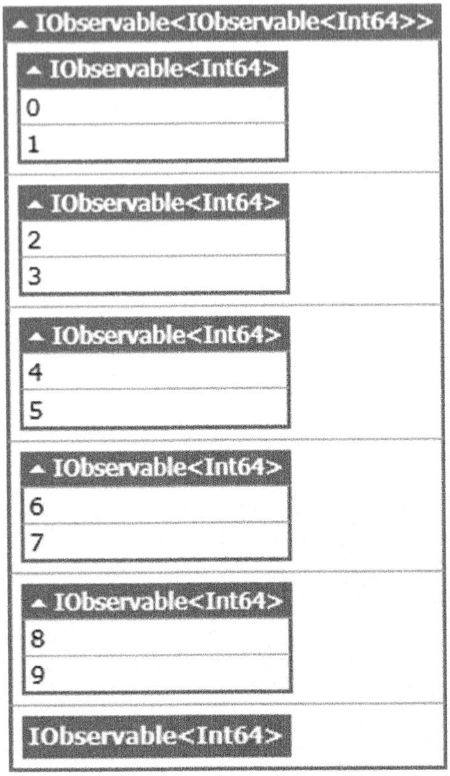

Figure B-18. *The result of Window*

As you can see, these sliced/buffered data values can now be passed to several servers for further processing.

Time-Tagging Observables

Sometimes it is important to know the timestamp of data as it arrives in the form of an Observable. Also it is important to know how long it took for the generator sending the Observable to generate each set of values. The methods described in the following sections help to do that.

Timestamp

The Timestamp method adds a timestamp for each generated value:

```
var slow = Observable.Interval(TimeSpan.FromSeconds(2)).Take(10);
slow
    .Timestamp()//Adds a timestamp value for each generated value
    .Dump();
```

This code generates the output shown in Figure B-19.

▲ IObservable<Timestamped<Int64>>	
Value ≡	Timestamp
0	10/20/2014 4:19:37 PM +00:00
1	10/20/2014 4:19:39 PM +00:00
2	10/20/2014 4:19:41 PM +00:00
3	10/20/2014 4:19:43 PM +00:00
4	10/20/2014 4:19:45 PM +00:00
5	10/20/2014 4:19:47 PM +00:00
6	10/20/2014 4:19:49 PM +00:00
7	10/20/2014 4:19:51 PM +00:00
8	10/20/2014 4:19:53 PM +00:00
9	10/20/2014 4:19:55 PM +00:00

Figure B-19. *The values and their associated timestamps*

TimeInterval

TimeInterval shows the time between two generated values in an Observable.

The example from the Timestamp section works fine—just change the method call to TimeInterval. The output I got is shown in Figure B-20; your results will be different.

▲ IObservable<TimeInterval<Int64>>	
Value ≡	Interval
0	00:00:02.0088604
1	00:00:02.0087423
2	00:00:02.0095363
3	00:00:02.0103909
4	00:00:02.0196927
5	00:00:02.0096906
6	00:00:02.0101853
7	00:00:02.0097747
8	00:00:02.0200047
9	00:00:02.0103498

Figure B-20. *Showing results of TimeInterval*

These two methods can be handy. Imagine that you are using Rx.NET for processing orders that are being received from a website and you see a surge of orders coming in a surprisingly fast time interval. That's a sign of a fraudulent transaction. Maybe your customer's account is compromised. A technology called *anomaly detection*, in simple terms, finds the "odd one out." Using the output from Figure B-20, you can run anomaly detection to find fraudulent transactions or faulty products.

Rx.NET Showcase

Rx can be used for a whole array of problems where the data is streaming. It is being made available on several frameworks; for example, Windows Phone 7.1 has it.

This section contains three examples that I think capture the beauty and power that Rx brings to event-stream processing.

Creating a Signature Capture Screen

This example is a small Windows application for capturing signatures. Here's the scenario. Courier companies want to get digital signatures from their customers, who—in the real world—use a stylus to write on a screen. This simulation replaces the stylus with the mouse for convenience.

Create a new LINQPad tab and add the following code:

```
Form sigCapture = new Form();
List<System.Drawing.Point> points = new List<System.Drawing.Point>();
bool draw = false;
sigCapture.Show();
var moves = Observable.FromEventPattern<MouseEventArgs>
                    (sigCapture,"MouseMove")
                    .Select(x => x.EventArgs);
var mouseDowns = Observable.FromEventPattern<MouseEventArgs>
                    (sigCapture,"MouseDown")
                    .Select(x => x.EventArgs);
var mouseUps = Observable.FromEventPattern<MouseEventArgs>
                    (sigCapture,"MouseUp")
                    .Select(x => x.EventArgs);
mouseDowns.Subscribe( x => { draw = true; });
mouseUps.Subscribe( x => { draw = false; });
moves.Subscribe(p =>
        {
                points.Add(p.Location);
                if(points.Count >= 2 && draw)
                {
                        sigCapture.CreateGraphics()
                                .DrawLine(new System.Drawing.Pen(
                                    System.Drawing.Color.Purple,5.7f),
                        points[points.Count - 2],
                        points[points.Count - 1]);
                }
        });
```

This code creates a Windows form that you can draw on with the mouse. When you click the form, the flag Draw becomes true, and subsequent mouse movements draw a line. The video at https://www.youtube.com/watch?v=KV4r_gyg424 shows me signing the form. That's not my official signature! For an exercise, try adding functionality to save the signature and redraw it.

The code is simple. As the user moves the mouse over the form, the event stream generates data; and thus the mouse points get added to the points collection. As soon as there are two or more points in the points collection, the example uses GDI to draw a line between the last two points collected. This example uses GDI to draw a line.

However, you don't always want to draw a line whenever the user moves the mouse. There has to be a notion of "pen down" or "pen up." The draw flag fulfills that purpose. On MouseDown, the flag is set to true, and on MouseUp it's set to false. That way, whenever the users presses the mouse button and moves it, the example draws a line (or rather, multiple lines, one after the other), much like Microsoft Paint.

Live File System Watcher

By watching events on file systems, a system administrator can create a live dashboard that reflects file events happening in that directory.

For example let's say you want to know whenever a file is created, deleted, changed, or renamed in a given directory. Using Rx, you can do this very easily.

Here is the complete code. Paste this in LINQPad and set the Language drop-down to C# Statements. Provide the path to a folder that you want to monitor.

```
System.IO.FileSystemWatcher w = new
//Set the folder you want to monitor.
System.IO.FileSystemWatcher("C:\\Apress");

//start the File System Watcher to watch events
w.EnableRaisingEvents = true;
//Find the files that have been created
var fileCreated = Observable
    .FromEventPattern<FileSystemEventArgs>(w, "Created")
    .Select(z =>
            {
              var file = new FileInfo(z.EventArgs.FullPath);
              return new
              {
                      FullPath = z.EventArgs.FullPath,
                      Created = z.EventArgs.ChangeType,
                      Name = z.EventArgs.Name,
                      DirectoryName = file.DirectoryName
              };
          });
//Find the files that have been changed.
var fileChanged = Observable
                .FromEventPattern<FileSystemEventArgs>(w, "Changed")
                .Select(z =>
                    new {
                      FullPath = z.EventArgs.FullPath,
                      ChangeType = z.EventArgs.ChangeType
                    });

//Find the files that have been renamed
var fileRenamed = Observable
                .FromEventPattern<RenamedEventArgs>(w, "Renamed")
                .Select(z => new
```

```
                {
                    OldFullPath = z.EventArgs.OldFullPath,
                    NewPath = z.EventArgs.FullPath,
                    ChangeType = z.EventArgs.ChangeType
                });
fileCreated.Dump("Created");
fileRenamed.Dump("Renamed");
fileChanged.Dump("Changed");
```

When you run this, you will see how the data gets surfaced as you create, rename, or change files in the specified directory.

Summary

Be warned! Rx.NET is not a replacement for the existing .NET eventing system. You should use Rx.NET only when you want to pass around the event arguments and process them in some way using the composable nature of LINQ and related frameworks. I hope you have already started thinking of how Rx.NET can help rewire some of your legacy code.

Index

■ S

■ T

Get the eBook for only $10!

> Now you can take the weightless companion with you anywhere, anytime. Your purchase of this book entitles you to 3 electronic versions for only $10.

This Apress title will prove so indispensible that you'll want to carry it with you everywhere, which is why we are offering the eBook in 3 formats for only $10 if you have already purchased the print book.

Convenient and fully searchable, the PDF version enables you to easily find and copy code—or perform examples by quickly toggling between instructions and applications. The MOBI format is ideal for your Kindle, while the ePUB can be utilized on a variety of mobile devices.

Go to www.apress.com/promo/tendollars to purchase your companion eBook.

Apress®
THE EXPERT'S VOICE™

CPSIA information can be obtained
at www.ICGtesting.com
Printed in the USA
LVOW03s1723190416

484356LV00005B/127/P

9 781430 268451